LET GO AFT
The Indiscretions of a Salt Horse Commander

In the Spellmount/Parapress Military List:

The Territorial Battalions – A pictorial history
The Yeomanry Regiments – A pictorial history
Over the Rhine – The Last Days of War in Europe
History of the Cambridge University OTC
The Fighting Troops of the Austro-Hungarian Army
Intelligence Officer in the Peninsula
The Scottish Regiments – A pictorial history
The Royal Marines – A pictorial history
The Royal Tank Regiment – A pictorial history
The Irish Regiments – A pictorial history
British Sieges of the Peninsular War
Victoria's Victories
Heaven and Hell – German paratroop war diary
Rorke's Drift
Came the Dawn – Fifty years an Army Officer
Kitchener's Army – A pictorial history
On the Word of Command – A pictorial history of the Regimental Sergeant Major
Marlborough as Military Commander
The Art of Warfare in the Age of Marlborough
Epilogue in Burma 1945-48
Scandinavian Misadventure
The Fall of France
The First Victory – O'Connor's Desert Triumph Dec 1940-Feb 1941
Blitz Over Britain
Deceivers Ever – Memoirs of a Camouflage Officer
Indian Army of the Empress 1861-1903
Heroes for Victoria 1837-1901
The Waters of Oblivion – The British Invasion of the Rio de la Plata 1806-07
Soldier's Glory – 'Rough Notes of an Old Soldier'
Craufurd's Light Division
Napoleon's Military Machine
Falklands Military Machine
Wellington's Military Machine
Commando Diary
The French are Coming! – The Invasion Scare 1803-05
Military Marching – A pictorial history
Soldier On! – Testament of a Tom
The Glider Soldiers
Sons of John Company – The Indian and Pakistan Armies 1903-91
A Guards Officer in the Peninsula
Gentlemen's Sons – The Guards in the Peninsula and at Waterloo 1808-15
Fuzzy-Wuzzy – The Campaigns in the Eastern Sudan 1884-85
Overlord Coastline – A Guide to D-Day Locations

In the Nautical List:

Evolution of Engineering in the Royal Navy – Vol 1, 1827-1939
In Perilous Seas
Sea of Memories
Ordinary Naval Airmen
Haul, Taut and Belay – Memoirs of a Flying Sailor
Keep Your Head Down – Falklands Notes by Pen and Fiddle

In the Aviation List:

Diary of a Bomb Aimer
Operation 'Bograt' – Memoirs of a Fighter Pilot
A Medal for Life – Capt Leefe Robinson VC
Three Decades a Pilot – The Third Generation
Bob Doe – Fighter Pilot
The Allied Bomber War 1939-45
Inn of the Few

LET GO AFT

The Indiscretions of a Salt Horse Commander

Henry Graham de Chair DSC★

WITH TRUTH AND HONOUR

PARAPRESS LTD
Tunbridge Wells

© Henry Graham de Chair 1993
ISBN 1-898594-02-3

First published in the UK by
PARAPRESS LTD
12 Dene Way
Speldhurst
Tunbridge Wells
Kent
TN3 0NX

A catalogue record for this book is available from the British Library

Printed in Great Britain by
The Ipswich Book Co. Ltd.
Ipswich
Suffolk

Contents

Introduction

The main object of this book is to show the modern generation why world-wide service in the Royal Navy was considered the best career for those fortunate to be selected.

I joined the Royal Naval college at Osborne as a member of the first of the small teams. Thanks to the post World War I Geddes axe, it was the end of an era.

What was I to call the book covering a relatively undistinguished, if varied career? 'Indiscretions of a Salt Horse' was ruled out, and 'Secure Cable' was discarded in favour of 'Let Go Aft' since as far as possible ships prefer not to anchor, but berth alongside the dockyard wall to avoid running boats. Seamen will know that to 'let go aft' is generally the final act of slipping the last rope before a ship leaves for its voyage. The reader must decide whether the 'Indiscretions' sub-title would be suitable.

I have pleasure in acknowledging the assistance given to me in the preparation of this book, particularly by my daughter Anita Lockett and her Issy; my son Colin and his wife for their unstinting help; my nephew Rodney and his wife Sarah de Chair for much topical naval advice and encouragement, and lastly my loving wife for putting up with me and tolerating my nautical obsession for so long.

Graham de Chair

Commander H. G. de Chair DSC* RN

1

Early Days

I was born at Clifton Lodge, Winchester on 10 September 1905. My parents had returned to England after three years in the United States of America, and were living at West Lodge, West Meon, in Hampshire which was my grandmother's house, so that my father could be near Portsmouth and HMS *Bacchante*, his first Command as a Captain in the Royal Navy.

In 1910, on his appointment to command the new cruiser, HMS *Cochrane*, we moved to Chatham, and in 1911 to a house called Ballancrieff, in Sunningdale, where my brother Somerset was born. My father was at that time the assistant controller at the Admiralty, but a year later, in 1912, he was appointed to command HMS *Colossus*, the latest of the 'Dreadnoughts'. My mother then took the family to stay with her parents in South Africa for ten months, after which my father was promoted to Rear Admiral, and appointed Naval Secretary to the First Lord of the Admiralty, Winston Churchill. Winston was then only thirty-seven years old, a sore trial to the Sea Lords and the Naval Secretary in particular.

In 1914 we had a German governess, Fraulein Cremer. Our relations were somewhat strained, and one week before war broke out she gave notice, saying she felt she was not giving satisfaction. My mother was then contacted by the War Office who said, 'We understand that you have a German Spy in your employ.' Fraulein Cremer had moved to the Military Secretary's family, but her real grievance with my mother was that she had all meals with the children in the nursery and consequently was able to learn no naval secrets.

We moved house on 4 August 1914, the day war was declared, to Lynnwood Chase, Bracknell, which was to be our home until 1923 when my father was appointed Governor of New South Wales in Australia. He did not see his new home again for I believe two years, being responsible for the blockade of Germany with the tenth Cruiser Squadron until 1916. My mother says she instructed me to crawl along beams in the attic with a bag containing fifty gold Sovereigns and secrete them in a corner away from prying eyes in case of invasion. We never found this bag.

At the age of nine, and not before time, I went to a school called Hill Brow in Bolsover road, Eastbourne, where the joint Headmasters were named Thornton and Hunt. Mr Thornton taught Scripture and was very popular; Mr Hunt taught carpentry and maths and put me in charge of the workshop. A Mr Croome taught Latin, history and drawing and gave me a bar of chocolate on Mondays for sharpening the drawing pencils. He also taught boxing, and gave me a Toby jug of Lord Nelson. One of the other masters, Mr Scallon, joined the Army and came back after being wounded. Mr Schulthess, who was German Swiss, taught German and French to such good effect that all boys entering the Navy became interpreters. I studied the piano and worked hard at it for a year, getting full marks at all my practices, by which time I decided that music was not for me and I would learn German instead, possibly in a fit of patriotism. We all learned singing, and many of us sang in the choir at St John's Church during Evensong.

Our games were played on Larkins field, a long walk from the school, and back up Granville Hill, so we only played three days a week. For swimming we walked to the Devonshire baths – also a long way – where I was initiated by going down the chute before I could swim, and had to be fished out after going under for the third time. Later I was given a shilling for swimming the width of the baths. More than a year later I was presented with the Royal Humane Society Certificate on vellum for rescuing my sister frm the sea at Port Holland.

For supper during the war we were given hunks of stale bread, thinly covered with black treacle, which was scraped off before it had time to soak into the bread.

In 1917, after representing the Navy on Lord Balfour's mission to the United States, my father was appointed in command of the third Battle Squadron based at Sheerness, in Kent.

When I was aged twelve my father took me to sea in his flagship, HMS *Dreadnought*, for a sweep of the North Sea; this was a great thrill for a small boy in war time. Even more exciting was the fact that we shot down a Gotha – a German aircraft. I slept in a hammock in my father's day cabin and I remember being left on the Admiral's bridge, furtively watched over by a staff officer, while papa paced up and down on the shelter deck far below where I could see him. This was probably his last time at sea in the *Dreadnought*, as shortly after he was relieved of his command for refusing to serve as a member of the Board of Admiralty with Lord Wemyss, as he was disgusted at the underhand way in which Admiral Jellicoe had been sacked from his post as the First Sea Lord.

My last year was spent working hard to prepare for the entrance examination into the Navy. When I had my eyes tested they failed me for being colour blind – I knew the difference between peacock blue and green and called a bead blue, however my father insisted on a further examination which I passed.

Before entering the Board Room for interview I was given three minutes in which to write an essay on 'What are good manners?' I had expected to write an essay on Nelson, or Napoleon or something like the Southern Railway and was completely unprepared for such a subject. However, all was well, and the interview passed off amicably. Asked what my hobbies were, I said painting and stamp collecting, whereupon I was asked if I had any stamps from North Borneo. Fortunately I could not remember where Borneo was and I said 'No'. Admiral Patey, the President then said, 'Have you any stamps from the Leeward Islands?' and I said, 'Yes' and was able to point them out on the map behind me. Perhaps it was Captain Charles Royds who asked how far I had got in arithmetic. I said, 'Simultaneous quadratic equations, Sir.' Luckily I was not asked to demonstrate! Sixty-six of the two hundred and forty candidates passed the interview and were summoned to the Russel Hotel for a written exam, which twenty-six passed. My desk number was thirteen, and I passed tenth into the Royal Naval College at Osborne, in the Isle of Wight. My Latin paper was a mess, but I was able to name all the rivers in Canada. French was no problem thanks to Mr Schulthess, and I enjoyed geometry.

A representative from Messrs Gieve, the well known naval tailor, was in attendance at the hotel to measure us all for our uniforms, and even before the formal announcement in the papers, my parents received a telegram 'Congratulations on your son's success – Gieve'.

In May 1919 we thirteen year old cadets joined the Royal Naval College, Osborne, as 'Exmouths', the first of the post war smaller terms. Lieutenant John Knox was our term officer, with Lieutenant Commander Mitchell, an engineer officer who supervised our engineering training and rugger – one third of our training was spent in engineering. Discipline was extremely strict and minor offences earned one tick; an accumulation of three ticks meant a beating, and I got three of the best once for having my toothbrush pointing east instead of west. I was also beaten for taking two buns at tea one evening. Everything was done to order: one gong meant 'say prayers', two gongs 'stop saying your prayers'.

We cadets learned to be tidy, with our uniforms and clothing laid out strictly in regulation fashion, on and in our chests: cap on top in the middle with one sock either side, monkey jackets on the shelf at starboard and trousers to port for rounds, by which time – 9 p.m. – we were lying at attention in bed. Reveille was followed by a stream of naked bodies jumping into the plunge at the end of the dormitory, we were then allowed five minutes to dress.

The cadets' 'gunroom' – the place where we lived, was on one side of a long corridor. We had to double past senior gunrooms, and were not allowed to speak to any cadet in a term a senior to ours, unless spoken to first. The key of our chest was on a lanyard, which as Juniors we were not allowed to swing, nor were we allowed to wear our cap on the back of the head. Any infraction of such customs constituted 'Guff' which was punishable. The chief cadet captains normally dealt with such relatively minor offences by administering a beating, but our term lieutenants dealt with our welfare and more serious breaches of discipline. For very serious offences 'official cuts' were administered by a physical training instructor over a box-horse in front of the whole term. Such punishment was very rare, and was never carried out in our term.

Mention of box-horses reminds me that I was good at gymnastics and games and was selected as a special vaulter, no doubt thanks to my prep school where I had earned a medal for gym. I also learned fencing and earned three points for my term as a 90% boxer.

Our only connection with the cadets in other terms was during our 'tutor sets'. Mr James Watt was my tutor whose set consisted mainly of Admirals' sons, who attend with him on Monday evenings and wrote essays. He took a great interest in each of us and was pleased when I took seven wickets as a slow bowler in a tutor set cricket match.

For my voluntary subjects I opted for 'Bird Watching', which entailed lectures on Sunday evenings with Mr Piggott; but we never got down to Osborne Bay for practical work, as only Senior Termers were allowed there. Any Juniors found there were made to 'Sing a Song' or suffer such other indignities as might be imposed by Senior Termers.

There was a high mast at Osborne, and all cadets had to climb the rigging; the most intrepid going up over the Futtock Shrouds, which I saw no point in attempting. Most of us clambered onto the platform by passing through the lubber's hole, instead of being suspended in space as one reached for a hand hold to haul ones self through the upper shrouds.

2

HMS *Iron Duke*, Midshipman 1923–1926

Patrick Boyle and I were sent to HMS *Iron Duke*, Flagship of the Mediterranean Fleet, with Admiral Sir Osmond de Beauvoir Brock as Commander-in-Chief.

We took passage to Malta in HMS *Ajax*, being inspected at Devonport by the Commander-in-Chief Plymouth, Admiral Sir Montagu Browning (Hookey Browning, a great friend of my father's) but that day he was very fierce and angry because Midshipman Ouvrey had not cleaned his dirk properly and there was hell to pay for this neglect of duty.

Captain Dunbar Nasmyth commanded the *Iron Duke*; the sailors loved him but he never smiled, although in later years I found him always cheerful and most friendly. Sadly he left the *Iron Duke* shortly after we joined and was relieved by Captain Biff Rose, a cousin of Boyle's. Patrick and I were the most junior midshipmen in the ship and were consequently the lowest of the low. The Commander, Herbert Fitzherbert ran a very efficient ship. The maxim 'Routine is the essence of efficiency', headed the Routine Board. The quarter-deck scuppers were of polished brass, which we called the Fitzherberts. No one could spit on the deck with impunity, and different coloured spitkids were placed in each part of ship or top for cigarette butts, and for sailors to use when spitting – a common practice then.

Captain Rose was generous with praise and blame, and given to forceful expression when irritated. I was in the second cutter trying to secure the head ropes to a buoy in a strong wind on arrival at Port Said. We had just left Alexandria after a pleasant week, and the Captain had toothache, so there was quite a flap on. No doubt I deserved his outburst: 'Stop his leave for a year, damn him; stop his leave for ever; stop all their leaves for ever.'

From Port Said we went to Beyrouth. It was very hot but the Captain was good enough to take the Midshipmen's gig's crew away at 0600 for instruction and practice, so I felt we were forgiven.

General drill was an occasion for quick action. Everyone was supposed to know what to do and as long as we were seen rushing about, all was well. Often as Midshipmen we had no idea what was happening and found it convenient to double smartly round 'Q' turret amidships.

As Midshipman of 'X' turret, Lieutenant Richard Mack, my Divisional Officer, sometimes allowed me to take charge and spot the fall of shot. During night defence exercises I was in the foretop with Lieutenant Commander Marx, controlling searchlights. One night there was a shout from the Captain up the voicepipe, 'Are you ready Marx?' Reply: 'Pretty well sir, pretty well'. Actually we had not even started to get lined up, but Marx knew how to keep the peace.

Lying at anchor off Kotor one night a bora struck the ship and the duty watch was called out to secure the quarterdeck awning with frapping lines. Orders were being shouted, the awning was flapping, and the wind shrieking. The Captain came on deck and in stentorian tones shouted: 'There's too much noise. Damn it, I'm making it all myself!'

On another day in Catarro Harbour after a sailing race had earlier been cancelled, because of the likelihood of bad weather, it was decided to hold it after all. The course was round a mark being laid to leeward, with orders to start the race as soon as boats got away. My dipping lug cutter was first away and in the prevailing strong wind soon overtook the picket boat, which was laying the lee mark buoy. My cutter was making about 12 knots as we rounded the marker buoy and luffed up for the return. As we turned, I looked back and saw a band of light green light on the north horizon with a suggestion of white water, and gave the order 'Shorten sail, down masts!'. The crew had the sails down but not the masts before the bora struck with sheets of hail and rain. We took shelter under the sails and the storm was all over within a few minutes, so we made sail again and won the race. Meanwhile some awnings in the fleet had been split or carried away by the unexpected wind.

A similar thing happened off Venice, and all boats lying at the *Iron Duke*'s booms were sunk by the storm except the *Benbow*'s launch, which Keith Walter took into Venice, where the Commander-in-Chief's yacht *Bryony* was lying. Lady Brock gave him breakfast in his pyjamas and oilskins. None of the Midshipmen was allowed leave until the boats were recovered. The *Iron Duke* lay in 42 foot of water and every time she swung at her mooring the keel caught the funnel of my picket boat and pushed it over. It took us two days to salvage her and pump her dry.

One Sunday morning in Malta, Boyle and I took two boats from Dockyard Creek with church parties to French Creek, where many *dghaissas* were lying at a mooring. To get alongside it was necessary to pass over the rope moorings and I naturally stopped my engine to slide over them. Not so Patrick Boyle, who went astern on the engine and was rather surprised to see a dozen or so *dghaissas* coming together and towards him with much zobbing and cursing by their owners, who were thus rudely awakened. Boyle's propeller was inextricably entangled with the ropes which he had to cut and then be towed back to the ship.

The Boat Officer was not amused and told Boyle to dive and clear his propeller. Patrick, nothing if not resourceful, did not relish diving on a cold winter's day and persuaded a crane driver the other side of the creek to lift his stern out of the water, which made it much easier to clear the propeller.

An important part of the Midshipman's duty during night watches at sea was to make cocoa for the Officer of the Watch. Patrick Boyle was engaged in this congenial task in the chart house but, finding the kettle slow in coming to the boil, decided to see if there was something wrong with the electrics. The Fleet Navigator's dividers lying on the chart table suggested a promising solution, as he promptly inserted the points into the two holes providing power for the kettle. There was a bright flash and both the points of the dividers were fused; then, as if by magic, into the chart house came the Fleet Navigator just in time to see the demise of his precious dividers. 'Mr Boyle, unless you can produce another pair of dividers for me within five minutes, I'll have your leave stopped for a month.' Patrick calmly put his hand into his pocket and produced his own dividers.

Patrick Boyle continued to show individuality during his brief service career. Later, during our gunnery course at Whale Island Patrick had to double around the island several times as a punishment. Finally, when he reported for his pay, the paymaster said 'Boyle, Boyle, you're not a naval officer, you failed the course at Greenwich, you shouldn't be here.' But no-one had told him. In 1942 who should I meet as an excellent instructor for anti-submarine operations in HMS *Vimy* but Lieutenant P.S. Boyle RNVR.

The Fleet Navigation Officer (Freddy Nuts for short) must

have been kindly disposed towards Midshipmen. He either gave or lent St John Tyrwhitt three pairs of white duck trousers which were carefully folded three times and stored in his chest. Someone playing with a loaded pistol in the chest flat fired it by accident and the bullet went through these white duck trousers, making 12 holes in each pair, 36 holes in all. I forget what the outcome was. Perhaps I should explain that Tyrwhitt was 'Tanky', the Fleet Navigator's assistant, whose duties included winding the chronometers daily.

With the Fleet at Pollensa Bay, I was sent at the Commander-in-Chief's request to his yacht the *Bryony* and the destroyers with bread before sailing. The weather deteriorated and *Bryony* was forced to sail with Lady Beatty and Mrs Duberley on board without the bread; as *Bryony* passed the flagship the officers pointed at their open mouths to indicate their anticipated hunger without their loaves of bread. The sea was very rough and the gale increased in strength, half way through my bread round my steering gear jammed and had to be disconnected, but the coxswain manned the tiller aft while I shouted steering orders, holding the wheel for support. We finished our deliveries safely, and returned to the ship and hooked on to the main derrick. Lieutenant Friedberger hoisted us from the crest of a wave and said, 'I never expected to see you again.' Captain Rose sent for and congratulated me on my seamanship after I had had a bath.

The Midshipman's cutter race was an annual event. The race started with the boats anchored in a line with awnings spread. The starting gun was the signal to furl awnings, up anchor, up masts and sail half a mile, then shorten sail, down masts and pull half a mile, then sail for the next half mile and down masts, out oars and pull the last half mile. I was stroke oar for the second race which we won, having been badly beaten by midshipmen from *Benbow* term in the previous year.

In 1924 Boyle and I with other midshipmen from *Anson* and *Benbow* terms went out to Ghain Tuffiqh to camp; after about five days we received orders to strike camp and by forced marching covered the twelve miles to return to the ship, starting at 4 a.m. The Sirdar of Egypt, Sir Lee Stack, had been murdered and our battle squadron was ordered to Alexandria. Sailing was delayed until after the weekend and I remember that Barry Bingham took his polo ponies in one of the ships.

General (Bull) Allenby was at Alexandria; his brother Claude was my sister's godfather and Boyle and I were invited to tea with the great man. We missed the boat sent to collect the guests and had to be pulled over to HMS *Marlborough* by three senior midshipmen who did it in fine style. We were not popular with them or our hosts when we arrived late.

Soon after arriving at Alexandria we landed a Brigade of Seamen and marched through the town with bayonets fixed in a show of strength. The officers all carried revolvers loaded in holsters. A few oranges were thrown at us but otherwise there were no visible demonstrations.

Midshipman 'Sally' Singleton's father was a Colonel on the staff in Cairo. We hoped that the four river gunboats would be manned during the crisis and I got Sally to write to his father, promising that, if the gunboats were commissioned, he would be one of the First Lieutenants. To our disappointment the Colonel wrote back to say that 'nothing short of martial law' would get the gunboats manned. So we settled down to a semi-peace routine, with golf and a visit to Cairo, where an Engineering Sub-Lieutenant showed us around, including a brothel where the beer was doped. Fortunately, being tee-total I managed to rescue my friends, to the chagrin of the management and surprise of the occupants.

We played rugger on a very hard ground against the locals in Alexandria, and I broke my collar bone, as did Alderson with whom I later stayed.

After three days in sick bay I was given leave to stay ashore in a magnificent house owned by Mr Harry Barker (the Cotton King); my room had its own bathroom with a marble bath to step down into, and I lived in the lap of luxury.

Recovering my strength after a week with the Barkers, I went to stay with my friends the Aldersons where his sister Christine acted as my nurse. They invited most of the midshipmen from HMS *Iron Duke*'s gunroom to lunch on Christmas Day and locked all the pistols, which every officer carried, in the safe. After the festivities, some were left behind and we had to send instructions how to unload a service pistol, before they were returned to the ship.

When the Fleet was anchored outside the harbour I used to take my picket boat through what we called 'the hole in the wall', a narrow tortuous channel through the breakwater by Ras el Tin lighthouse, with a rock in the middle of it. This was a good short cut and saved a long trip to the end of the harbour round the western end of the breakwater.

HMS *IRON DUKE* AT MALTA, MARCH 29th – APRIL 5th

I was in a whaler recovering a torpedo when HMS Volunteer *collided with HMS* Iron Duke

HMS *WIVERN*

In 1924 after a week onboard HMS *Barham*, assisting the gunnery department with super elevation strips for their six-pounder sub-calibre guns, it was a relief when destroyers of the Third Flotilla anchored in Plateali Bay, and Boyle and I joined for three months' small ship training.

I was fortunate in being sent to HMS *Wivern* (Lieut.-Commander Harcourt). We sailed for Patras with mails as soon as we midshipmen were aboard, and on arrival I was instructed to load the mail from the whaler.

Harcourt took me under his wing, and kept me up to the mark with instruction; he was a very taut hand and I was generally on

1925 COMBINED FLEET MANOEUVRES

THIS IS AN UNEXAGGERATED VIEW GOING FROM THE WARD ROOM TO THE BRIDGE. H.M.S. WILD SWAN ON RIGHT.

LOOKING ASTERN FROM THE COMPASS PLATFORM

H.O.D. de Chair

the bridge with him or in the chart house plotting during exercises. I also kept the morning watch with the First Lieutenant at sea, so on a number of occasions I was on the bridge for over 18 hours out of the 24.

During Red and Blue Fleet manoeuvres with the Atlantic and Mediterranean Fleets, we had a very rough time and were hove to for eight hours to the north of Majorca. The Captain's idea of amusing a Midshipman during lunch was to have a bowl of gruel sliding between us on the wardroom table as we sat at opposite ends; as the ship rolled we dug at it with our spoons.

The last of my three months in HMS *Wivern* was spent in the Engineering Department, and when the Engineer Officer went sick, I was nominally in charge. After some nine hours in the engine-room I was not feeling too well myself one day at sea, and retired to my cabin under the bridge to rest. It was not long before the Chief Engine Room Artificer came to my cabin and asked where the Chief (Engineer Officer) was. I realized that the Chief ERA knew that the Engineer Officer was on the sick list and suspected trouble, so I went back to the engine-room where I found two artificers standing round an oil fuel filter, the bearing of the port propeller shaft being hot. I ordered 'stop the port engine', and went to the bridge to report to the Captain, who fortunately said I was quite right in my decision. Half an hour later the Engineer Officer, having been raised from his bed, felt the bearing which was by then cool, and said we could safely continue with port engine. Not surprisingly it was not long before we ran the bearing and were lucky not to strip the turbine. At the subsequent Court of Enquiry, the Engineer Officer said, 'Now we will call the Midshipman.' However, Captain (D), Captain Gordon Ramsey presiding, said 'No we won't. The Midshipman knows nothing about engineering, is not meant to know anything about engineering, and is only doing training.' Thanks to him I was not required to give evidence.

The Sub was Jack Eaton, later my Admiral as Flag Officer Reserve Fleet. He was most entertaining, and his main job was as Correspondence Officer. He used to say 'Only two kinds of correspondence. What's on the desk which has got to be dealt with and what's on the deck which has been dealt with.'

Later during our cruise, HMS *Wivern* was sent to Levkas in Greece to recover the Fleet mails and I was sent into harbour with

13

a whaler. We found the mail lying in a disused shed in the main street of this hot and dusty town; there was no one about, so I got a carrozzi and with my crew loaded all the bags into it and thence into the whaler. On return to Malta the Destroyer Command paraded in the Corradino and I was called out to report to Rear-Admiral Addison, the Rear Admiral in command of Destroyers. He, in front of the assembled company, congratulated me on my resource and initiative in saving the Fleet's mails. I suspect Harcourt suggested that he should do so, but it was a nice gesture.

After three months in the *Wivern*, I volunteered for a short air course in HMS *Eagle* together with midshipmen Dennis and Boyle. Lieutenant Gerald Langley was our instructor, and we felt very grand being accommodated in cabins. I shared a two-berth cabin with a Pilot Officer RAF, and was taken up in an Avro Bison (known as a bullock) by Flight Lieutenant Venmore, whose nickname was 'Little Bigness'; (tee-total, non-smoker and very strong in the arm). His after-dinner parlour trick was to take you by the seat of your pants with one hand and hold you up above his head. The new Commander-in-Chief Mediterranean, Sir Roger Keyes, decided to fly from HMS *Eagle* and was taken up by Venmore in his bullock. In the aircraft were the Fleet Aviation Officer and Fleet Gunnery Officer, as well as the Commander-in-Chief who occupied the gunner's seat behind them. No sooner had they taken off than the pilot fired a Very light, turning to make an emergency landing because of a cracked water jacket. He was on his second bank when the engine cut and the aircraft spun into the sea. No one had thought it politic to warn the Admiral of action to take in the event of a crash, and they hit the drink like a brick wall, the Admiral being knocked unconscious and sustaining severe injury to his chest and skull.

The other officers managed to scramble clear as the plane started to sink nose first, but the Admiral was trapped with his head down in the sea. Then assisted by the two officers with him, Venmore seized the Admiral by the seat of his pants and held him up above his head (his after-dinner parlour trick). In so doing he saved the Admiral's life, although he was three months in Bighi Hospital recovering from his injuries. According to his daughter Katharine, the Admiral recovered consciousness when someone trod on his foot and he expressed himself forcibly. Presumably this was in the boat taking him to the recovery destroyer in the prevailing rough sea, referred to in Cecil Aspinall-Oglander's Biography.

In 1924 the oil burning (slush wofflers) *Queen Elizabeth* Class battleships came to Malta, and Vice Admiral Michael Hodges came to HMS *Iron Duke* as Second-in-Command of the Mediterranean Fleet, and Flag Officer of our squadron of coal burners (the clinker knockers), comprising HM ships *Iron Duke*, *Emperor of India*, *Marlborough* and *Ajax*. Our Grenville term Midshipmen all transferred to the *Queen Elizabeth*, leaving me as Senior Midshipman of the *Iron Duke*.

Commander Harry Daniel was our Squadron Gunnery Officer and Commander Bent the Executive Officer; Captain J.C.W. Henley took over from Biff Rose as Flag Captain. Towards the end of my time in the ship, the Captain's Secretary lent me his cabin to prepare for my seamanship examination, necessary for promotion to sub-lieutenant. Thanks to that, Bertram Thesiger's 'Queries in Seamanship', and Mr Barber the Bosun who was always ready to answer questions, I came out top of the Fleet with 944 marks out of 1000.

After shipping my first stripe, Commander Daniel asked me to obtain a suit of armour for the dance he was running. I tried Verdala Palace, but there all the suits were too small, then in a small shop I found part of a Japanese suit of armour.

Finally I visited the Malta Tin Works and asked if they could make a suit of armour. 'Oh yes,' said the manager, 'we make very good suit of armour, we make for Wembley Exhibition.' So I said, 'How soon could you make one and how much would it cost?' Reply: 'Three months and it would cost £50.' To which I said, 'Well, I want one for five pounds by tomorrow.' The manager seemed surprised, but said he would see what could be done, and in my new uniform I proceeded to shake hands with every man in the factory. They worked all night and by the next morning had made the helmet and arm pieces – all for five pounds. Such was the goodwill of the Maltese in 1925.

We blacked the helmet and stuck a red feather in it, so that Daniel could appear as a knight in armour at the dance, which was a great success. Each ship's wardroom with their ladies arrived in period costumes according to their fancy. Queen Elizabeth and her cortege from the Flagship, Madame Beaucare from HMS *Barham*, an Indian Potentate from *Emperor of India*, and the Duke

15

and Duchess from the *Marlborough*. All the acceptances for the dance were illuminated, and displayed in the Admiral's cabin under glass for several Sundays running before the event, and great excitement was the result. I had to appear as a mystical figure by the screen door in period costume before lunch one Sunday.

Captain and Mrs Henley very kindly invited me to stay with them in Valetta before I returned to England, and later I often stayed with them at Lamberhurst in Kent, as did many other homeless members of the *Iron Duke* gunroom.

Rudyard Kipling had been a friend of my mother's family and one day while staying at Lamberhurst, I rang to ask if we could call on him. He said 'come to tea', so I said 'there are rather a lot of us'; then he said 'come as many as you can get into one car'. We went to Burwash in three cars, parked two round the corner of Batemans and arrived with all fifteen of us piled high, some on the bonnet and some on the running boards. The old man was delighted and well prepared with fireworks in his garden after tea.

In January 1936 I returned to the UK overland. The SS *Lubjana* had a rough passage to Catania where I spent the day sightseeing with Mrs Miles and her friend before taking the train to Paris. There I stayed four days with Mr and Mrs Prince, American friends of my parents, visited the Louvre and other tourist attractions, and finally reached my grandmother's home in Twickenham after descending from a bus with eight pence in my pocket.

After my leave, two terms were spent at the Royal Naval College at Greenwich, which was supposed to be a sort of University course. Being near London we sub-lieutenants were expected to broaden our minds by visiting the museums and art galleries, many sub-lieutenants experienced the delights of the unaccustomed bright lights but at the expense of learning.

At Greenwich I was one of six in our term recommended for the Staff Course in due course, as a result of an essay; but the Staff Course never materialised. From Greenwich we proceeded to Portsmouth for the Torpedo Course in HMS *Vernon*, being accommodated in the Navigation School in the Dockyard. There again I only achieved a Second Class Certificate.

This was followed by a six weeks' Gunnery Course at Whale Island. My only distinction there was to be Captain of the Rifle Team and the only Sub-Lieutenant in the Pistol Team when we beat the marines, my father's seven-inch Webley Target Model with a light pull-off being partly responsible.

We only had two days to learn 15-inch turret drill before the Gunnery examination, and decided that we could each concentrate on a few of the duties of a turrets crew. All went well until about the fifth change round, when being in the working chamber I opened the breech of a misfired gun – a serious and potentially dangerous mistake – so only got a Third Class Pass in Gunnery.

The final course was Navigation, by which time I was obviously stale and tired. During the examination my nose bled all through the Tide paper and I got another Third Class Certificate.

Out of the 36 cadets who had entered Osborne in May 1919, the term was now reduced to 24, of whom 15 were required for submarines. Only six volunteered, and I was appointed to New Zealand, far from submarines, probably to be near my parents who were then in Australia.

3

HMS *Laburnum* New Zealand Squadron
1927-1929

My appointment as Sub-Lieutenant to HMS *Laburnum* took effect from 23 July 1927, but the Admiralty allowed me to break my journey in Sydney where I spent seven weeks with my family whom I had not seen for four years. Passage in RMS *Orama* of the Orient Line took six weeks, so that I did not join the ship until three months later.

While taking passage to Australia, I was appointed as King's Messenger, and was entrusted with several large sealed packages of confidential books for Columbo and the Australian and New Zealand Navies, which were locked in the *Orama*'s safe.

Captain Matheson kindly allowed me to visit the bridge and encouraged me to take sights, which I generally did when Gerry Martin the First Officer had the morning watch. We became close friends and he was an honorary member of our young circle which soon got together, about twelve people, self-styled the Suerats. We must have given the Captain some misgivings when we returned onboard late at Marseilles and Columbo as the ship could not sail without the King's Messenger! He persuaded me to box every morning with Forbes McHardy, the New Zealand Light Heavyweight Champion, and I also ran the ship's sports programme, which kept me fully occupied.

I sat at Dr McIlroy's table with a Mr Boyce who had been Director-General of Survey in the Sudan for 23 years; Mr and Mrs Maslin from Canberra and their nephew Fred Maslin, a sheep farmer; Forbes McHardy and his sister Joy from Palmerston North, and a honeymoon couple, Ian and Mrs Campbell of Hawkes Bay; they kindly asked me to stay with them in New Zealand, having insisted on mending socks and washing things for me among other passengers. On arrival in Sydney we chartered the *Alice Rawson* ferry, named after my Godmother, in which our party all went across the harbour to the zoo.

After a very pleasant time with my family at Government House, I sailed for Aukland in the *Aorangi* which rolled heavily for four days. Mr and Mrs Graystock, promoters of leading singers, and Mr Burton, President of the Bread Bakers' Conference, were very complimentary about the Governor of New South Wales, and I had to make a speech after a concert onboard.

Relieving Lieutenant Knowling in HMS *Laburnum* was made easy as he took endless trouble to brief me, having come across the harbour in the early morning to meet me on arrival in Aukland, and stayed with me for a fortnight before returning to UK via Sydney.

The Graystocks asked me to a party on my first night in Auckland which I accepted, as most of the Officers were ashore and there was nothing doing onboard. After a very good dinner, I was taken out to the local country club known as Dixieland, for a dance. Despite the galaxy of partners, this was probably my first and last contribution to the Auckland social whirl. Instead I joined the Tramping Club and found the exercise at weekends with such fine views in the hills very rewarding.

The New Zealand Squadron consisted of two cruisers, HM NZ ships *Dunedin* and *Diomede*; two sloops, HMS *Laburnum* and *Veronica*; *Philomel* a cruiser as depot ship, and *Wakakura* for target towing and Fleet duties. Commander F.N. Attwood and his delightful family arrived a few days after me and he relieved Commander Brooke in command of HMS *Laburnum*.

My duties comprised Gunnery Control, Signals and Wireless, Confidential Books and Correspondence, Intelligence, Messdecks, Cable Officer, Watchkeeping, and Divisional Officer.

Commodore G.T.C.P. Swabey DSO RN, flying his Broad Pendant as Commodore New Zealand arrived at Auckland with *Dunedin* and *Diomede* a month after I joined, and I reported on board the *Dunedin* as Officer of the Guard as soon as the gangway at Sheerlegs Jetty was out. The Captain called on the Commodore an hour later. The Commodore returned Commander Attwood's call on Sunday two days later, but sent a verbal message saying he would not require a guard. I should have known that this indicated the official nature of the call which was planned to take place after church in the dockyard shed, but knowing we had no guard to give him, I omitted to mention this when I slipped the note to the Captain during the service. Result – the Commodore and Captain of the *Diomede* arrive onboard wearing swords and my Captain and the First Lieutenant are without. The only bugler is Wesleyan

Church Party and out of the ship and we cannot sound the 'Alert'. My Captain has to repair onboard *Dunedin* to apologise. My name is MUD!

My first effort at control of a full calibre shoot was on our way to Whangarei and the Bay of Islands. With only two guns most of the salvos were short, ten rounds a gun firing at eight rounds a minute.

At Russell in the Bay of Islands we were persuaded to hire Zane Gray's launch and caught two mako sharks, including the record for the year, a shark weighing 411 pounds which involved a very exciting chase lasting nearly two hours. The *Laburnum* ship's company, not to be outdone by their Officers, saw a grey nurse shark alongside and caught it with a meathook on the end of a heaving line, which was then brought to the capstan and hove up. Finally the Gunner had to come and shoot it with a pistol.

At Onerei, *Laburnum* was severely defeated at cricket by the local club of which we were made Honorary Members, all four of us Officers having been out for ducks. This in spite of the special autographed bat which Rudyard Kipling had given me as a Cadet. I often wonder what happened to that bat and hope it has been preserved with his autograph.

Whilst at Auckland, the Captain was asked by the Professor of Biology at the University if we could let him have some cockroaches for the students to dissect. As Messdeck Officer I was happy to oblige and put five in a matchbox but forgot about them until a month later, when we were able to present one rather fat cockroach and four perfect skeletons.

HMS *LABURNUM* BACK AT AUCKLAND, 1928
GISBORNE. DUNEDIN. WELLINGTON TO PICTON

After Christmas festivities, a treasure hunt resulted in several people getting wet, as I had laid clues in tobacco tins in the shark-proof swimming pool alongside the jetty; which reminded me that swimming instruction was needed for several members of the ship's Company who were encouraged to learn to swim before they could go ashore.

A certain amount of social activity resulted from a dance given by the sloops at which I acted as Pier Master. My sister and some friends came over from Sydney and toured the North Island while we swept for Northumberland Rock with *Wakakura*'s Oropese sweep and our Dan buoys off Gisborne Roads.

Our next port of call was Dunedin in the South Island, a delightful place where we were made very welcome. After three days visiting Omaru, Timaru and Lyttleton, we went to Wellington where the sloops landed range parties at Trentham Camp and I took charge of the rifle butts. Captain Gage Williams lent me a very good racing hack on which I took great pleasure in doing rounds of the camp when all was quiet.

A week at Wanganui was followed by Picton where Mr Tripe and his family entertained us. He lent me a beautiful horse called Rampion which I rode from Koromiko 16 miles to Tuavereina, the site of an English detachment massacred by the Maoris as the result of an accidental rifle shot. We cantered three quarters of the way and finished by rounding up the cows for milking. After insisting on giving me supper, I was loaded with jams, mushrooms, apples and scones, all home-made, to take back to the ship.

After World War I, the ladies of the Picton Branch of the Navy League provided a hall in which to entertain visiting ships' companies, there being very few local men after the terrible losses at ANZAC. At the final dance the Captain made a speech and presented a clock from the ship's Company.

We left Picton on 17 April for Napier in Hawkes Bay. It came on to blow during the first watch and I had to sing during the middle to keep awake. Several people were sick, spray coming over the bridge and the wind force eight to nine. From Napier, Neil Campbell drove me through Hastings to his station 'Awanui' in the hills where I enjoyed a few quiet days leading the pastoral life. I was initiated into the job of holding a mob of cattle together while he cut out steers, and we had a day's hunting with the Hawkes Bay.

Two years later I received a heartrending letter from Dorothy Campbell, telling of the ghastly upheaval of the earthquake on 3 February 1930 which changed Hawkes Bay from a happy and prosperous district to a ruined and bloody shambles. I believe the *Laburnum* was washed onto the beach at Napier by the tidal wave and washed off it again by another.

On 19 May, *Diomede* sailed for UK, passing close to us as we cheered ship. Her paying off pendant caught in our rigging and parted, so we sent some of it to the *Philomel* for Yeoman Bunch whose wife made it, and some to Paddy Boyle's fiancée, Margaret Tripp from Timaru. When her father called onboard the *Diomede*, he is reputed to have said to Boyle, 'Well, young man, what are your prospects and what are your assets?' To which Boyle replied, 'The answer to both questions is Nil, have a gin.' Ronnie Hunter-Blair was First Lieutenant of the *Diomede*, and got engaged to Nan Colbeck living at Auckland. They were dining with me and some others onboard when *Laburnum* was berthed alongside the *Diomede* on 27 November. We all decided to go on deck after the soup and look at the eclipse of the moon when a signal arrived from *Diomede*, '*Laburnum*, too much noise', to which I replied, 'Submit noise is being made by Nieces who are uncontrollable, request advice and assistance.' Then came a hand messages from Nutty Wells, the Captain of the *Diomede*, 'I think I had better come and have a look at the Tawdry Bauble.'

Two regrettable incidents occurred onboard about this time; on going rounds I discovered a lot of water in the four-inch magazine, possibly caused by some mischief maker, and a fire in number two store which had to be flooded to extinguish the fire, and was subsequently pumped out three weeks later.

Lieutenant-Commander O'Callaghan, the First Lieutenant, owned a fine hunter called Captain which he lent me after we had been out with the Pakaranga Hunt together. Captain jumped bare wire and everything in sight until we came to a barbed wire fence where four horses baulked in succession. Captain sent me over but declined to follow.

Monday 4 June was the King's birthday, and the Army and Navy paraded in the Domain assisted by thousands of Boy Scouts. His Excellency the Governor-General, General Sir Charles Fergusson, inspected and we marched past. I carried the King's Colour for the Navy, but had it at the Order instead of at the Carry during the inspection. The Domain Battery was singularly erratic in its timing of the 21-gun salute and I had to hold the Colour at the Clip during the operation, as it had a staff with a heavy brass knob in the form of a crown on the end of it. The Squadron Gunnery

Officer gave me a bottle for not dipping when the Governor-General passed!

We sailed for Fiji the following day. On 6 June, Captain Kingsford-Smith landed at Suva in his now famous aircraft *Southern Cross* after taking off from California, and two days later on 8 June took off and landed at Brisbane – three and a half days flying from San Francisco to Australia. He was presented with £5,000 for the finest flight in history.

EXTRACT FROM HMS *LABURNUM* NEW ZEALAND SQUADRON
(1927–29)

HMS Laburnum at Fiji and Apia (British Samoa)

Coaling by native labour at Suva was a slow business and the Captain called a conference to ensure a future rate of at least 30 tons an hour. In my journal I noted: 'The Fijian lives for the moment, but he is tired; leave him to do a job and he will languish.' For this reason Indians were imported for the sugar industry in Fiji in 1904. The two black races have a supreme contempt for each other. The one strong, of fine physique but little mental capacity, and the other possessing all the brain and cunning of India. It is necessary to have police of each nationality.'

Before sailing for Apia we were invited to dine with three bachelors, known as the Batch. A band of Fijian singers behind a beaded screen in the dining-room gave us a delightful concert during the meal. Pilot and I joined them with our uke and guitar respectively and were initiated into a Kava Ceremony. Our navigator, Lieutenant Maxwell Richmond, had to drink a full bowl of the stuff, lapping it up like a dog, but one small bowl was enough for me. At a subsequent visit the Batch came to dinner onboard and brought the words of their songs which we were able to copy out and put to music which our Engineer Officer Mr Thomas had written down tonic-sol-fa by listening to the natives singing in the fields. On returning to New Zealand, Pilot and I, as Rusty and Rastus, would black our faces and play during the interval at dances.

We only stayed a day at Apia where the new Administrator, Colonel Allen from New Zealand, had taken over. We had tea with

23

Mrs Allen at Vailima, Robert Louis Stevenson's old home, and she came to dinner with Major Bell before we sailed for Fakafou with the Meteorological Officer and collector of Customs for Atafou.

Earlier the *Dunedin* had arrived from Apia (British Samoa) while *Laburnum* was breaking the sloops' coaling record with 220 tons at 47 tons per hour at Wellington, and we heard about the trouble with the Mau, most of whom are over 55 years old and quite friendly. Apparently the Governor was alarmed and failed to deal with the situation. It seems the Mau were hurt at not being arrested and told their friends to come along and make a party of it. Then there might be 100 or more stragglers having heard the buzz who came to be arrested. The Governor panicked and told the Commodore to land every available man from both ships as Apia was being attacked. Then one of the matelots said, 'Look 'ere, you boomin' Maus, you pack up and go 'ome out of it', and the entire so-called attacking force dispersed! Later, Colonel Allen took over as Administrator in time for the King's birthday parade which the natives had organised without orders. At five minutes to 0800 Colonel Allen's wife's maid told her of the parade, and Colonel Allen managed to be on the dais, taking the salute, as the leading column was giving Eyes Right. There was no more trouble.

HMS *LABURNUM* VISIT TO TOKELAU ISLANDS.
PAGO PAGO AND DANGER ISLAND

Landing with the Captain, Doctor, the Meterologist and Mr Bates, our leading Telegraphist and a couple of interpreters, on Fakofou, meant getting very wet as we crossed the reef in canoes to reach the beach. Three hours later we returned to the ship loaded with presents from the 300 inhabitants, being skilfully propelled over the reef breakers; we then sailed for Nuko Nono where we repeated the process. Thence to Atafou leaving the Meterologist with two hydrogen cylinders and rubber balloons etc to spend a month observing the upper air and trade winds. The water round all these coral islands is about 200 fathoms deep and the ship has to lie off, it being too deep for anchorage. Each island has a different religion depending on which missionary got there first.

We returned Mr Bates to Apia late on 22 June and proceeded to Pago Pago in American Samoa, a US Naval Base governed by a US Navy Captain, in Tutila. Customary salutes were fired and official calls exchanged, after which we were lavishly entertained. Commander Le Bourgeois took me sailing in his outrigger canoe; very thrilling, 20 knots reaching and close hauled within two points of the wind. After a lot of bailing and a couple of upsets, a squall struck us and Commander Le Bourgeois jumped over-board, I honestly believe to see what I would do. This time the sail was in the water but we were near home in shallow water.

The French sloop *Cassiopée* arrived from Apia on 28 June and we became firm friends. She was rather more up to date than *Laburnum* with the difference that their magazine and shell-room, adjacent to the wardroom like ours in a similar position, was tastefully decorated with divans and soft lighting for entertaining. I imagine their ammunition was in store in Tahiti!

Coaling by native labour at Pago Pago was a very slow business and I found time to buy a lot of things at the Commissary Store at trade prices. Unfortuately the water we embarked was chlorinated and we were short of drinking water, only 13½ tons to last the next 19 days before reaching Tahiti.

Two days at seven and a half knots saw us at Puka Puka, Danger Island, where we deposited three bags of mail from Aukland, some originating from Raratonga. Payment of the 570 population is communal. Each man gathers 200 coconuts, each woman 100, and each child old enough 50 a day; they get one penny for each coconut, so the money is distributed in proportion to the size of the family by the German trader Herr Nikau, and everyone is happy. The natives had three months' warning of our visit and presented a lot of gifts, hats, mats, sticks, shells, bags and 70 live chickens. Nine mats from the three villages were dedicated to the *Laburnham*, spelt variously, or to '*Manua Dangerouse*' for Man of War. The women from each village sang a song as they presented their mats.

Eventually after a large feast and watching a wrestling match, we were paddled back to the ship, being dragged across the reef and precipitated into the boiling foam when the right wave at last condescended to arrive.

I presented the King with a tin of tobacco and we set off for Manahiki.

I note that the son of the Administrative Agent for Raratonga came to breakfast and the Captain landed with the Doctor, after which we departed for Rakahanga. I took five star sights on the way and during these trips fixed the ship every day when at sea. In six months cruising in the South Pacific, we never sighted a single other ship at sea. Keeping a standing middle watch I often played my ukelele to keep awake.

Landing on Rakahanga was really exciting; coming over the reef, the boat was literally suspended in mid-air on two oars whilst the backwash from the surf crashed into the sea and we anxiously awaited the next breaker which all but broached us to. The Captain made the usual speech and enough presents were handed out for every member of the ship's company to have one, and the officers two, each.

Entering the West Pass to Penryhn Lagoon with the current rushing through the narrow channel was a thrilling experience for me in the crow's-nest, stationed there as I was, to point out any shoals. When I reported 'shoal right ahead', the Pilot who had come onboard said 'there's no shoal there'. It was a rock, probably eight fathoms deep but easily visible in the crystal clear water.

As we entered the lagoon we could see a host of sailing craft coming across to meet us to trade pearls for what we had to offer. The Chief Stoker did a roaring trade with the ship's tobacco and soap, and I had four natives sitting on my cabin floor bidding for my football jerseys and other surplus items, for which I netted two boxes of pearls, admittedly not all matching. Five days in the lagoon gave us a useful opportunity for general drill and ship's maintenance work before sailing for a look at Starbuck Island which I did from the crow's-nest to see if there were any signs of life ashore. There was nothing, only windswept low-lying ground with some scrub.

Malden Island on the Equator was as far north as we went during this cruise. There I did a sketch of the foreshore where the Captain and company landed to survey gear left by the Fiji Government for New Zealand. Rolling-stock, sheds and a mast and 12 coconut trees comprised the report. My journal sketch of it must be unique, since the island vanished after our early explosion there of an atomic bomb.

We lay off Vostock all one day rolling heavily and left for Flint at sunset. Bad weather came on during the middle watch with rain squalls. When not on watch I was pitched out of my bunk twice. The First Lieutenant landed on Flint and brought off a turtle weighing 265 pounds. So we had turtle eggs for supper but could hardly taste them.

Continuing our southerly track we came to anchor at Papeete on 20 July and saluted the French nation with 21 guns, the salute being duly answered by the *Cassiopée* from her berth, moored stern to the wharf. The normal calls were paid, including the various foreign Consuls, and the Captain called on the Governor of Tahiti with the British Consul.

HMS *LABURNUM* AT PAPEETE (TAHITI) 20th-27th JULY 1928
BORA BORA. ATIU. RARATONGA

The combination of Penrhyn pearls, Tahitian cheap champagne and beer had a depressing effect on some of our men. One could understand how the mutineers of the Bounty succumbed to the charms of the local women, many of whom were of mixed parentage. We averaged three leave breakers a day, and I claimed one shilling (five pence) a day for making substantial use of my knowledge of the French language with the Police! The net result was only too apparent and kept our Doctor busy at his vocation. Hitherto he had found life onboard a Flower Class sloop an excellent opportunity to learn the various jobs done by Executive Officers, and mastered gunnery, navigation, signals, and cable work besides watch-keeping. Doctor Pollard could be described as a proper Naval officer. Previously his day had consisted of about five minutes writing up the Wardroom wine books, ten minutes to complete the Times crossword puzzle, and not more than twenty minutes in the sick bay.

Coaling with basket hoists at Papeete took 15½ hours over two days before we could leave for Bora Bora, entering Teavanui Pass and anchoring off Vaitape Village in 17 fathoms with the usual spring on the cable to provide as much ventilation as possible in the heat. I went ashore in the skiff under sail to call on the Agent Speciale, a French Army Warrant Officer. I recalled that it was here that Von Spee coaled *Scharnhorst* and *Gneisenau* and entertained the French Sergeant-in-Charge under British colours, before the Battle of Coronel against Admiral Craddock's light cruisers early in World War I.

Cassiopée brought Governor Bouge from Papeete and the Administrator of a neighbouring island complete with wife and retinue. Calls were repeated as at Papeete and lunch and dinner parties were given ashore.

In a flat calm sea, *Laburnum* carried out her three-fifths power trial lasting eight hours and called at Harvey Island. After repairing the Resident Agent's motorboat, Chief came with me for a delightful bathe and run along the sands wearing helmets and gym shoes. Here Mr Bunting, ex-Royal Naval Reserve, as the Agent kept everything in good order, bungalow whitewashed, etc., and was making a garden. Next day we steamed round the uninhabited island of Takutea and on 13 miles to Atiu where 20 of us landed, being carried ashore from the reef on the backs of natives. They gave us a big feast and many presents, garlanded us with beads and flowers, and loaded us up with oranges which grow wild as do limes and candle nuts. Mr and Mrs Scott gave us tea, he being the Resident Administrative Agent, and she made a lot of cakes herself.

With 800 inhabitants, 20,000 cases of oranges were exported annually. There are three denominations of churches there and as it was Sunday they refrained from demonstrating their prowess at sports and spear throwing or their rather unique style of cricket which saves having to run!

After another night at sea we anchored in the roadstead off Avadnua Harbour in Raratonga on a ledge, two cables from the reef, and kept steam at one hour's notice. Calls were exchanged with the Resident Commissioner, Mr Ayson, who was saluted with eleven guns under the Red Ensign on leaving the ship.

· HMS *LABURNUM* AT RARATONGA, NIUE, PAGO PAGO
14-22 AUGUST 1928. WALLIS ISLAND. SUVA

Entertainment at Raratonga included a ball and garden party for the Officers and a dance for the men, and drives round the Island with bathing, cricket and tennis. Our departure was somewhat delayed on account of the anchor fouling the coral.

Heavy rolling during a night trip with a heavy swell and wind on

28

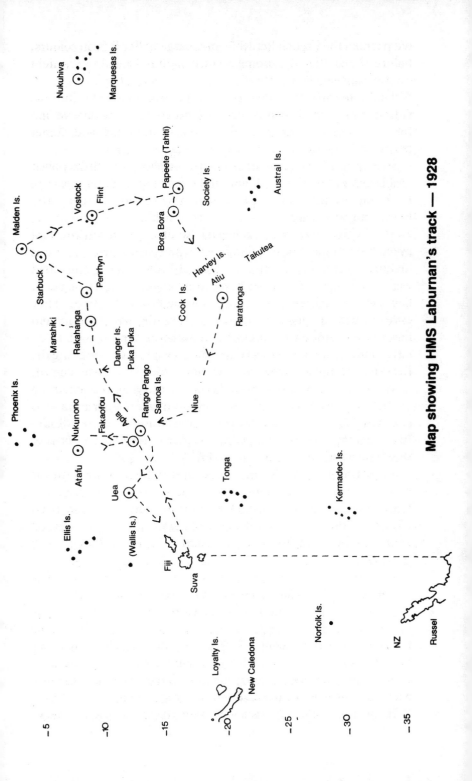

Map showing HMS Laburnan's track — 1928

the port quarter, course south 75 west at seven knots brought us to Nieu and anchorage in Alofi Harbour. Mr Luckham the Resident Commissioner called and was saluted with the customary 11 guns. We collected mail and delivered one from Raratonga. This is a famous place for bananas and straw hats. After a day there we left for Pago Pago once more, just like coming home after our island cruise. The Governor was away and Commander Le Bourgeois was acting for him, so apart from our salute to the national flag, official calls were dispensed with. Commander Le Bourgeois took me sailing again in his Pau Pau canoe and we swam on the coral bottom wearing goggles.

My last few days were somewhat spoiled as a result of a late night, regatta practice and a mile swim, which gave me 'flu. I was unable to keep watch until we reached Wallis Island three days later. Arriving at Uea we entered the lagoon and proceeded by devious channels ten miles from the entrance and anchored in five fathoms with a spring on the cable. The French Resident and wireless operator came onboard and asked us to tea the following day, Sunday. They were the only white people on the island apart from two Roman Catholic missionaries. We took their mail for Suva where we anchored on 29 August. RMS *Niagara* arrived on 31 August (my father's birthday), with him, my mother and sister, and Miss Bavin, daughter of the Prime Minister of New South Wales and Mrs Attwood onboard. The Captain and I went to meet the ship on arrival, and my father left in the *Niagara* for a month's leave in England. The Captain gave me 48 hours leave with the family at Government House, ostensibly to recover from 'flu! HMS *Brisbane* and HMNZS *Dunedin* arrived on 2 September and I boarded them both as Officer of the Guard, with my formal pendant flying. On the 5th, Commodore Swabey invited me and the family to dinner onboard and there was a dance at Government House afterwards. He inspected the *Laburnum* with his Staff the following day and gave us a very good report before sailing.

Richmond and I went with the Government House party in the launch *Adi Beti*, four hours' steaming inside the reef and via the Rewa river to the Island of Bau. The Governor, His Excellency Sir Eyre Hutson, was presented with a whale's tooth, and we saw a Kava ceremony, a Mecci and a war club dance. We were met by a fleet of sailing canoes and went out in a big one belonging to Rata Pope the Chief who gave us an excellent dinner and concert, with girls singing the news in verse until he dozed off to sleep. Lieutenant Richmond and I returned to Suva on the mainland by taxi, which stopped at a cafe four miles up the road, and we had visions of having to walk 18 miles in the dark.

Back at Suva there was considerable social activity and *Laburnum* defeated the *Veronica* very handsomely, having accepted their challenge to a regatta.

HMS *LABURNUM* AT SUVA AND LAUTOKA

Later the *Veronica*'s fishing party deposited me on the quarantine island of Mukalouva where I spent a pleasant weekend with the Government House party.

On her way to Lautoka, SS *Endymion* hit a pinnacle rock in mid-channel in Nandi waters. The rock was hitherto undetected, and we were sent up to survey the area and chart the rock.

My first experience of surveying under instruction from Pilot (the navigating officer) started with me whitewashing a steep sandy cliff – and myself into the bargain – and covering a very prickly bush with a white tarpaulin.

We had two Fijian launches which steamed 100 yards apart, with a wire between them, and found the rock during our sixth sweep and buoyed it. I had to make accurate fixes using sextant and station pointer during the 10-mile sweep each way, giving helm orders to the coxswain of the launch in Fijian. The only Fijian word I knew was 'Benaka, Benaka', meaning very good, but it worked. I would say 'Benaka, Benaka Sou' Sou' West', and he would acknowledge with 'Benaka Sou' Sou' West', and when on his course ordered, would report, 'Benaka, Benaka Sou' Sou' West' and I would acknowledge with 'Benaka, Benaka', meaning very good. At the end of the run I would order 'Benaka, Benaka Nor' Nor' East', and he would shout to the other launch which then stopped while we went round in a circle until steering North North East and the coxswain reported 'Benaka, Benaka, Nor' Nor' East', meaning he was on his course, and so we proceeded like that for two days. We named our beacons and buoys for accurate fixing and easy reference, Rum, Hops, Gin, Fizz, Beer, Port, using two at a time for the station pointer. Reading the sextant angles in the bright sun to a minute of arc was rather trying for the eyes. We continued sweeping a channel for shipping six and a half miles long and half a mile wide, between the rock now named Turtle Rock and Curacoa Beacon. After recovering the mark buoys we proceeded to anchorage off Lautoka meeting Mr Farquhar, owner of the sugar mills, and played some golf and a good cricket match.

The idea was for the ship to carry out a bombardment by indirect fire at long range, using single line observation and Forward Observation Officer controlling. That was me. We took one and a half hours to reach Lovuka Island where the ship was anchored out of sight of the target, which was a sand cay. The range was 10,000 yards and I was 900 yards from the cay, which was meant to represent a cruiser taken by surprise at dawn. A whistle proved most useful to warn the engine driver of the generator to rev up before transmitting. My team were about 150 yards back in the bushes out of sight of the enemy. 24 rounds were fired, two of high explosive, two of semi-armour piercing, the rest practice shell which hit the cay five times; I brought back one shell brightly polished by the sand for a doorstop.

HMS *LABURNUM* AT LAUTOKA, SUVA AND AUCKLAND. LEAVE TO THE THERMAL REGIONS WITH MY BROTHER

After a picnic lunch and bathe I sent the bombardment equipment back to the ship in the motor boat and sailed the ten miles back to Lautoka in the whaler.

Returning to Suva the Captain handed out chocolates including some from the Governor for our work in Nandi waters. More socialising followed, including a progressive dinner party with seven different courses each in a different house.

On Monday 15 October, we left Fiji for Auckland, carrying mails, and did a futher three-fifths power trial for eight hours with 130 revs at 12 knots. Hands turned out in blues on our second day out and I had to disguise the fact that my uniform had two stripes when I would still be a Sub-Lieutenant for some weeks. All my blue uniforms had been sent home to Messrs Gieve for second stripes, assuming that they would not be required for at least six months.

On the third day out the wind veered from South East to North East Force five, and we set the foresail. At times we had been under sail with three sails to steady the ship and help us along.

Back at Auckland, we secured on *Veronica* at Devonport at 0515 on Saturday, 20 October and sent 40 men on first leave.

Surgeon-Lieutenant Frankie Quinn was there to relieve Pollard, who we took out for a farewell dinner and cinema, followed by an impromptu party onboard.

My mother and sister arrived from Honolulu on 4 December and I took them with half the passengers of the *Niagara* to the Cargen Hotel and then over to Takapuna. My brother Somerset came over from Sydney on 17 December. Meanwhile, after various gunnery exercises and some rough weather, *Laburnum* moored ship in Port Fitzroy, a very fine harbour.

My mother took a house at Takapuna, then a quiet village. We had a tennis party followed by a cabaret with Gwen Fullerton and June Craig who stayed the night with us. Onboard, Christmas Day was celebrated in fine style with many callers before I got rid of them before my family arrived for lunch and to spend the day onboard. I allowed the men to have their rum mixed one-and-one* as a treat. Somerset and I stayed a night at Dr Fullerton's house and developed films before going to Rotorua where Rangi the well-known guide showed us round, and then to a Maori concert which I liked so much I attended twice.

We drove to Wairaki, visiting the Aratia Rapids and Huka Falls en route, saw the Karapiti blowhole and bathed in the hot sulphur baths after supper. Thence to the National Park, via Lake Taupo, passing under Mt Ruapehu which I sketched. From the Vice-Regal train we were driven to Waitomo and Arapuni to see the dam and hydroelectric scheme and the Glow-worm Caves at Waitomo. A fascinating sight. Any noise and they stop glowing so we had to be quiet to see them.

HMS *LABURNUM* AT AUCKLAND. JANUARY 1929 AND
COMBINED OPERATIONS. FEBRUARY

Laburnum sailed for Tauranga and anchored off Mt Maunganui until slack water allowed for going up-river to within two miles of

---

*One part rum and one part water, instead of the usual one part rum and three parts water. This mixture is properly called grog.

Tauranga where we moored ship. We dined with Commander Fell, Rtd., at his farm and bathed in the river. I rode back in a bathing dress. Ferry boats ran liberty trips for us until 6 p.m. and we gave leave until 11 p.m. From all accounts Mt Maunganui would be an ideal place for a holiday – good surf. Our Signalman gave the Boy Scouts lessons and I took some of them sailing in the whaler. After four days we unmoored and proceeded to Kawau where four of us landed after tea for a bathe.

After various drills and combined exercises with the cruisers, we returned to Auckland and Pilot and I took our girlfriends to a very well-acted play. The family left for Sydney in the *Niagara* on 29 January. After various parties I noted that Gold Flake (Gwen Fullerton), GF for short, and I sat in the dicky of June Craig's car, rather cold, but the end justified the means. Lieutenant Richmond and June sitting in front were soon to become engaged. GF was an expert photographer and a very good friend to me, and we put up a good smokescreen for the happy couple until the announcement was made.

COMBINED OPERATIONS AND THE BATTLE OF WOOFIT

An opposed landing planned after the model of Gallipoli at Orewa in Whangaparoa Bay a few miles north of Auckland was code-named WOOFIT. The beach was defended by Blue Force and the two cruisers and sloops followed by Wakakura as Red Force were manoeuvred by wireless as they approached in line abreast two and a half cables (500 yards) apart. When one and a half miles from the beach, anchors were lowered by capstans to four fathoms and all ships anchored by veering three shackles to avoid the rattling of cable running out as usual. When troops were embarked, tows formed up astern of the ships and motorboat engines all started together by signal from the Commodore in *Dunedin*. They then all went ahead keeping station on the centre. Because of the complete darkness it was only possible to see the nearest tow, and I was hailed by the *Diomede*'s leader. Despite all the noise of cable being lowered and motorboat engines starting up, this hail was the first intimation that Blue Force had of impending invasion, but by the time tows were slipped and boats were approaching under oars, the alarm had been given and a fierce fire was opened on the troops and boats during the landing, with rockets lighting us up. Without the element of surprise it was obvious how futile the attempt would have been.

However, despite the shambles, Red Force claimed a glorious victory, having gained their three objectives ashore.

My own contribution was not without some personal satisfaction. As Cable Officer, I had always maintained that cable on deck should be whitewashed and not painted; cracks would show through whitewash but were easily hidden when painted over. Having lost my battle with the First Lieutenant, who preferred paint, I saw the 31st link in the ganger on the starboard cable with a gap of an inch between the ends. It must have opened up when the anchor was sheeted home after marking the four-fathom mark with white paint. Fortunately we used the port anchor, or I could never have convinced my superiors of being blameless for loss of the anchor. Another quarter of an inch and it would have gone.

After a sleepless night for the Pilot and one hour's sleep for me, I was late for a party organised by Gold Flake and self for him and his fiancée. Then *Laburnum* departed for Lyttleton carrying out the routine three-fifths power trial en route. It came on to blow, decks awash and shipping green seas over the fo'c'sle, 'bouncing up and down like a bloomin' rockin' 'orse', as one sailor put it. The ship was virtually hove to at four knots during Sunday afternoon and night. We had a very good collier and winchmen for coaling at Lyttleton, and Pilot and I were taken out to dinner and a theatre by Betty Rutherford from Canterbury. Eight years later she wrote in astonishment to congratulate me on my first command.

After only one day at Lyttleton, we proceeded south to Dunedin again, my favourite port of call. The Captain went to meet Mrs Attwood at Oamaru, and she was able to join in with the considerable festivities and entertainment. Apart from nuisance from small boys while the ship was open to visitors, the visit was a great success. Dr Williams lent me his Buick in which I drove his daughter Lettie in a treasure hunt organised by Pilot. About 50 people took part, but the hills are very steep and I had to cool the brakes with two buckets of water when they were smoking at the bottom of one hill.

Our week at Dunedin passed all too quickly and we made our way to Timaru where, after complicated manoeuvring, we secured to the jetty with huge hemp springs because of the heavy swell in the harbour. General drill was exercised and Commander and Mrs Attwood took Mr Thomas, the Chief, and me with their two children for a 150-mile drive towards Mount Cook where we picnicked. A delightful day 30 miles from Mount Cook, passing Lake Takepo, the deepest in New Zealand and very beautiful, a sort of verdigris green. Whilst at Timaru, a signal arrived announcing the expected arrival of my relief, Sub-Lieutenant Thew, who had left England in SS *Tainui* on 1 March, and saying the sloops were due to recommission. More entertainment with the proverbial New Zealand hospitality which we tried to reciprocate.

After nine days at Timaru, we departed on 11 March for Paterson Inlet in Stewart Island at the extreme south of New Zealand.

HMS *LABURNUM* AT STEWART ISLAND.
BAD WEATHER, LYTTLETON, PICTON AND WELLINGTON

We anchored between *Dunedin* and *Diomede* which was just as well, because the whaler in which I was endeavouring to coach a Leading Seaman capsized during a fierce squall and we were picked up by *Dunedin*'s motorboat. The Captain met me on the gangway and said, 'What happened, Mr de Chair?' and I said, 'I'd rather not tell you until I have had a bath.' The water was very cold, 54°F.

The week's programme, including a convoy exercise, was cancelled on account of the bad weather, and ships were ordered to sail as convenient. Our plan was to visit Milford Sound on the West coast and I knew the Captain was as keen as I was to see these beautiful fjords. The wind increased to gale force from the North West during the middle watch and there was a sudden drop in the barometer. I did not call the Captain as I knew if I did we would have to turn the ship round. However, the matter was decided, because he was pitched out of his bunk and we made for Nelson, but the harbour authorities there could not give us a berth. Commodore New Zealand gave us permission to go to Lyttleton where we berthed on *Veronica*, to that ship's intense annoyance. However, we combined efforts to return hospitality and Mrs Attwood and Gold Flake arrived from Hokitika. They had been walking up the glacier there with a guide called Al. After three hours' climbing, they all sat down to rest and Al felt impelled to entertain the ladies. Suddenly he said, 'Bet you I can tell your ages!' Mrs Attwood said, 'well, Al, how old am I?' 'I should say you was between 36 and 38', says Al. 'Quite right', she says, 'I'm 37'. So Gwen pipes up and asks 'And how old am I?' 'Well,' he says, 'you've got a full mouth, I should say you was 27', which was accurate. So they both say to Al, 'Al, how can you tell?' 'Well,' he says, 'you see, I've lived with sheep!'

After a week of jollification in Christchurch, we wended our way to Picton against a heavy sea and much pitching through the Tory Channel and a seven knot current into Queen Charlotte Sound.

The First Lieutenant and I went for a riding picnic with the Tripe family again, passing the monument at Massacre Hill where the Maoris had tomahawked the party sent to survey the land purchased from them by the British Government. We rode about 20 miles.

The Navy League gave a dance for the sailors attended by Commander and Mrs Attwood. This function was sadly marred by bad behaviour and some fighting, which resulted in several arrests and some lovely black eyes had developed by the time we got to Port Nicholson for Wellington. Ronnie Hunter-Blair met us there as the First Lieutenant's relief and on 8 April, five days after our arrival, Pug Thew joined as my relief and had rather a rush turnover. On 9 April I ceased Naval duty and left for Sydney in RMS *Makura* to be Aide-de-Camp to my father.

4

Aide de Campe to the Governor of New South Wales 1929-1930

My mother and sister met me, after an enjoyable trip in the *Makura* with congenial company. The Captain, Commander Springbrown RNR, made me an honorary member of the bridge and the Second Officer, Lieutenant Todd RNR, invited me to bring three bachelor friends to sit at his table. On arrival at Government House, I relieved Lieutenant-Commander Lowther as Aide de Campe (ADC) and soon got the feel of what the Signal School describes as 'Bell hop'.

The Prime Minister and Mrs Bavin and their daughter Shirley came to lunch and I went to the opening performance of Pavlova's dance opera on the first day. We then called on the Governor-General, Lord Stonehaven, and Mr Bruce, ·Prime Minister of Australia.

On the second day, Sunday 14 April, after tea at Admiralty House, Kirribilli, with Lady Stonehaven, I went to Moss Vale with the family for two days in the country. Returning to Sydney, I was invited to travel on the engine for part of the way. My father, hereafter referred to as His Excellency (HE), and the family attended a Pavlova matinee and Captain and Mrs Springbrown of the *Makura* came to tea.

On Thursday, 18 April, various dignitaries called, and HE inspected HMAS *Albatross* and the submarine *Otway*. Anna Pavlova and friends came to lunch and we were shown round the new Dutch liner, *Nieuw Zeiland*.

And so it went on with my father and mother engaged in continuous official social functions, most of which I attended. Brigadier-General Anderson was the Private Secretary, seldom seen after lunch, and Mr Budge was the Parliamentary Secretary. I was responsible for issuing and keeping the record of all invitations and doing the introductions.

ANZAC day, 25 April, required the Governor to be in two places at once and I represented him at St Andrew's Cathedral where, escorted by the Police Inspector, I arrived two minutes

38

late, having been held up in traffic by men who had returned from Gallipoli.

Our visit to the Riverina on the Murray River was the first by a Governor for twenty-three years, when my father's uncle, Sir Harry Rawson, was Governor of New South Wales. The combination of wheat and wool industry and great loyalty was most impressive. Most of the trade is with Victoria across the Murray River, and great rivalry is only to be expected between the two States. They even have differing gauges for their railways.

The Riverina is the most fertile part of New South Wales and raises between one and a half and three sheep to the acre, in comparison with parts of Western Australia, where it is one sheep to 50 acres. They say the sheep there eat the wool off each other's backs! At Wanganella Estate, Mr Otway Falconer showed us David, a ram he bought from Mr Fred McMaster for £5,000. His son Mac took me across country in a sports car, chasing emus and kangaroos. One wallaby jumped over the bonnet and I shot an emu with my pistol at 40 mph. Otty Falconer was reputed to have turned over four times in his Rolls, doing this sort of thing, but suffered no ill-effects to himself.

During one week in the Riverina from 29 May to 6 June, HE made 42 speeches, my mother 33, my sister Elaine four, and I escaped with two mostly at schools.

As ADC I received no emoluments from Naval Funds, but my father gave me £200 a year and all found, including the use of the Crossley touring car which I often drove to Bondi Beach to surf before breakfast.

A three-valve short-wave set and buzzer installed in my office enabled me to keep in practice on Morse, having been recommended for the long signal course in England.

My father had brought twelve members of domestic staff from England; Turner the Butler was already there and coped with many odd situations, from a lady calling herself the 'Queen of England – just going up to my rooms', to a rather aggrieved Second Footman whom I reprimanded for speaking to the Governor with his hands on his hips.

The New Zealand Squadron visited Sydney on 29 June, and I was able to arrange for the Officers to be Honorary Members of the Australia Club and Rose Bay Golf Club of which I was also an Honorary Member. I played a good deal of golf, and after three months of lessons, the Pro said to me, 'I'll make a golfer of you yet, Sir.'

My sister Elaine and I represented our parents at various functions in Newcastle, arriving on 9 July, being met by the Mayor and Mayoress and Town Clerk before going to stay with my cousin Dymphna and her husband, the Dean of Newcastle, Bill Johnson (later Bishop of Ballarat). At Walsh Island dockyard I launched a train car and saw the mid-section of a floating dock which I also launched. Thence to the steel works and after some golf represented HE at a Military Ball. Our last of the three days was spent on Lake McQuarie, followed by a private dinner and a smoke-oh with the soldiers. During this time HE was acting as Governor-General in the absence of Lord Stonehaven who was in HMAS *Albatross* visiting Papua.

KOSCIUSKO ON LEAVE. THEN SYDNEY AND SOME HOLIDAYS

Elaine and I spent the next ten days at Kosciusko where I won a two-mile ski handicap race by dint of falling down at the right places and rubbing my skis in mud for the hill climbs. We shared a sitting room in the hotel with 14 other people, and drove back to Sydney in Jack Gunn's car, staying with the Osborne family at Currandooley. Margaret Osborne, commenting on their name, said it was very common in Australia, 'but rabbits are our worst pest!' Four days later, Elaine and I returned to Kosciusko for another ten days with the ski club, where I made a trip to the summit on skis. Leaving the girls of the party at Betts Camp, Dr Peter Braddon, Flight-Lieutenant Dennis Moore and Dr Cato with George Aalberg, the Norwegian professional, and I, set off up Charlotte's Pass towards the ridge. Pounds Hut provided a very welcome rest where we had a cup of tea and half-frozen tinned peaches. The hut had been built to commemorate the loss of three men who perished in a blizzard there the year before.

The final ascent was a sore trial to me. The ridge was all knob ice and my friends refused to let me take my skis off and carry them. Between us and the summit was a valley with a snowdrift at the bottom, I belive covering the snowy river, called Rawson's Pass after my great-uncle. The descent consisted of slabs of sheet ice, with a short drop between each. Being the worst skier in the party,

40

I watched them go. George Aalburg reached the bottom, and I could see him as a little black speck, hopping and still standing. Then the others disappeared and it was my turn. Very steep with no possible means of control, I threw my sticks away in good time, and tried to do a telemark stop at the bottom. The result was apparently spectacular, and I did two or three somersaults, landing head down in the drift with nothing but a pair of skis showing. My friends dug me out with no ill-effects and we side-stepped up the steep slope to the summit, from which we had glorious views, and could see Mount Buffalo 85 miles to the south. Side-stepping down was more difficult for me than going up, but we eventually all met again at Pounds Hut and had a wonderful run back to Betts Camp from Charlotte's Pass, where a hotel has since been built.

Back in Sydney I was taken over the southern portion of the Harbour Bridge under construction by Dorman Long at a cost of £4½ million.

The end of July was marked by a visit by the French cruiser *Tourville* and a dance given by Donald Anderson on board the Orient liner *Orama* for sixty friends. The Governor-General came to stay for five days and we spent a weekend at Canberra with him and Lady Stonehaven. Then I went with my mother to Lismore where she opened a musical festival. It is a very fertile and rich area of dairy farms.

Race Week in Sydney from 4 to 14 October included dances and social engagements without a break, and I was glad of a chance to stay a couple of days with Doug and Gordon Munro at Keera, near the Queensland border. We entered for every event in the Bingara Show, bending races, tent-pegging, jumps, and a bucking bullock competition to finish with. In view of press reports, my father was not amused at my taking part in the latter event.

October ended with a three-day stay for us with the Hore-Ruthvens at Adelaide, and with the Stonehavens and all State Governors and their Staffs for Melbourne Cup Week, dances every night, and much entertaining by the Baillieus, Hunters and Shackells.

Hamish MacDonald asked me to stay at Wanterbadgery West, Wagga Wagga, and lent me his prize horse Robkin, a beautiful jumper. We mustered two paddocks and did some sheep work before attending a cattle sale.

41

In December we stayed with the Fred McMasters at their show sheep station, Dalkeith, probably the best in New South Wales, and very well run. Unlike some owners he lives there and does not leave everything to a Manager. I heard a certain station owner living in England was not satisfied with the financial returns and wired to his Manager 'start shearing'. Back came a reply 'can't start shearing, lambing'. To which he retorted 'stop lambing at once and start shearing.'

A LONG WAY HOME. QUEENSLAND, MACASSAR, BALI AND JAVA TO SINGAPORE

I returned to Melbourne for Christmas with the Baillieus which was spent at their hill station at Masterton. A very skilful drive by Bill Baillieu up the hills on very skiddy roads got us there safely and a good time was had by all.

Rear-Admiral Evans invited my father and me to visit Hobart in HMAS *Australia*, his flagship, and we stayed with Sir James O'Grady, the Governor, a delightful character who had been an Irish cabinet-maker and ran Government House with a staff of one and his daughter as secretary. Tasmania had asked for a Labour Governor but were surprised to find that they had to provide a car and pay for all entertainment.

Federal Ministers had been told what a fine place Jervis Bay was after we visited the Naval College there, and decided that it was much too good for budding Naval Officers. Accordingly it was requisitioned as a holiday resort for Federal Ministers and their families. I gather the decision was reversed by saner counsels in due course.

ANZAC Day was on 25 April, shortly before our departure from NSW. I think twenty-one VC's were invited to lunch at Government House. One gallant soldier felt he could not come as he had no suitable clothes, so a new suit was provided. 'Well, Ryan,' I said, 'how do you like your new suit?' 'Best suit I ever slept in, Sir', he said.

Five days later we left by train for Brisbane where we visited the Governor of Queensland, Sir John and Lady Goodwin, and stayed with the Bells of Coochin, where I was initiated into the art of stopping a mob of cattle with a stock whip. After 12 days we boarded the Dutch ship *Nieuw Holland*, KPM, Captain Bauer, travelling under the name of Johnson, as far as Macassar. Three days in Bali and a fortnight in Java included attendance at a Garabeg Bezar and two days as guests of the Governor-General, Jonkheer De Graeff at Buitenzorg. We had a wing of the Palace to ourselves and only met him twice, at dinner the first and last nights of our three-day stay.

From Batavia we took ship in SS *Insulinde* at Tanjong Priok, arriving at Singapore after 36 hours on 22 May, and a sleepless night while unloading went on. Captain Sillitoe, ADC to the Governor, Sir Cecil Clemente, took us to Government House where we stayed for two days. Mr Jacob, the Chief Engineer, showed my father and me round the Naval Base under construction and we went to the races in the afternoon, followed by high jinks later.

ADC, ACCOUNTANT AND STAFF OFFICER (PLANS) TOURING THE ORIENT. SHANGHAI, PEKIN AND WEY HAI

My mother had spent a profitable day in Singapore, Chinese bed-hunting inter alia, which the ADC sent home in a crate. She sent a telegram to the Governor of French Indo-China, asking if an aircraft could take us to Angkor Wat, but the air age had not so far reached this tourist attraction, and after a leisurely passage to Saigon in SS *Porthos*, Messagerie Maritime, the Governor's ADC arranged transport to Phnom Penh by car. There, the Governor of Cambodia called after 11 p.m., having taken his sweetie to the cinema, and said he was instructed to provide two cars to take us to Angkor and back, and then to Saigon. My journal contains 12 pages about Angkor Wat and Angkor Tom, including its ancient history and the decline of the Khamer Empire.

The *Porthos* took us to Shanghai and the French doctor took HE and me round the Chinese city. Going for a walk later with the doctor, we crossed a bridge and looked into a building to the surprise of a meeting of Communists who rose up and chased us back across the bridge, where we felt safe. HM Gunboats *Gannet* and *Petrel* were near our berth and John Waldegrave had a party for Elaine and me with Singleton who had already played the piano for the orchestras of 75 cabarets. After three jolly days with our friends in Shanghai, we embarked in the Blue Funnel Liner SS *Hector*, doing a trip round the Gulf of Pechilli. She was like a breath of spring after the smoke-laden *Porthos*; spotless white decks and smartness personified. Made one proud to be British.

The Editor of the *Tsingtao Times* showed us round the German Defences after we had gone to the top of Lao Shan, the first range of hills captured by the Japanese, from the Germans in 1914.

Friday, 13 June at Wei-Hai-Wei, Elaine and I left our parents with Lady Pearce and went by launch to the mainland where we climbed Pinnacle Hill with Thea Meyer, a charming Danish girl, leading without shoes, and her two sisters.

Next day the *Hector* anchored off Taku bar, 16 miles out, and we went ashore by launch, running aground on the bar, where we were restrained from accepting lifts in a junk by the Customs Officer, so only caught the train to Pekin by the skin of our teeth.

Three days of feverish shopping in Pekin at bargain prices occupied most of our time including lunch in the British Legation with Sir Miles Lampson who had an array of carpets laid out for our inspection. To me my father said 'you mustn't let them buy another thing.' Eventually seven pantechnicons of furniture etc. reached England. Of course we visited all the possible tourist attractions including what an American writer described as 'a woman's fifty miilion dollar whim', the Summer Palace built in 1860 for twenty-four million taels by the Empress Dowager, money allocated for building ships for the Chinese Navy; the marble boat by a lake being the nearest approach to a ship the old lady wanted.

HOMEWARD BOUND. DAIREN. JAPAN

At Dairen we left the *Hector* and by a smart evolution Elaine and I secured four double-berth cabins on board the Japanese liner *Hong Kong Maru*, bound for Kobe through the Inland Sea, after a visit to Shimonoseki. The ship berthed alongside with a White Ensign at the fore as compliment to HE. Admiral Kobayashi sent his ADC, Lieutenant Kaseda Cho IJN, to meet and look after us to Kyoto, where we stayed at the Myako Hotel. Meanwhile the Manager of Messagerie Maritime arranged for all our baggage to be landed from the *Porthos* and sent to Kyoto.

After ascending Mount Hior by funicular and on foot, with the ladies in chairs, Kaseda took me to the oldest restaurant in Kyoto, 'Sumiya' by name, an interesting experience to say the least. After several apparitions appeared, mine host informed me that, if I gave a girl nine glasses of Sake, I would be expected to marry her. I was sorry to disappoint him.

Professor Sadler in Sydney had arranged for the Master of the Tea Ceremony in Japan, San Tan Tan Sei, to invite us to a ceremony in his own home, an unsual privilege for foreigners. His ancestors had been Masters of the Tea Ceremony to the Emperor's Household for fourteen generations.

At Nara, Elaine nearly had a fight with a roe deer after feeding it. There we saw a three hundred-year-old tree which, by grafting with seven varieties, bore six different leaves in different places. In the Todaiji Temple, Elaine had to be hauled into Paradise after passing through a small square hole at the base of one of the huge wooden pillars of Daibitsu; the hauling was undertaken by three strong men.

From Nara by train, car and walking three miles, we put up at the Sho-jo-Shin Temple at Koya San, the centre of Zen Buddhism. I was kept awake most of the night by two members of the Imperial Household jabbering away in the next room, separated by a paper screen. This was followed by a somewhat uncomfortable Prayer Ceremony from 5 a.m.

Sunday, 29 June. Prince and Princess Takamatsu were welcomed in London by the King and Queen, so that our visit to tombs of the Emperor Meiji and Empress Shoken in great ceremony was well timed.

We had a delightful train journey to Kozu, exquisite scenery including a clear view of Mount Fujiyama. From Kozu we drove to Myonoshita, through Odawa by the sea, completely destroyed in the 1923 earthquake. It received no relief for three weeks until a British gunboat from Hong Kong arrived. At Myonoshita, our guide, 'Nishi', left his Will at the desk, considering our walk into the valley dangerous.

The Vice-Minister of Marine, Vice-Admiral Kobayashi met us on arrival in Tokyo. Mr and Mrs Shimidzu who had travelled with us in the *Nieuw Holland* from Brisbane were also there. I stayed with Captain Legge, our Naval Attache, and the family stayed in the Embassy with Sir John and Lady Tilley.

On Friday, 4 July, my parents were received in audience by the

Emperor and Empress after the Ambassador, and spoke for about ten minutes through an interpreter.

HOMEWARD BOUND. JAPAN, CALIFORNIA AND HAWAII

Baron Sakatani, President of the Japan-Australia Association, gave a lunch party for us at which I was seated between Admiral Takarabe, the Minister of Marine who also entertained us at the Naval Club, and Vice-Admiral Kobayashi, both of whom spoke English. My only indiscretion was to get them both to autograph my menu card, but they seemed pleasantly complimented.

Admiral Kobayashi took us to a theatre where we met our old friend Mr Shimidzu. We had been reluctant to accept all his offers of hospitality, but thought it would be nice to introduce him to the Admiral. To our surprise, the Admiral turned his back on him. Possibly something to do with a building contract and, we thought, rather snobbish. Eventually, to make up for his loss of face, we accepted Mr Shimidzu's offer of a drive to Nikko in his Lincoln car to see the cherry blossom and the Toshogu Temple, and various other beauty spots.

On 10 July, Kaseda took HE and me to Yokosuka and the flagship of the First Fleet, HIJMS *Mutsu* which was at that time refitting, and round the harbour in the Port Admiral's barge. All very interesting, not least in the ships and things we were not shown. The new cruisers were at sea. Baron Harada took us to the Ju Jitsu School where the instructor gave an enthralling exhibition of the art in the afternoon. That evening, Mr Yonosuki Shimidzu took me to see the first revue ever held in Japan. I finished the evening by sitting on his hat! Price Y 1.50. In a note, I see 'Lieutenant-Commander Thatcher will provide another.'

Next morning we went to say goodbye to Admiral Kobayashi and were received by Flag Commander Oka and taken to the office of the Minister of Marine where we talked with him and Kobayashi; despite Admiral Takarabe's known antipathy to Admiral Togo, he became quite enthusiastic over my father's eulogies about the Battle of Tsushima in the Russo-Japanese war.

From Yokohama, we embarked on board the SS *Asama Maru* (Captain Shinomiya) calling at Honolulu where we stayed two days, having crossed the date line on Christmas Day. With typical

46

Japanese hospitality, Christmas was celebrated on two days running to keep to 25 December – presents, turkey and all.

Somerset came over from Oxford to join us in San Fransico, whence we proceeded to Los Angeles to stay at the Biltmore Hotel and visit Yosemite Valley. We were entertained by Douglas Fairbanks and Mary Pickford in her dressing-room (lunch for 17), and at their beach home, Pickfair. After three weeks' holiday we returned to San Francisco for a conference at Berkeley University, for which Somerset came as a Delegate from Australia, and I as one from New Zealand. Thanks to an article by Admiral McGruder, USN, in the *Christian Science Monitor*, I was able to debunk some scurrilous remarks by a Commander regarding Britain and the 5:5:3 ratio of warships with the USA and Japan agreed at the International conference.

It saddens me to think that, after all the apparent good will in Japan, within 11 years we should be fighting each other to the death.

CALIFORNIA AND CANADA

Whilst still at Los Angeles I called on my Godfather, Dr Lyndley, who gave me a lovely Longines wrist watch; I also spent a very interesting day with Major Burnham, fishing for tuna off Catalina Island. We caught nothing but I never spent a more interesting seven hours with one man. His book 'Scouting on Two Continents' says it all.

My brother Somerset and I spent a day on board the ferry from Los Angeles to San Francisco, reclining near the stern amid coils of rope and young people enjoying the sunshine. From San Francisco we took the train through the redwoods to Seattle and rejoined the family before crossing Canada in the Canadian National Railway with the help of the Chairman, Sir Henry Thornton. We stayed two days in log cabins adjoining the hotel at Jasper Park by the lake, where a mock raid by Red Indians was provided for our benefit. At various stops, including Winnipeg, I left the stations and ran for up to twenty minutes into the cities taking photographs, causing some anxiety on the part of the family lest I be left behind.

My father and I stayed four days in Montreal while the rest of

47

the family visited Boston and New York. I went down to Lennox-ville to see the house my father was born in and lived in until he was six years old. On a window I found his name which he must have scratched before leaving for England, DUDLEY DE CHAIR. At Montreal he was made Hon. LL.D. of McGill University and an Honorary Chief of the Hopi Tribe of Red Indians.

After a year as ADC in Sydney and keeping the accounts and planning for our trip home lasting six months, my father evidently considered that I had a flair for organisation!

As an Acting Sub-Lieutenant, I had chosen as my subject for a lecture during the Divisional Course, 'How Canada Was Won', and I was very keen to see the Anse du Foulon or Goat track, up which General Wolfe's men climbed to the Heights of Abraham. My father agreed to look after the luggage while I took the night train to Quebec, with breakfast at the Chateau Frontenac, and duly set off on my quest with camera, binoculars and map. Instead of a goat-track, I found a main road going up the hill and was proceeding up it, hot and dusty, feeling rather lost. Suddenly out of a side road shot a sports car with a pretty girl driving it, so I doffed my hat and said 'excuse me, but can you tell me where the goat-track is?' She looked hard at me and said 'If you really want to know, get in', and she took me to her aunt's house, old Miss Price. At the bottom of the garden was a wooden cliff where the goat-track had been. Curiosity being satisfied and finding that my companion Jean Price was some sort of relation, I was only too happy to spend the rest of the day with her family. As it happened, Quebec was playing polo against Montreal that afternoon, and I think Jean's brothers were in the team, so after watching that and tea, I got a speedboat and joined my father in the *Duchess of Richmond* as she steamed past, climbing up a jumping ladder to a side port, evidently quite a normal procedure. The first thing I saw on board was my father's portrait over the door. This ship had been his flagship of the 10th Cruiser Squadron as HMS *Alsatian* of the Allen Line, during the blockade of Germany. Captain Freer now in command, had been his First Lieutenant, so it was a great reunion and privilege being at the Captain's table with Mouse Bromley, whose father had been Captain of the *Camponella* in the same Squadron.

We reached Southampton on 6 September 1930.

5

HMS *Nelson* 1930-31

My appointment to the Flagship of the Home Fleet duly arrived and I joined HMS *Nelson* at Portland on 4 November 1930.

Shortly after joining I relieved Tyrwhitt as Senior Watch-keeper, and my duties covered successively six-inch gun control, 'A' Turret and After 16-inch gun control, besides being number three of the Fo'c'sle Division with most of the paperwork and Divisional lists, messdecks and flats, and Queen Anne's Mansions, the nickname of the bridge structure.

A good deal of social activity occurred before we sailed for the West Indies on 7 January 1931, carrying out exercises with the Fleet as far as Cape Finistere.

My first night watch on the bridge, except for one middle watch, coincided with a night encounter exercise in heavy weather. As everyone else was busily engaged with the enemy, all handling of the ship devolved on me, without much previous experience, but under direct observation from the Admiral's bridge. Many orders were given for alterations of course, but the rain poured down and the wild winds blew a gale on the port quarter causing the Quartermaster to steer with 10-15° of helm. Before I knew where I was the ship was swinging, and refused to stop swinging until she was 15° past her proper course, and the Admiral was asking for the name of the Officer of the Watch. I felt very much under a cloud and must have shown it. Dick Pugh, an Aviator, gave me some friendly advice, and explained that the *Nelson* is a funny ship to handle and pivots about B turret.

By 14 January we had passed the Azores, but still had a wind force eight on the port quarter. HMS *Nelson* was rolling 12 degrees each way, with heavy seas washing down the upper decks. HMS *Hawkins* in company was reporting 40 degrees of roll which reminds me of a signal from that cruiser's Admiral to *Shropshire*: 'How many shores in *Shropshire*?' Reply: 'Dunno, how many Hawes in *Hawkins*?'

I took great pride in Queen Anne's Mansions, the bridge structure, for the cleanliness of which as number three of the Fo'c'sle Division I was responsible. The bad weather presented a heaven-sent opportunity of employing all 64 fo'c'sle ratings at hands fall-in the following morning, scraping, rubbing down and painting, provided the foul weather held; and I sent a chit to my Leading Seaman Pulford for extra scrubbers and scrapers, and put down for a call in time for hands fall-in. Not only did my chit never reach Pulford, but I was not called, and so was not present at hands fall-in at 0540 as arranged with my Divisional Officer, to claim my hands. Naturally he was furious and I was relieved of my command of Queen Anne's Mansions. More mud!

HMS *Nelson* moored ship off Bridgetown, Barbados on 22 January, with the cruisers to seaward of us. HMS *Despatch*, flying the flag of the Commander-in-Chief West Indies was in harbour with Captain Atwood, my old Captain, in command. They gave me an 'At Home', and I had a private yarn with him in his cabin. The usual calls were exchanged, and the Governor, Sir William Robertson gave an 'At Home', which was followed during the next week with much entertainment and sight-seeing, interspersed for the likes of me with Regatta practice and watchkeeping day and night.

Passing St Lucia and Granada at daybreak was a beautiful sight, and during Divisions we were off HMS *Diamond Rock*, and stood in silence in honour of the historic stand for ten months against the French Fleet based in Martinique.

The ship was open to visitors at Dominica and we were entertained ashore. Two of us visited a plantation, riding two very scraggy horses which galloped over rock and root with never a slip, up the narrow pathway to South Chilton. The gig's crew went away the following morning feeling like death, and we sailed in the evening, giving a searchlight display before passing the Saints, a group of rocks close to the waters where Rodney defeated de Grasse on 12 April 1782.

Our next anchorage was in Frigate Bay, St Kitts. Officers had several bathing picnics and there were two dances, the first given by the ladies of St Kitts. There was no love lost between them and the ladies of Dominica, and after they had called for three cheers for HMS *Nelson*, the Senior Officer present must have forgotten which island we were in and called 'Three cheers for DOMINIQUE!' There was a deathly hush.

The Governor of Jamaica, Sir R. Stubbs, was saluted with 17 guns when he returned the Commander-in-Chief's call, and a magnificent programme of entertainment for our visit was worked out. Dances every night and every kind of sport. Four char-a-bancs full of the fo'c'sle men went to Dunn's River about 60 miles from Kingston, and five officers also went there in a taxi. We were so tired that we slept nearly all the way there and back, despite the beautiful scenery.

VISIT TO PANAMA

We picked up a Pilot off Colon breakwater, with the British Naval Attaché and US Liaison Officer, and Dressed Ship with Masthead Flags as we passed through the Gatun Locks, as it was the anniversary of George Washington's birthday.

Arriving at Balboa we dressed ship overall as the first wire went out alongside the pier. Between Gatun Reach and the Culebra cut, our speed was progressively reduced from 15 knots to two, with engines stopped. There we were taken in two by two electric tram cars called mules, running along the sides of Pedro Miguel locks. The locks were only 110 feet wide and we only had two feet to spare either side. I was in charge of fenders starboard side, consisting of long spars, and as we progressed, one of the mules on the port side was pulled into the canal, causing damage to the ship about ten feet above the water line. HMS *Nelson* was probably the biggest ship to transit the canal and the Pilot standing on the bridge smoking a fat cigar, had no direct communication with the upper deck. His only comment was: 'Well, you played up Hell with Our canal.' After proceeding along Miraflores Lake and two locks, we entered Balboa reach and saluted the US Nation with a 21 gun salute, after which HMS *Nelson* secured astern of USS *Texas*, Admiral Chase's Flagship of the Pacific Fleet. Calls were exchanged between the various Admirals and the British Minister, followed by the Foreign Secretary and Governor of Panama, and there was a continuous stream of boats passing the *Nelson* all day from the US Fleet lying off Panama in the Pacific. Their men were immensely impressed and the Officers wanted to know our paint recipe. (Atlantic Fleet grey enamel from top to water line, with the mainmast covered with silver paint!)

Our wardroom officers were each allocated to one US Navy ship during our stay, and I went to USS *Idaho*, the crack gunnery ship

51

where the Assistant Fire Control Officer, Lieutenant-Commander Jess Kenworthy, looked after me. He and his charming wife Lorna became really good friends, so much so that I was constrained to embrace Lorna on the Union Club steps in front of a large audience.

With such a large number of enlisted men in the port, the US Navy Patrol consisted of a Post Captain wearing brown gaiters and belt and 250 men. They also had what was known as the Officers' Patrol, with a strength of about six extremely staid men, whose duty it was to ensure that any Officers unfortunate enough to succumb to the wiles of the local harpies, should see them safely back to their ships. Our own Patrol consisted of one Lieutenant and six men, as far as I can remember.

350 American Officers came to our Theatrical Show, and our visit ended with 32 American Admirals and all the Officers and their wives at our 'At Home', followed by boxing on board USS *California*, Jess Kenworthy refereeing.

Our return through Gatun locks caused further damage to the ship, for which the US Government paid. Total costs were probably about £560 for both trips.

After calling at Bridgetown again, we proceeded to Gibraltar, carrying out war routine and exercises all the way. Gibraltar lived up to its name for get-togethers and entertainment, including our show, 'Between the Bollards', by Officers, and 'The Curate's Egg' by the *Queen Elizabeth*. There was a gymkhana at North Front, in which I won the Pig-Sticking Competition and the Gretna Green Race with Myrtle Jellicoe on the Governor's horses. This was followed by a point-to-point out by San Roque, a fairly stiff two and a half mile course, in which my hireling horse preferred to barge its way through, rather than over, the hedges, and I believe we barged at least two Admirals off the course. There were 20 in the field and several crashes. I came seventh.

Our return to Portsmouth covered a full power trial and more war routine, Action Stations being sounded off while I was in my bath.

On Sunday morning, 29 March, in fog, we were hit by SS *West Wales* on the starboard side, abreast B turret, causing a dent in the side and a crack two yards long in the Topmen's messdeck.

A bitterly cold wind greeted us and we secured at South Railway jetty on All Fool's Day. A change from the West Indies.

Lieutenant-Commander Grantham (Granny) took over as fo'c'sle Divisional Officer and a remarkable improvement in morale and efficiency was soon evident with our 240 men.

During one of our many war routine exercises I was controlling the port six-inch gun battery in the Director tower. Below me was the trainer whose duty it was to follow the pointer on his dials by keeping two pointers in line. John Cowie, as the Principal Control Officer on the bridge, called down: 'Are your Pointers in line?' My operator assured me that they were. Actually they were in line, but only at the side of the instrument, and the guns were 40 degrees off bearing. Cowie, the Torpedo and Electrical Officer came down and without a word went through the narrow hole to see for himself, after which I did likewise and corrected the mistake. When I got to my cabin and was off watch, I sent a note to Cowie quoting 'Habbakuk 2, verse 1' which reads: 'I will stand upon my watch, and set me upon the tower, and will watch to see what he will say unto me, and what I shall answer when I am reproved.' His answer came in another note quoting Psalm 121, verse 4: 'Behold, he that keepeth Israel shall neither slumber nor sleep.' Nothing more was said.

It was not often that young Lieutenants were allowed the privilege of doing jobs which might attract attention, but I was allowed to work the main derrick occasionally, to deputise for the Boat Officer, Beaky Armstrong. The derrick was controlled by a topping lift and four guys worked by their respective electric winches, in addition to the purchase for actually hoisting and lowering boats. Each winch was manned by men from its appropriate part of ship, Fo'c'sle-Starboard Fore, Main Top-Starboard After, Fore Top-Port Fore, and Royal Marines, on this occasion, the Port After. It must have been the Marines' first time when I gave the customary orders for plumbing a picket boat before hoisting it out:

'Tend your guys.
Derrick Topping, up Topping life,
Haul away Starboard Fore,
Haul away Starboard After,
Check Port After' (meaning easy away)

Did the Marines Check? Not on your Nellie! They hung on like grim death, with the result that the Starboard Fore (malleable cast iron) block carried away and knocked me and the Warrant Shipwright over, hitting me in the chest. I dimly saw this blur hurtling towards me and the accident bell rang, as I gave the order 'still'.

Fortunately the force of the blow was broken by the bight of the wire rove through the block being caught by the four-inch ammunition lockers on the boat deck, or I would not be writing this now. Neither of us was seriously hurt.

Our main concern, and certainly that of the Commander, was the Regatta, for which we had been practising hard. For the last six months the wardroom gig's crew went away for pulling practice whenever possible, often morning and evening. All boats were rubbed down and painted by volunteers during passage to Scapa Flow, where we moored ship on Saturday 30 May. The crews were conditioned like race horses. Months before, the Commander had planted a huge tin of Beemax in front of me at breakfast, saying: 'Beemax for you, me boy – makes old men young and young men furious!'

Regatta Day on 2 June dawned fine but with a strong head-wind down the course which made pulling difficult. Our Chief Petty Officers' gig won the first race and our two Marines' cutters trained by Lieutenant Watson RM came in first and second. After that we couldn't go wrong and the band turned out to play the winning crews home after all but five races. The wardroom race was delayed starting, but we won by five lengths ahead of *Malaya*. The cold wind froze my hands, so that I was pulling mechanically for the latter part of the race, and quite pulled myself out. However, Beaky Armstrong's exhortations forced me to get up and carry my oar up the gangway where the Commander-in-Chief was clapping each of us as we reached the quarter deck. We were all presented with large medals which had been cast by the Warrant Ordnance Officer the week before in anticipation of our success. In a speech to the Ship's Company, the Commander was in very good form and said, 'Personally I wouldn't call King George my Uncle!' He then called on all the Admirals in the Fleet who had congratulated him.

Lieutenant Fletcher, later to be my best man, added a touch of humour to the events by winning an impromptu race for Drifters' dinghies, wearing a top hat and tails, with his crew in various fancy dress clothes, male and female. He brought the *Sundown* alongside at a great rate, having forgotten to go astern, but did so just in time and we turned the band out for him as well.

The Commander-in-Chief inspected the ship at Stornoway, our next stop, and congratulated all concerned on their behaviour at Panama, on the shoots and the Regatta, not forgetting a very satisfactory inspection, which made him very proud to fly his flag in the *Nelson*. After a call at Lamlash the ship went to Guernsey where our landing parties paraded and marched past the Governor on the King's birthday. Considerable entertainment and sporting activity took place.

HMS *NELSON* AT PORTSMOUTH AND LEAVE WITH THE ARMY

Back at Portsmouth, *Nelson* de-ammunitioned, half-yearly promotions were duly celebrated, and the Captain got married. The Jellicoes very kindly invited me to accompany them to the first Court Ball held by Their Majesties for several years. It was a brilliant scene with 200 people present and all the Court Ladies dressed in white except Princess Ingrid of Sweden, who wore pink. The men in Ball Dress.

In answer to an Admiralty Fleet Order inviting Officers to apply for paid leave with an Army Regiment, I consulted my father's cousin, George de Chair, then Brigade Major at Aldershot, and he arranged for me to spend three weeks with the 5th Royal Inniskilling Dragoon Guards. I had a grand time and the Officers went out of their way to keep me interested. Polo when I wanted it, a three hundred guinea hunter to ride in the morning, with a different horse in the afternoon; and they put me in charge of a Troop on manoeuvres. I designed my own uniform, consisting of hunting boots, blue breeches and monkey jacket, with white cap cover, it being summer. What they did not tell me was that only Chief Umpires wore white cap covers, and my friends having told me my objective, a hill to be captured, waited to watch the fun. As I galloped up followed by my Troop, I was rather surprised to be greeted by two Generals galloping up to me, saluting and then hurriedly saying, 'Oh, good morning Navy' and returning to their respective forces.

A Cavalry Regiment in peacetime before the war must have been an ideal life for the lucky selected Officers, with three months' hunting leave a year, and their chargers for hunting and polo. Glittering messes and apparently very little work except perhaps once a fortnight by turns, supervising muck out and early morning exercise. The Adjutant seemed to do all the work and it seemed incredible to me that these gallant Officers should so successfully transfer their allegiance to tanks when war came. After hunting with some of them with the Old Berks, they presented me with a nice picture entitled 'A gallop with Jem Hills from Bradwell Grove' to commemorate a sailor remaining on board his horse for 15 miles over stone walls. My son, now a Major in the same regiment, is its proud possessor, tho' he doesn't know one end of a horse from the other, being a tank expert.

HMS *NELSON*. PORTSMOUTH AND SUNDOWN TO INVERGORDON. 1931

Admiral Hodges took ill and at 3 a.m. on 7 September, was taken to Haslar Hospital with pleurisy, so the sailing of the Fleet was delayed. The regatta being over, I was given orders to take the Drifter *Sundown* to Invergordon, but first of all had to get her out of the floating dock and thence to the coaling depot, all on a Sunday. Fortunately, Lieutenant Popham, in charge, had been instructed in Torpedo by my father, when he was an able seaman in 1893, and kindly let me go on coaling with dockyard labour during the dinner hour. Meanwhile I had a bath and lunch back in the *Nelson* and sailed after adjustment of the compass off Port Gilkicker.

We had a bad night in the Channel and put into Lowestoft where I was made an Hon Member of the Yacht Club, and Johnnie Lee-Barber's father very kindly took me to his home for dinner.

The following day found us wallowing past the Wash, with my two midshipmen prostrated with sea sickness; later a deputation arrived from the Engine Room asking if we could take shelter. Accordingly, I anchored in the dark close under Flamborough Head which provided a good lee, and was reassured to see the lights of some cruisers and destroyers sheltering off Bridlington. By 0800 when we awoke, they had all sailed and we were left snugly sheltering, with breakers outside to the south, as far as the eye could see. Then it was raise steam for full speed as we charged the wall of breakers; the last wave before it broke looked as high as our mast, and crashed on deck without smashing the wheelhouse windows.

We made the Tyne by nightfall and moored up at the Fish Quay, among the fishing drifters at North Shields. There I left the Coxswain in charge and took my two midshipmen up to Newcastle for a comfortable night in a hotel, as they were about all-in.

It appeared that various agitators had been on board in our absence trying to persuade my crew to mutiny, but Petty Officer Crouch, our excellent Coxswain, kicked them out and we left for Rosyth, little realising that HM Drifter *Sundown* was probably the only ship in the Fleet that had not mutinied.

Invergordon, where we arrived after a week at sea, looked its normal self, full of ships, but I was surprised to find no one except the mate to take our lines by the forward gangway. Clambering up it in my seaboots, I was in time to hear the Commander addressing the *Nelson*'s Ship's Company the other side of the deck. He was explaining that a Committee of Officers would investigate any cases of hardship which the men brought to them, as a result of the Labour Government's arbitrary cut in pay by 25%, which meant starvation for some families.

A letter to my father shows the impressions made on me, a young Naval Officer at the time.

17/9/31 Thursday   HMS Nelson
                                                  Atlantic Fleet
                                                    c/o G.P.O.
                              Invergordon to Spithead at Sea.

My dear Father,

An extraordinary state of affairs prevails in the Fleet. I brought my drifter alongside during evening quarters on Tuesday evening and was just in time to hear the Commander addressing the Ship's Company.

As you have doubtless seen, a spirit of unrest prevails, owing to the drastic cuts in pay which in many cases impose extreme hardship and downright poverty.

On Sunday night the men held a meeting in the Invergordon canteen and decided that they would not go to sea until they obtained justice. They realised that the Officers could do nothing for them unless pressure was brought to bear, and so when the

First Lieutenant went up to weigh the anchor they sat on the cable and refused to work. When the Commander went up they cheered him, but said it was impossible. He had been fully alive to the danger and had been instituting enquiries into specially hard-hit cases as soon as the new rates were made known. These the Chief of Staff took with him to London to represent to the Admiralty. Next day the Fleet Accountant Officer, accompanied by the Director of Victualling, followed with more, and all the time a Committee comprising, first Divisional Officers and then the Captain, Chaplain, Commander and Paymaster, were hearing cases of men whose families would be quite unable to live on the new rates of pay.

There has been nothing like it since 1797, but now the men know they have our sympathy and as far as normal ship routine goes, carry out their duties as smartly as ever.

On Wednesday I kept a day on as O.O.W. and we gave the men a make and mend. Then about 6 p.m. we got a signal from the Admiralty saying all ships were to return to home ports, and it became a question once more of whether the men would obey orders.

The Commander went for'ard and helped matters a lot but it was a great pity Admiral Hodges was ill at home. Rear Admiral Tomlinson commanding the Battle Cruisers was Senior Officer in the Fleet and very wisely ordered *Nelson* to lead the Battle Squadron out of harbour at 11 p.m. He realised that this ship's company have a better spirit than the others, many of whom have had meetings on their fo'c'sles all the forenoon and done no work.

Now we are on our way back to Portsmouth. Carrying out no exercises and proceeding at economical speed, whilst the Midshipmen, eleven of them, and Officers' wives, follow in Officers' motor cars! This was the only humorous touch of the whole business, sending eleven Midshipmen ashore at half an hour's notice, each with £5, to drive Officer's motor cars back to Portsmouth. We all went to the gangway to see them off.

It seems very little thought has been expended on the actual distribution in reduction of Navy Estimates which are not very large, so that I am confident some better solution will be arrived at.

If, for example, a P.O. could be reduced 1/– instead of 1/6 it would made all the difference, and I sincerely hope those in office will come to their senses. It is so awful to think of the Navy, which one regards as the last word in integrity, coming down to this, and I'm afraid its effect will be felt in many other directions. I suppose things are not looking too rosy as regards Income Tax either, but I hope not too bad.

This letter may be of interest in years to come, at any rate to me, for never shall I forget last night, 16th September, and the relief we all felt when the anchor came up and all ships pointed towards the Souters. I felt almost like repeating Ld. St Vincent's words – 'Discipline is preserved Sir' – but fear we are not through the wood yet.

Best love to the family,

Your devoted son Graham.

Several Naval Officers' wives had arrived in Invergordon and as all leave was stopped, were at a loss to know what to do. Accordingly the Admiral made a signal to the Fleet stating – 'Those Officers and men whose wives are here may be granted leave to go ashore and settle their affairs.' I was Officer of the Watch and knew that the only boat for this purpose would leave in ten minutes' time. No one in authority above me was in a mood for troubling about wives or boats, and to have approached the Commander on the subject when all nerves were on edge, would have been extremely tactless. I therefore took it upon myself to broadcast to Officers' quarters only, that the boat would be leaving in ten minutes' time. Several Officers were thus enabled to go and see their wives, but the Commander heard the pipe and blew me sky-high for a bone-headed idiot, as he thought the pipe might upset the troops. I had thought of that, but decided that as the signalmen knew all about it, no harm would come from three Marine sentries in the Officers' quarters also knowing about it.

After leading the battle fleet out of harbour, *Nelson* took station astern of the Admiral flying his flag in the *Renown* or *Repulse*, I forget which. I happened to be Officer of the Watch about lunch-time when, in low visibility, we were approaching a sandbank called the Cockle near the Wash. The Battle Cruiser suddenly altered course to port without signal. Instead of following in her wake, I turned with her. Had I not done so the *Nelson* might have been swept onto the Cockle by the strong westerly set of the tide. What a story for the press after the Invergordon mutiny. The

Captain commended my action when he arrived on the bridge. We had already heard enough about the Nelson which went aground on the Hamilton bank, outside Portsmouth Harbour.

The Fleet remained in home ports for about a fortnight, but as soon as Admiral Sir John Kelly hoisted his flag on 6 October the wires began to hum. He visited all the big ships and addressed the Ships' Companies. In the *Nelson* he said substantially: 'I suppose they keep a list of Admirals at the Admiralty, and they say: 'Who shall we send to the Home Fleet?' And they look at their Service Certificates to see who would do. 'Here's a good bloke, VG.VG.VG* Nelson – oh, he's dead, so we can't send him.' And they look down the list and see this one, VGI.VGI.VG.VG. Jellicoe, a brilliant Officer – 'Oh Lord, No, we can't send him either, he's dead.' And they go on looking till they come to this one. Bad. Mod. Indifferent. Joe Kelly. 'He's a proper Bird. We'll send him.' So here I am. I know I'm no oil painting. Have a look at me . . .' And so in this vein. He soon had the men eating out of his hand and they trusted him.

The Fleet sailed for Rosyth on 8 October and I took the Drifter *Sundown* up in record time, non-stop with a following wind, arriving at 0205 in a howling gale alongside the water boat. The Admiralty queried our time of arrival. I was christened Graham the Greyhound (9½ knots).

The Commander-in-Chief conducted General drill on 5 November, envelopes having been distributed the day before, not to be opened until ordered. As I had the middle watch, I looked carefully at our envelopes, and spotted the word 'Egg' in one and told the Commander. Sure enough after the various evolutions the order came to open this envelope 'Send Poached Egg to *Rodney*.' The Signalman of the watch shouted down to the galley 'Cookie Egg!' The Cook expecting the order was so excited that he dropped a whole box of eggs. However, in record time a tray with poached egg, toast, butter and marmalade was delivered to the Midshipman of the picket boat, already at the gangway, which he duly presented on *Rodney*'s bridge, wearing Round jacket and Dirk, an easy first for *Nelson*. The only thanks we got for our initiative was a signal from the Commander-in-Chief to his Flagship, 'Your egg was bad and the dish was dirty', and a dirty old dish was returned in its place.

Later, Lieutenant Fletcher was running the drifter and

received the following signal from the Commander-in-Chief (Joe Kelly). 'Judging by the smoke issuing from your stack, your dinner must be over-cooked.' Reply from *Sundown*: 'I am just toasting the forenoon's catch of herrings. Could you taste one for your tea?' Answer from Commander-in-Chief: 'Put the herrings where the monkey put the nuts. This signal is not to be logged as if it is, you will be!'

For my last trip in *Sundown* I was ordered to take her with the drifters from *Rodney* and *Hood* under my orders. The others were very slow and I kept trying to jolly them along by signal, until a plaintive wail came from one during the middle watch 'Can my signalman turn in?' It never occurred to me that he had to be there to answer signals which I had been making myself.

After a very eventful year in the Fleet Flagship, and despite my Captain's kindly efforts to dissuade me, I persisted in applying for the long Signal Course, for which I had been recommended from my last ship HMS *Laburnum*.

I could not have asked for a better job as number three of the Fo'c'sle Division with Granny Grantham as Divisional Officer and Brian Scurfield the number two, and as Senior Watchkeeper I had begun to get the feel of the ship.

Having passed the preliminary examination I was appointed to the Signal School for the next long course, and was relieved by Padfield at the end of November 1931.

6

HMS *Victory* for the Signals Course, 1931

Our course of twelve Officers included two Observers, Nigel Weymouth and Ted Unwin, and Tom Inglis, Millar, Amie Cox, Alwyn Lennox-Conyngham, Conrad Rawnsley, Neil McKinnon RAN, Harry Reid, and Christopher Bonham-Carter and myself. Our instructors were Lieutenant-Commander Toby Everett and an Instructor Lieutenant who taught mathematics and Wireless Telegraphy theory. He was engaged to be married and so was not available to assist after working hours.

We were all issued with a set of secret and confidential books and were expected to learn the Fleet Codes and Fleet Signal Books word perfect by heart, which in my case took a bit of doing, not being as quick on the uptake or having the type of photographic brain which was ideal for the job. Consequently I very soon discovered that my evenings were fully occupied very late into the night, and whereas it would have been nice to join Everett and others in the wardroom and attend mess dinners, I contented myself with very occasional visits to the mess and a quick informal supper.

We all carried black walking sticks, most with silver knobs, mine with a curved handle and gold tip, a Buna cane presented to my father in New South Wales.

Our days started with morse on a buzzer and writing down. After a while one could read at 25 words a minute and was writing down two words after reading each one.

Everett took us at 'mast' which entailed sending and reading messages by flags to another mast, the meaning of which we learned by heart from the Fleet Code. We all had our own telescopes for this exercise. Marching manoeuvres with answering pendants were conducted by word of mouth to the rest of the class, who acted as a fleet of ships, from the manoeuvring table. A flashing exercise every evening, with partners writing down concluded the official day's work.

A short session on the 10-inch signal projector was considered sufficient, but when Pat Matheson asked me to demonstrate a repair, I had forgotten its existence, by that time being thoroughly

62

tired and struggling to master advanced mathematics involving the square root of minus one etc., used for thermionic emissions.

However, by the time leave was due in August, I had successfully qualified as a Signal Bosun, but felt I needed an extra two months to complete the course on wireless, and informed the Captain accordingly. I received a polite note whilst on leave, saying I need not return to complete the course.

Lennox-Conyngham was awarded the Jackson Everett Prize for being top of the signal course and Rawnsley and I did not complete it. Everett did his best to help me but could not stop me overworking, so that by the time I left I was thoroughly worn out and stale.

Going home for weekends at Wentworth should have helped, as there was a saying that the married Officers did best because their wives could hear them reciting the colours and meanings of flags in bed! I was seriously contemplating marriage to a near neighbour during this time, but not for that reason.

7

HMS *Achates*. Third Destroyer Flotilla.
1932-34

When I reported to the Admiralty, Commander Halsey offered me a job as First Lieutenant of a local Destroyer Flotilla, but I asked if I could go instead as the number two of a running destroyer in the Fleet, where I would gain better experience. I was subsequently appointed to HMS *Achates*, bound for the Mediterranean. Captain Tovey told me: 'If your new Captain is half as good to you as your father was to me, you will be very lucky.' This proved true and I could not have wished for a better Commanding Officer than Commander McCall.

My appointment to HMS *Achates* was for 26 September 1932 and Vice Lawford and I arrived on board the day before. I had not been there long before John Cuthbert called on the Captain and asked if I would like to go to Dartmouth as a Term Officer, under Captain Wodehouse. However, I gratefully declined and settled down instead to learn my new job, as number two of a Destroyer, which included the duty of Navigator.

On 4 November, being in all respects ready for sea, the Captain said to me: 'All right, Pilot, take her out.' This was understandable, HMS *Achates* being his first command, and no doubt he wanted to see whether I had mastered the new helm orders. As *Achates* approached Drake's Island, a sharp turn to port is required; I was a little late with my order to turn – my first 'boob' in the ship. After that we proceeded out of harbour to number two buoy where we swung compass, then sailed for a rendezvous with HMS *Codrington* and HMS *Acasta*, en route for Gibraltar.

We spent the following Saturday in the Bay of Biscay and for the first time in my experience it lived up to its reputation. A large number of the men were laid out, but it did them good and blew away the cobwebs. On the Sunday the weather cleared and we rounded Cape Finisterre about noon. The *Queen Elizabeth* flying the flag of Admiral Chatfield passed us and the Flotilla closed in perfect station. Three long strings of flags went up in QE's main

64

topmast halliards; a message to 3rd Destroyer Flotilla wishing them luck in the new commission and saying that the Commander-in-Chief was very sorry he was leaving the Mediterranean. Captain (D) 3 replied: 'We deeply regret we should not have the honour of serving with him.' Then came a private message to Commander McCall '*Achates*' from the QE's midshipmen, his old term at Dartmouth, wishing him every success.

In a letter home, I wrote: 'If all destroyers are as good as this one I never want to go to another big ship!'

After a month at Gibraltar, getting acquainted with the rest of the Flotilla and the local authorities, not to mention voluminous station and local orders, we proceeded to Malta doing full power trials along the North Africa shore. Our arrival in Malta on 18 December 1932 was somewhat marred by the after guard letting the stern wire foul the starboard screw, requiring divers down for two days. This was a pity, since the Captain had brought the ship up Lazaretto Creek stern first in fine style at 12 knots.

Lazaretto Creek woke up in the forenoon on Christmas Day and after the officers and families had been round the messdecks to admire the decorations, the usual sailors' funny parties were in full swing. In the afternoon all was quiet and in the evenings the patrols got busy as the sailors celebrated.

I was in general charge of the church parties at the destroyer depot and met the Admiral and Mrs Rose, who was very friendly, and who asked me up to tea. I told her I had promised to super-intend the broadcast of the King's speech at the Castile. It came through very well and was well worth giving up the afternoon for.

Commander and Mrs McCall invited the Officers to dinner on Christmas night; we cooked the meal and did all the work, the servants having been allowed a holiday. I provided and also filleted the fish, which the First Lieutenant ably cooked; two nice John Dorys. Fish was scarce in Malta unless you were satisfied with Dendici or Lampuki, so these were much appreciated. After dinner we played 'Priest of the Parish' and sang songs; a very pleasant evening.

The New Year 1933 followed with the usual harbour drills, and the First Lieutenant's wife Mrs Maud, having just arrived, came to watch our general drill. She was sitting on Manoel Island opposite the ship with her child where she could witness all our evolutions at close hand. One of the orders from Captain (D) by signal was: 'Erect signal mast on Manoel Island and hoist the answering pendant'. I went ashore with my signalman, taking bearing out spar and stick for a yard, and the necesary lines and shackles for halliards, all in our *Dghaissa*, and they had it erected before any of the other ships had even landed their gear. Not having called on the newly arrived lady, who I had to pass, I stopped to say 'How do you do?', which resulted in a voice of brass from the Captain on *Achates*' bridge: 'Mr de b . . . Chair,. are you too b . . proud, or too b . . . tired to run?' No doubt Mrs Maud was suitably impressed.

Our next cruise took us to Port Drepano, in Greece. The platoons from *Achates* and HMS *Anthony* under my tender care had succeeded in reaching an eminence some 1,500 feet above sea level and three miles inland, when we got the signal 'Landing cancelled. Return to "A" beach.' It then began to rain very hard and we returned rather disconsolate, especially as none of the attackers had landed. We were supposed to be insurgents ensconced in the hills, who had given trouble to the British colony, being led by a fanatical priest in the person of our First Lieutenant, with a black hessian cloak and fez. I also wore a red beard! The exercise was repeated in fine weather and showed very clearly the advantage of position and the difficulty of advancing in force up a hill with rough country and little or no cover.

The following is an extract from a letter home:

'We left Port Drepano and proceeded down through the Greek Islands inside Cephalonia to anchorage near Missollonghi, of Byronic fame. The whole fleet is here, less aircraft carriers. We are Red fleet being attacked at an open anchorage by Blue force aeroplanes.'

We anchored inshore of the *Codrington* where there was more shelter and again kept anchor watch all night, this time in the pouring rain. Ship was darkened at 0600 in the morning and we stood by for the main aircraft and gas attack.

About 1100, I sighted a submarine breaking surface and we had our pendants up in all ships, which mitigated the monotony a bit, and very soon afterwards the intrepid birdmen started coming. During the attack we gave the gas alarm and the First Lieutenant lit tear gas bombs, threw them into the messdecks and shoved them into the engine and boiler room fan intakes. Being Officer of the Watch, I directed the anti-aircraft fire and cooked up a record of it afterwards, consisting of lovely red and black lines and squiggles. A bomb target was moored quite near us, so we got a fine view.

The submarines did well on the Monday, getting inside the close screen and popping up 300 yards off the battleships in some cases.

The night encounter was most instructive and realistic, but again we never got nearer than within 8,000 yards of the battle fleet. I fired eight dummy torpedoes at a cruiser 3,000 yards off, thinking it was one of the battleships, but we and HMS *Anthony* were the only destroyers in the division not under fire and should have pressed home our attack by turning straight for the searchlights.

VISIT TO THE RIVIERA. APRIL 1933

The spirit of *entente cordiale* was epitomised by our Spring cruise to the south of France. The following are extracts from letters home:

'Most of my time has been taken up when ashore, with arranging French parties either by or for us, as I find I'm the only interpreter in the Flotilla. The officers of the 20*eme* *Batallion des Chasseurs Alpins*, a very nice lot, gave two At Homes for us, one in the forenoon and one at the Casino on Saturday night. Wine books seemed to take up a good deal of my time and all our bills are near the five pounds limit, after our *entente* visit this month.

P.S. Am getting quite French now. Just had to write all the "chocolate letters" for Captain (D).'

MALTA. 1 MAY 1933

'The review was at the Marsa today. The Governor took the salute and the First Lord and Commander-in-Chief inspected the front rank of the Brigade. It was very hot but the troops did their stuff well and we got a lot of 'chocolates' from the First

Lord and Rear Admiral (Destroyers). I had the *Achates* and *Anthony* platoons and we were told we were as good as any of the battleships', which, considering we had only one day's practice on the fo'c'sle, was not bad.'

We had a pleasant visit to Rimini, where I was acting First Lieutenant in Maud's absence (for interview in London for Chief of the Fire Brigade). This was followed by earnest preparations for the regatta at Split, at the beginning of August. The regatta took place and *Achates* came in rock bottom.

The officers' race came at 11.45 and all the sailors came aft on the quarterdeck to see something worthwhile – real 'scientific' rowing instead of their brute strength and b . . . ignorance. 'For Gawd's sake, break the spell, Sir', the Gunner's Mate said. A typical 'westo' remark! The Captain said we never pulled better and Captain (D) and several other Commanding Officers also thought we were far and away the best pulling crew in the race, but did we win? No. *We* came in seventh and crew from HMS *Active* who had never given up drinking or smoking and were quite bolshie about practising, walked away with it. I called them the 'drunky's express'!

In Kotor, we anchored in the main harbour with the whole fleet. This place was captured for the British by Captain William Hoste in 1814 with two ships; the *Bacchante* (38 guns) and *Saracen* (18 guns). They proceeded to capture and dismantle Fort Spagnuolo, another at Eregnovi and another at Sveti Juraj, in the same lake as Kotor. The difficulties were tremendous and when the French General saw them trying, he first laughed and said it would take six months to get one gun up the hill above Kotor. However, Hoste got it up 2,500 feet in only two days and mounted it at the top in six. The General said 'It was a very unmilitary proceeding.' Hoste then told him: 'English sailors do nothing like anyone else, but they will astonish him before they leave him!'

Before leaving Kotor, several 'At Homes' for the departing Fourth Flotilla culminated in a very good one in the *Queen Elizabeth*. Lieutenant Kostobadie, who acted a Stanley Holloway-inspired scene of an RNVR man from Wigan joining the Navy for two days, came and dined with me afterwards, so we dressed him up again and he re-enacted it, with a lot more besides.

On 9 August, we were emergency destroyer and at 0700 on the

Thursday got a signal to raise steam for 27 knots and proceeded with all despatch to the assistance of SS *Treci*, reported to be sinking about 35 miles from Brindisi. When we approached the reported position towards noon, we saw first one ship and then another and turned from our course to investigate, so causing a slight delay. However, we finally found the *Treci* about ten miles west of the reported position, with two ships already standing by. She had a heavy list to starboard and the sea which was calm had risen to within two feet of her afterdeck. Maud and I went over in the whaler to investigate but we found none of the crew of the *Treci* on board, but only some of those from the other steamers, so we then boarded another Yugoslav ship, the *Bosanka*, which was the nearest to the *Treci*. There we found the master of the *Treci*, a nice, open countenanced man, engaged in saving his personal luggage, apparently very unconcerned for the loss of his ship, and the master of the *Bosanka* evidently quite decided as to who should get any salvage or insurance money going.

We offered to help but were assured that no assistance was required and that they could do very well without our Engineer! We suspected jiggery-pokery and went back to the *Achates*, who then lay off and watched the proceedings for a couple of hours. The after-hatch of the *Treci* was half uncovered, but, on observing us scrutinising her, the master ordered it to be covered up. This was later removed again when it was thought we were not looking!

About 1430, finding nothing happening, the Captain went over in the whaler himself and I accompanied him. First we boarded the *Bosanka* and interrogated the master, taking his name and any particulars necessary for a court of enquiry. Evidently both he and the master of the *Treci* hailed from Dubrovnic and were personal friends. We next proceeded to board the *Treci*, which was about two feet lower in the water than when we first arrived. The Captain talked to the master, who, whenever he thought we were about during the day, made a great show of sounding his wells. We were both prepared to dive and swim for it, as the list seemed to be getting worse and she was certainly settling down. After a while the master of the *Treci* gave his account, which I took down in writing.

It appeared that the *Treci*, at 3,817 tons gross whilst loading aluminium ore worth £6,500 in Sibenic, had touched the bottom but divers who investigated reported no damage and the ship proceeded for Rotterdam. About midnight the following night the chief reported a leak aft, and an hour later, 26 inches of water in numbers three and four bilges. By 0200 a further 40 inches had gained and an hour after that the ship took a list. At aboout 0400 the bulkhead between numbers three and four bilges collapsed, and the crew took to the boats in which they were picked up some two miles from the abandoned *Treci* by the Italian steamer *Chilena*, who then made the W/T report to Klinci radio which we received and acted upon. This was at about 0800 and apparently the master of the *Treci* had persuaded the *Chilena*'s master not to attempt to salve the *Treci*, as it was not safe to board and she might go any minute. At about 1100, along came the *Bosanka*, bound from Cardiff to Ancona in Italy. We wondered whether it was bad luck for the Yugoslavs that she was adrift on the rendezvous, or whether it was coincidence that she and *Treci* should both be off their courses and that seeing a fellow countryman foundering, she immediately rushed up to the sinking vessel and planted a salvage party on board.

It was bad enough to be reported and picked up by an Italian merchantman, but when an hour after his friend arrived, a British destroyer appeared on the scene, we imagined the master of the *Treci*, if he had any evil designs, to have cursed his luck. His whole conduct and the collection of circumstances throughout the day pointed to a clear case of 'barratry', if not 'bottomry'! The former means wilfully destroying your ship so as to get the insurance money and the latter mortgaging her with a similar end in view. At all events, had we been able to take her in tow as soon as we arrived, or shortly after noon, we could have, I am sure, got her into Brindisi which was only 25 miles away. Luckily we did not try, as there is a clause in King's Regulations and Admiralty Instructions forbidding men-of-war to take merchantmen in tow (or claim salvage) if there is another merchantman standing by. We were itching to do it, as the Captain's share alone would have been about £500 and mine I suppose between £100 and £200, and about £30 for each man.

The master of the *Treci* had apparently made no effort to beach the ship (the last point made in my report) and subsequently, while we were laid off, still did little or nothing about getting in the tow of *Bosanka*. The *Chilena* meanwhile, fed up with the delay, requested permission to proceed, which the Captain granted. At about 1600 the master of the *Treci* came over and told me he had entered into a written agreement with the master of *Bosanka* (all 'my eye') to be taken in tow, the terms being 'No cure, no pay', which is usual. After that he pulled leisurely over to the *Treci* and had a look round and then went back to the *Bosanka*. After a further delay two hawsers were brought across and made fast but in such a dilatory fashion as to confirm our worst suspicions.

The *Treci* had bluff bows and as no attempt was made to put the rudder over, she sheered off as soon as the *Bosanka* went ahead and very soon parted both hawsers. Our Captain then suggested putting the helm hard over but they put it the wrong way and soon the master of the *Bosanka*, having surreptitiously uncovered the after hatch, came over and told us he thought it unsafe to keep any men on board the *Treci* any longer, seeing that towing operations were very dangerous (the sea was flat calm) and that he expected the end soon.

Just after that we got a signal from the Commander-in-Chief, with whom we had been continuously in touch, to return to harbour which was about 100 miles away. Five minutes later when we were a mile away the *Treci*'s bows lifted and the air pressure blew up both fore and one of the after hatches. Then she slid gently backwards and quietly subsided below the swell.

Our cruise ended with massed torpedo attacks on the battle fleet, by three flotillas engaging battle-practice targets at the same time, representing counter-attacking flotillas. Malta was in sight and evidently the noise of 27 destroyers each firing 48 rounds of full calibre was enough to impress the inhabitants with the fact that we had come back!

RETURN TO MALTA

Back in Malta, one settled into what for me was a good routine. The Captain and First Lieutenant lived ashore, leaving me free to work for the Destroyer Command examination in the evenings, tell off the hands in the morning, and play polo in the afternoons when there was any. With £150 a year and my Lieutenant's pay, I could afford to run two ponies and a car, with groom and a stable which I had built at the head of Sliema Creek. Carlo Ghigo, my groom, would bring the ponies to Manoel Island at about 6.30 in the morning and Robin White, First Lieutenant of the *Antelope* and I would exercise them on Manoel Island, before returning on board by our Dghaissa in time for breakfast and the day's work.

On our next cruise, during one breakfast a signal was received from Admiralty calling for volunteers from Lieutenants of four years seniority to command a topsail schooner for the Royal Geographic Society, bound for Graham Land in the Antarctic (a nice, cool place). This seemed the answer to the maiden's prayer as far as I was concerned. I turned to the Sub and said: 'Will you come?' Weston replied: 'Yes, I'll come as a deckhand, for no pay.' Then to the Chief, 'Will you come?' Yes, he replied, 'I'll come.' This looked rather like mutiny, but I went to the Captain, who had also seen the signal and said: 'We want to go sailing, Sir.' 'What do you know about sailing?' he asked. 'Well, nothing, Sir, but I'm going to Denmark to learn.' At which he replied: 'Well, you can't.' Over two hundred Lieutenants with the required four years seniority sent their names in, and Dudley Ryder got the job. I knew the leader of the expedition, John Rymill, an Australian, who told me I would have been selected had he known. As it turned out, I was spared a miserable three years. The Royal Geographical party treated the five Naval Officers like servants and Rymill refused to let Ryder be Captain, just sailing master, saying 'We are all gentlemen and don't need discipline.' He had an idea that Shackleton had been put under arrest by his navigator, which was quite untrue.

When they got back from the expedition, the schooner *Penola* berthed astern of my HMS *Wrestler* and I made Ryder and Rymill shake hands in my cabin. They had not been on speaking terms for over a year.

Writing from Skiathos in September, I noted:

'These Greek cruises have the very excellent effect, that there being *no* attractions on shore, officers dine in each others' ships much more and so build up the proper flotilla spirit.'

However, there was an occasion when the Flotilla was anchored in a long straight line, with *Codrington* the leader at the head and *Achates* and *Anthony* at the other end.

At two o'clock in the morning I was woken up by the First Lieutenant of HMS *Arrow*, Bunny Clitherow, who told me: 'Do you know your First Lieutenant is drowned?' I said: 'I don't believe it.' We looked into his cabin and there, sure enough, was

72

Colin Maud sleeping peacefully, starko and dripping wet. He had been dining with the Flotilla Gunnery Officer in the *Codrington* and when about to leave decided that the dummy wooden projectile displayed on the loading tray of *Codrington*'s number four gun on the quarterdeck rightfully belonged to the *Achates*. Without further ado he removed his clothes, seized the projectile and dived over the side with it, to the consternation of his hosts and some of his fellow First Lieutenants. When he did not reappear, all the emergency night boat crews in the Flotilla were called away, but Maud must have anticipated this and swum back to the *Achates*, a distance of about two miles, keeping inshore of the ships where he was unlikely to be seen. He was a very good swimmer, rather resembling a seal in the water. During the Second World War, he was, not surprisingly, the sole survivor from HMS *Somali* which was torpedoed in the Arctic, and during the assault on Normandy was a truly terrifying Beach Master.

On Wednesday, 27 September 1933, we arrived at Haifa and all the third Destroyer Flotilla berthed stern to the new south wall which had just been built. Getting in was rather tricky. We let go both anchors, one from the capstan and the other from the bitts with a complete turnround and two foot slack to get it going after letting go the anchor. The turns round the bitts jammed, but I was luckily able to put a slip on the cable and take the turn off before the ship gathered stern way. Then I knocked the slip off and, oh boy, what sparks! We went astern till both cables were out to a clinch, seven on each as I had changed two shackles over from starboard to port, then put on both compressors and hoped the cables would not part. They did not, but we parted a wire aft and I think the anchors started coming home as the bottom was sand and there was a strong headwind blowing. This harbour was very good, rather like Gibraltar's.

I think it was after the Flotilla efficiency test that we visited Gibraltar. As a member of the Torpedo Control Officers' union we did well, and were by a long way top of the torpedo proficiency list, with no bad runs and no torpedoes lost during the commission.

As wine caterer, I was able to profit by John Agnew's wife Lita Larios's connection with the wine industry. La Ina sherry, brought into Gibraltar from Spain in casks in the boot of their car, was sold in the wardroom at two pence a glass, and I think we had as much as four casks of it.

Admiral Cunningham as Rear Admiral (Destroyers) in HMS *Coventry*, with *Achates* and *Acasta*, visited Bizerta, where we had a hectic time. I claimed five shillings a day interpreter's allowance and was quite hoarse from continuous jabbering! It was a French submarine and seaplane base and had a very nice crowd, but all our wine bills were well over the top that month. The Squadron was challenged to a game of football by the Artillery, and I as Sports Officer decided that a combined team from the two destroyers would be more than a match for the Artillery. I was wrong. I went along to the match with the team, which was in a huge stadium, packed with spectators, including all the Generals and senior French officers in the district. I sent a hurried note for Commander McCall with his brass hat and the Captain of *Acasta* to come and support me, and collected a dozen cap ribbons to present to the French team after the match. They beat us hollow (I think, 12 nil) and of course won the huge imitation silver cup. They were so pleased with the cap ribbons which I handed to each of them, lined up, that they insisted on our taking the cup back on board.

Writing from Malta on 25 January 1934, I noted:

'I have suddenly had to take on a good deal more than usual as Heap is going home for the navigation course and I am taking over correspondence, confidential books, Captain's Secretary and Pay Master, in addition to my other duties. All most interesting and valuable experience.'

Admiral Cunningham wanted to see what would happen if destroyers steamed at full speed in a gale from astern. Returning from the Riviera in a northerly gale, he disposed his 27 destroyers in line abreast five cables (half a mile) apart, course south, and orderd us all to proceed at full speed. A big sea was running and my Captain said we must not use more than five degrees of wheel. The ship was yawing up to 45 degrees each way as we overtook each huge wave, but suffered no damage. HMS *Bulldog* on the other hand probably used too much wheel and at one point broached to, about 120 degrees off course, burying her lee rail and smashing boats. Heywood-Lonsdale, the First Lieutenant, had cleared all hands off the upper deck, but was himself caught in a green sea and washed aft, catching hold of the torpedo davit, but was washed away from that, bashing up against the after screen and thence onto the quarterdeck, catching his leg in the depth charge trap. By a superhuman effort he managed to get back on board with the next roll of the ship, but with three torn ligaments in his leg.

The Shrimps were due to play against an Army team next day when we arrived in Malta, and Mountbatten had to look round hastily for a number one with a low handicap, and I was lucky to be selected. He lent me two beautiful ponies, of which, riding Bannerback, I remember, was like sitting in an armchair. For six weeks I played in his team, consisting of Charles Lamb and Major Thomas, besides him. We used to meet in his cabin every day and discuss tactics. What we were not going to do to the Army was nobody's business!

Having passed all the examinations qualifying me to command a Destroyer, it was time to go home, with all my certificates signed by Rear Admiral Rose and Andrew Cunningham as Rear Admiral (Destroyers). The wardroom dined me in the mess. I did not want it, but it was an amusing evening and we made speeches. The torpedo party presented me with a dummy model of a crushed head and two poems. Eventually I returned to UK in SS *Strathnaver*, arriving about 27 June 1934 for leave at Wentworth, awaiting my next appointment. I kept one of the poems as a souvenir:

> The battle o'er the tumult died
> But TCO was anxious eyed
> A 1000 fish he'd fired, some said
> But never had he crushed a head.
>
> The Captain swung the ship with skill
> The Gunner always knew the drill
> But still the prayer of TCO
> was just one hit before I go.
>
> At last the fatal night arrived
> When Graham skillfully connived
> to fire two SFPs beneath
> the *Coventry* and the *Keith*.
>
> The whaler's crew with joyous shout
> Announced the fish had had a clout
> and through the ship the word was passed
> Old Vasco's had a hit at last.

8

HMS *Venetia*, Second Destroyer Flotilla
1934–1936

I was appointed the First Lieutenant of HMS *Venetia* when the ship recommissioned, and relieved Chippy Stanford at Devonport, arriving on board on 13 July 1934, in time to make out watch bills before the new Gunner's Mate joined. Stanford kindly returned from leave to turn the refit over to me. After three years as First Lieutenant, he was intensely proud of HMS *Venetia* and I inherited a very smart ship, evidenced by funnel guys and guard rails carefully canvassed and enamelled white, mahogany beadings round the fo'c'sle to prevent streaks over the paintwork, and the ship's crest of the winged Venetian lion displayed in prominent places, including the lifebuoys.

Lieut-Commander R.G. Stewart ('Blossom') assumed command from S.E. Crew-Reid, and I stayed with him for two and a half years. He favoured red lifebuoys, which, with the ship's name in gold leaf and the crest on a white disc held in the centre of white cords, showed up well against the enamelled paintwork or in the sea when dropped for exercise, especially if there was any chop (white water). A black cat walked on board the day after commissioning which pleased the ship's company.

After commissioning, we went to Rosyth where we lay in pens in company with Commodore (D) during our working up period. Our stern light was half a minute late in being switched on one evening, and the Captain was ordered to repair on board. The air was blue for some time afterwards.

Apart from Fleet exercises, we spent the next six months on North Irish patrol. We were supposed to protect the Army garrisons at Fort Leenan and Fort George, but as long as we were within 100 miles of Lock Swilley, nobody asked any awkward questions. The Captain's mother lived at Largs and we spent most of the time on the west coast of Scotland, with plenty of opportunity for recreation, and the ship's company enjoyed many opportunities of going ashore.

During the fine summer weather with very little sea time, cleaning ship and routine work was generally completed by noon, so we had to devise projects to keep the ship's company occupied. We made a rifle range near Oban, and made good use of the hills for field exercises. I remember dressing up as an Albanian peasant, as a sort of terrorist to be chased and caught by landing parties.

During a visit to Lamlash, the Duchess of Montrose very kindly invited the officers to play tennis at Brodick Castle. There was also a party given by the Provost. It so happened that the farmer on Holy Island complained that the goats were eating his crops and he would appreciate it if we could shoot them, so I arranged for a landing party of some thirty men to land with rifles so that we could make a job of it. Fortunately, I asked the Duchess if we could send a party ashore on Holy Island to shoot goats. She said: 'Certainly, and I will send my keeper.' He arrived rather late, by which time I had the men spread out at intervals across the northern spur of the island, ready to advance when ordered. The keeper, a huge man in plus-fours, when he did arrive, said: 'You mustn't shoot a nanny-goat, and you mustn't shoot a kid, and you can only shoot one billy-goat after I have seen it through my telescope.'

At that, I took a deep breath and blew my whistle, and the party came scampering over the hill towards me with their rifles at the high port. I said: 'There seems to have been some mistake' and I told them what the keeper had said, adding, 'Any man who does not wish to continue can go back to the ship.' Seven, including the Warrant Engineer and I elected to stay, and to fire in the reverse order of what I felt was their assessed accuracy, beginning with the Engineer Officer who wore glasses. To cut a long story short, we panted up and down the two hills on the island, being observed by these fine, white-coated goats, who sensibly managed to keep out of range. We ended up behind a stone wall near the lighthouse at the southern end of the island, and prepared to open fire, whereupon the lighthouse keeper dashed out and headed off the goats, who made their way down a steep cliff onto the beach facing the Clyde. There, firing vertically downwards, one billy-goat was duly despatched and the executioners had the pleasure of carrying it the whole length of the island, for delivery to the Duchess, with many thanks for a good day's outing.

I do not remember meeting the Army at Londonderry, but we took the Duke of Gloucester and the Duke of Abercorn up the river to Belfast where the photograph shows them landing.

NORTHERN IRELAND, 1935

Frank Gilliland had been an RNVR Lieutenant in command of a coastal motor boat in World War I, and had a nice house on the banks of the River Foyle, to which he invited us to dinner. He told us that a destroyer flotilla of nine boats had come steaming past in line ahead, and he thought it would be nice to invite the Captain (D) to dinner. He manned his flag staff with three gardeners, and hoisted the international signal meaning 'Hope you will dine with me tonight'. Back went the reply from the Leader: 'WMP'*, whereupon Frank gave the order 'Down of all'. The head gardener gave a violent tug to the halyard, which promptly parted, leaving the signal flying for each ship in turn to accept such a kind invitation.

The Southern Irish Patrol comprised the other three ships of our division under Commander Caslon in HMS *Viceroy*. The Abyssinian crisis was soon to bring us together again.

THE ABYSSINIAN CRISIS

We were getting ready for messdeck rounds and looking forward to seeing the International Motor Bike TT Race, when the cypher signal arrived informing us of the crisis in Abyssinia. Rounds were cancelled, steam raised in two boilers and we were on our way to Liverpool at 23 knots within three hours, to recover a torpedo which had been hidden under sacks of flour, on a wall 50 feet high. The Gunner got it safely on board with the aid of some unemployed men, who were as usual sitting on the wall. We then proceeded to Devonport at 17 knots, where we were to be completed to war complement, embark stores and ammunition, and get ready to sail

*With Much Pleasure

on 13 September. Stokers and sailors arrived from out of the blue on 30 August, mostly at half an hour's notice, and I spent the following week shaking up the dockyard, embarking Mark IV torpedoes, fitting warheads, testing cable and painting out messdecks. We also embarked ammunition and sea store deposit gear, including Mediterranean awnings and stanchions.

On 10 September, which happened to be my birthday, there was a large tea fight at Admiralty House.

HMS *VENETIA*. PREPARATIONS FOR WAR WITH ITALY

Friday, 13 September, should have been the day of our departure, but to avoid any superstitious forebodings, sailing for the Mediterranean was put off until the 14th. Meanwhile, there was some disappointment that arrangements for our whaler to take part in the Rawson Cup at Portland had to be cancelled. My crew had given up some of their leave for it and had even made up the menu for every day of the return trip to Devonport.

Twelve Sick Berth Attendants arrived on board for passage to other ships, and I told them they would have to sleep in the wardroom or on deck, as we were already crammed full of men and stores. Eight bags of confidential books for the Commander-in-Chief, Mediterranean were stowed in the warhead magazine, and I scrounged cordite racks from HMS *Wescott* as she was not ready, fitted shell racks and cleaned up the upper deck as much as possible, before sailing for exercises with the 4th Division. We all knew we were going to Malta, and rendezvoused 24 miles south of the Eddystone and set course 210 at 20 knots. Very rough weather caused an uncomfortable night, which meant that I had to be on the bridge nearly all night.

The weather moderated the next day and by the time we reached Gibraltar we had shifted into white tropical uniform and rigged windsails. There was quite a reunion with the 4th Division after our five months absence in Irish waters and home ports. We left Gib the next morning and set course for Malta at 20 knots. In spite of spreading bridge and waist awnings, the temperature in the engine room was 127° Fahrenheit, with the wind astern keeping pace with us. Hands were exercised at action stations by day and night, with ship darkened for search light exercise by sub-divisions at 5,000 yards distance.

The 4th Division berthed in Sliema Harbour and was welcomed to a cocktail party in HMS *Keppel*, where we learned that we would remain in Malta under orders of Captain Baillie-Graham to act as local defence flotilla ('the suicide squadron'). It was decided that I would be Master Gun Control officer for the 4th Division. I wrote at the time: 'My Tels are delighted', and, later: 'The locals have proper wind up and everyone seems to expect air and Coastal Motor Boat attacks.' Notwithstanding the state of our sides, I gave a make and mend after the Captain had cleared lower deck, and explained the situation.

The next day we started hanging up splinter mats (lilos) and painting upperworks Mediterranean grey. They called us the Elizabeth Arden Division, on account of the dark hulls, light upper works and lipstick-coloured funnel bands

A floating mine was reported on Tuesday, 24 September, and 'Exercise Box' on Malta Black Out was staged for the benefit of the RAF. At 2100 the signal '*IMPORTANT*' – 'Blackout' was radioed, telephoned and telegraphed all over the island. Not a light was to be seen for half an hour. We had been six miles west of Filfola to warn ships approaching. None came and at 2330 we anchored in Marsa Scirrocco.

Extracts from my journal follow:

Bomber squadrons from Sicily were reported during black-outs on two successive nights, detected at 1500 feet. The usual teething troubles with Gunnery and new crews. A vast amount of VC-VF gear (visual identification equipment) fills the chart-house and bridge and I doubt whether any of us will ever know how it works.

Tuesday, 1 October. Sent in three gunnery analyses and played tennis on Admiral Cunningham's very nice court. Mrs Cunningham invites all and sundry to use it and have tea afterwards.

Seven months without a full calibre shoot, despite bi-weekly drills in Ireland . . . I mustered all the gunlayers and trainers and said I would ask for full calibre shoots every night until they could hit the target.

Tuesday, 3 October. Single ship and divisional concentration full calibre firing. The former bad on account of bad rate keeping. The latter, 41 hits within 100 yards. The best to date, and very gratifying for me, as it was my first effort as Master Control Officer.

Sunday, 19 October. Captain (D) of the nineteenth destroyer squadron came on board at 0930 and inspected the ship's company at Divisions, and walked round mess decks and upper decks. He paid no compliments, but said: 'I'll tell you how much I like you when I've seen the others.' I was rather disappointed, but I knew Captain Vian. On Monday we slipped after a violent hail squall, with hailstones as big as blackbirds' eggs.

We exercised with our Asdic (submarine detecting equipment) pinging all the morning, and ran PVs (Paravanes) in the afternoon. Several things went wrong while getting them in. Exercising paravanes once a quarter is too seldom to attain real efficiency.

Italian submarines have been hanging round Malta for some time and we nearly pinged one onto the rocks off Delimara, but he turned round just in time and took us about 15 miles towards Sicily. Good practice for our anti-submarine team.

Viceroy made us paint semaphore arms black and we have painted funnel bands black; otherwise, we still have a little pride left, though our side looks like an ashen grey sunset upside down.

19th Flotilla. Malta. When controlling divisional torpedo attacks or concentration firing, we hoisted a cone and lowered it when the other division took over. *Vega* failed to take over when I lowered the cone for his benefit. In the next run, the signalmen were too busy to deal with it and so I detailed an Ordinary Seaman for Run III, his sole duty being to hoist the ruddy thing. However, he had a much better idea and unhooked it first, got the halyards twisted six times, caught it up in the blue flag and then let them go. He was surprised when I jumped on top of him, to find the other end still belayed.

Friday, 8 November. General drill. *Venetia* first in every evolution and *Douglas* ('the leader'), last. They said they forgot to

81

hoist pennant one to indicate they had completed the exercise. We made several large holes in the skiff, hoisting it onto the fo'c'sle. Captain (D) asked if we would like a Shipwright. I didn't tell him his Shipwright was already up to his eyes in work for *Venetia*, but we replied: 'No thank you, as damage does not impair our fighting efficiency!'

Sunday, 10 November. Emergency destroyer. Played tennis with Mrs A.B. Cunningham.

11 November. Armistice Day. Cleared lower deck at 1045 and paraded a Petty Officer's Guard. Took a party sailing in the whaler to St Julian's. They got very wet beating back.

16 December. Our first week in harbour since September. Only two ships in the flotilla remain running – HMS *Douglas* and HMS *Mackay*. All the rest have broken down one way or another.

Christmas Day. The Captain came on board after four days' sick leave and admired the decorations, which were the best in the harbour. Divisions and church on the upper deck, with hymns accompanied by Able Seaman Tipton on the squeeze box, were followed by visits to the wardroom by the decorating party, followed by the Leading Hands and Petty Officers. Mrs Stewart came the rounds of the messdecks and had to unveil an enormous 'tiddy oggy' (Devonshire pasty), bedecked with streamers and rosettes and hidden by blue and white flags.

She was then elected Vice President of the Football Club and presented with a blue and white check elephant, with port and starboard ears and yellow feet.

1 January 1936. Rear Admiral (Destroyers) inspected the destroyer command on Manoel Island and made a very good speech, the gist of which was to dispel 'buzzes about going home', and that the present political situation was likely to continue with a crisis about once a month. During our absence the cash box was stolen from the cupboard in my cabin, and I had to make good about £80.

The Captain and I were sitting up late on our Emergency night, and towards 0330 I suggested it was about time I got a command!

'No 1,' he said, 'I'll go and see Captain (D) in the morning', which he did. Captain (D) Phillip Vian then passed his recommendation on to Rear Admiral (D), Rear-Admiral A.B. Cunningham, who forwarded it to the Commander-in-Chief. A week later, I was appointed in command of HMS *Stronghold* to relieve Stanford at Alexandria. However, the Admiralty stepped in and appointed Lieutenant-Commander Hadow in command. Stanford was furious and wrote: 'Rear Admiral (D) wanted you as his best First Lieutenant to take on this job.' About ten contradictory signals passed and I turned HMS *Venetia* over to Lieutenant Topp between 0530 and 1800, before embarking in HMS *Ajax* for passage to Alexandria, where, after calling on Captain (D) and dining at the Club, I was shown Vice Admiral Malta's signal 'Lieutenant de Chair is not to sail to Alexandria in the *Ajax* but is to return to the *Venetia*'.

I gathered that Vice Admiral, Malta wanted me for HMS *Worcester*, where I went next day to relieve Pleydell-Bouverie. He was first lieutenant of HMS *Echo* which had collided with HMS *Encounter* during a night torpedo attack. After a week's exercises driving *Worcester* manned from reserve with *Encounter*'s crew, we turned over to *Encounter*. Renfrew Gotto, her Captain, came down from Bighi Hospital where he was suffering from neurasthenia as a result of the collision and turned the books over to me, without signing for them. I was now in the highly unusual situation of being temporarily in command of HM Ships *Encounter* and *Worcester*, but was still required to go to sea in *Venetia* to control concentration firing for the Division. In *Worcester* we were four Lieutenants and 'tail-end Charlie' during a night attack on one of the battle cruisers being led by D19. This monster looming up in the darkness obviously caught Captain (D) by surprise. He turned to starboard without signal and fortunately we all did likewise, without orders. Signal '*Worcester* from *Venetia*: You could have had our straws for the asking!'

Lieutenant-Commander A.C. Stanford arrived in HMS *Woolwich* on 7 February and took command of *Encounter*, *Venetia* berthed on *Worcester* and both ships went into number four dock on 12 February, with *Venetia*'s ship's company living in *Worcester* and painting out their own messdecks. HMS *Encounter* then sailed for Alexandria.

HMS *Achates* had sustained damage to her side and cracked a turbine casing in a gale when alongside in Haifa harbour. On about 27 February, with only one day's notice, the officers and men of *Achates* and *Venetia* changed ships, those of *Venetia* bringing their beer and books with them as soon as *Achates* berthed alongside at 1330. *Achates* sailed for the UK at 1900, leaving our Engineer Officer Chiefy Truscott and six behind in HMS *Venetia*, with *Achates'* crew. We arrived at Devonport on 4 April 1936, after passage on one engine at 12 knots, and remained there until 24 September. Our turbine casing was lifted out and replaced by a new one and the ship refitted. We all had our leave due, mostly six to eight weeks which had accumulated during our time abroad.

Patricia Ramsey and I did a lot of sailing together during the summer and we all made the most of our time in the home port.

Our mutual friend Arnold Green, the Australian First Lieutenant of HMS *Cygnet*, decided to get a lap ahead while his Captain was on leave and received the following signal: '*Cygnet from D2. I observe that you are painting your funnels this Sunday morning. Why aren't you at Prayers?*' Reply: '*Cleanliness is next to Godliness: we prayed last Sunday.*'

After what my sister described as an interesting summer, Pat and I got engaged to be married on 7 September. Blossom Stewart left me in command on 19 September and took over HMS *Brilliant*. After a full power trial in low visibility, I took the *Achates* out to Gibraltar where we turned over to *Venetia* once more. Commander Fogg-Elliott was watching as I brought his ship into the dock at five knots, rather too fast on account of a cross wind, and had to order 'full astern', which started emptying water out of the dock!

THE SPANISH CIVIL WAR AND HOME

I had taken, as my guest, Major Hugh Ford of the 5th Royal Iniskilling Dragoon Guards and we duly installed ourselves at the Rock Hotel. We were having breakfast in our dressing gowns on our veranda and had a grandstand view of two Spanish cruisers steaming into the bay and bombarding Algeciras. It was my first view of guns being fired in anger. After three days I took *Venetia* back to England, leaving Ford behind, which was fortunate for him, as we had a rough trip.

I was not particularly concerned about the Spanish Civil War and we were not expecting action. Suddenly, as we were passing Tarifa Point, a Spanish aircraft from Huelva approached in a dive towards my bridge. I waved to the pilot and he waved back, zooming up over our fore stay, no doubt after having seen our white ensign.

On return to Devonport, I duly reported to the Commander-in-Chief and enquired from his Staff Officer (Operations) if I could expect a command. He rang the Second Sea Lord's office at the Admiralty and was told: 'Yes, he'll get a command.' I had visions of a China gunboat, which would not have been much help in my engaged state, but heard him say: 'You know who he's marrying, don't you?' I often wonder whether it was thanks to Pat, who was an Admiral's daughter, that I was given the plum 'makee learn' command of HMS *Wrestler*, in the HMS *Vernon* flotilla. Anyway, I paid *Venetia* off into reserve on 28 October 1936 and commissioned *Wrestler* from Reserve at Portsmouth on 17 November, for service in the *Vernon* flotilla and experimental torpedo running.

9

HMS *Wrestler*, the *Vernon* Flotilla 1936–7

My appointment to HMS *Wrestler* was considered a very desirable appointment for an aspiring Commanding Officer, which it certainly turned out to be, but with only two other officers in the ship, a commissioned Gunner and a commissioned Engineer, my time was fully occupied. Signal books had not been corrected for three years, and other confidential books for up to seven years. Charts had never been corrected, and despite my protests on collecting all these, I was told to get on with it. Pat and I spent the first three months of our married life correcting the books, and for a modest sum I persuaded the Navigation School to get the charts up to date. Mr Ven of 'Smeed and Smeed' (a wine and spirits firm) came on board most days and wrote up the Wine and Tobacco books; and Mr Pyle, the Foreman of Shipwrights, was a great help in getting our alterations and additions and other dockyard work done.

After two weeks experimental running at Portland, Pat Ramsey and I were married at St George's, Hanover Square, on Saturday 12 December 1936. Commander Berthon, the Senior Officer *Vernon* flotilla, kindly offered to take my ship to sea if required that day, but after one night at the Berkeley, I had to leave Pat and return to Portsmouth for another week's running at Portland, before Christmas leave and our honeymoon.

We eventually found a charming thatched cottage near Warsash and took it unfurnished for one pound a week. Commander and Mrs Richmond greatly assisted by lending us their furniture, which was duly conveyed from Alverstoke in the *Vernon* lorry. I was able to extend our small garage by means of the canvas cover of a set of torpedo tubes, and used a pair of oars for support to give our Rover and baby Fiat shelter.

The better part of each week was spent torpedo running at Portland. Lieutenant-Commander Lyn Taylor and the trials party would embark by noon on Monday and we sailed five minutes later, anchoring for the night off the breakwater at Bincleaves and returning at 26 knots on Thursday evening in time for a 'Friday while', unless HMS *Wrestler* happened to be duty destroyer over the weekend.

Pat and I spent most of the weekends sailing our 14-foot dinghy, for which I laid a two-arm mooring off the Crab and Lobster pub at Warsash. This and one laid by Mr C.S.D. Noakes were the first moorings in the Lower Hamble River.

Lady Jellicoe invited us to stay at Ventnor for a dance and the weather being fine, we sailed over to Cowes in the dinghy. My plan was to luff alongside the sloping camber by the Royal Yacht Squadron, and for Pat to jump out while I took the boat to a mooring. This she did as I went about and threw the suitcase with all our clothes in it after her. Of course, the inevitable happened, and it landed in the water, but was retrieved by onlookers, it being well and truly soaked. Our hostess rose graciously to the occasion, since it was clear that Pat's dress as far as the dance was concerned was ruined. As I recall, Lady Jellicoe took off the dress she was wearing, to reveal a very smart bright green silk slip, which she later removed, saying: 'There's your dress, Pat. Put a reef in it.'

CORONATION REVIEW 1937

HMS *Wrestler* was completed to full peacetime complement with reservists on 10 May 1937 and joined the 10th Destroyer Flotilla (*Vernon* and local flotillas) under Commander Berthon, our Senior Officer *Vernon* Flotilla. Captain B.C.S. Marten with the Portland flotilla, and ships from Devonport and Chatham as the ninth flotilla, took us all to sea for a week's exercise, which was very good value for the Commanding Officer. Some of the First Lieutenants found life rather hectic, and the then acting First Lieutenant of HMS *Wild Swan* (Lieutenant Victor Clark) will not mind if I quote him. On his ship's company noticeboard, he exhorted the men with: 'two hands for the King and tons of elbow grease.' During evening rounds he noticed the words 'Bul-Shit' scrawled over it. This represented a serious reflection on discipline and morale. After mature consideration, he sent for the offending document and wrote in red ink: 'This should be spelt with two Ls', signed First Lieutenant.[1] At hands' fall in the following morning it was all smiles and no more trouble.

We all took up our berths at anchor for the review at Spithead in time to clean up and paint ship. As we were approaching our allotted berths, in formation, a man fell overboard from the ship astern of *Wrestler*. However, he was seen in time for the two following ships to avoid him by turning in opposite directions, without reducing speed, so that HMS *Vidette*[2] was able to pick him up and still remain in station.

20th MAY

Day broke fine but rather misty, brightening later when the course was cleared for HM Royal Yacht *Victoria and Albert*, preceded by SS *Patricia*, to steam down the long lines of ships about eight miles West and back eight miles East, followed by SS *Strathmore*[3] and SS *Rangitata*.[4] By kind permission of Their Majesties we were allowed to invite guests on board for the occasion, provided that ladies wore dark colours and no sunshades or umbrellas, and men refrained from wearing cloth caps.

Experimental torpedo running was never dull. Sometimes a torpedo gyro pivot broke and the torpedo ran ashore, to be retrieved before admiring children. We were spared an unpleasant accident on 16 June, when, owing to gyro failure, a 35 knots torpedo turned 180° and was struck by our stem post between the air vessel and head. It was a miracle that at 25 knots we struck it there, and that the torpedo floated upright minus its head, contrary to expectations.

On the following day we took part in a demonstration for the RAF Staff College, Andover. HMS *Iron Duke* was attacked with torpedoes by six destroyers and six aircraft, and then by submarines. Ships from our squadron recovered the torpedoes, and after embarking ten RAF Officers each from *Iron Duke* and five Cadets from HMS *Erebus*, carried out depth charge attacks and picked up a lot of stunned fish, which impressed the Cadets. Manoeuvres before and after the attacks included gridirons, in one of which we narrowly avoided collision with the Senior Officer of the local flotilla in HMS *Verity*. My senior officer supported me, but I felt we were both at fault, and later I went over to apologise.

The half-yearly promotion on 1 July included Commander to Captain our Senior Officer, Lyon Berthon; Jock McCall, my Captain in *Achates*, and Lord Louis Mountbatten. Admiral Cunningham advised me to take the staff course.

Commander P.N. Walter assumed command of the *Vernon*

flotilla at 0800 on Wednesday, 13 July and took us all to sea for a coast defence exercise. Captain and Mrs Berthon were on the jetty to see us off and we cheered them as we had done before, after he spoke to the ship's company.

Further demonstrations were carried out for Camberley Staff College and the Imperial Defence College during the ensuing weeks. Captains Cedric Holland (my old Captain (D)) of Second Destroyer Flotilla and the Hon Guy Russell, came out in *Wrestler* for the last one, and seemed pleased with the exercise. The next day, Commander Walter came on board and walked round the ship. He seemed suitably impressed, except for the guns, which was hardly surprising with two-fifths of her proper complement. All holding down bolts and shell racks had needed scraping for months.

My father came out in *Wrestler* one week for down swell trials in rough weather and some 10,000 yards direction runs. One torpedo ran ashore on the beach west of Warborough tout and had to be recovered through a ten-foot surf. He appeared surprised by the manoeuvrability of a V and W class destroyer, and I think our efforts were a revelation to him. Two stories he told may bear repetition.

Queen Victoria expressed a wish to witness a torpedo attack while she was staying at Osborne. Accordingly, four torpedo boats, each with one torpedo, approached her, probably in line abreast, and fired in her direction where she was standing on the beach. The idea was for her to be able to see the torpedoes being fired and for them to shut off in good time before grounding. However, one torpedo came straight at her and shot out of the water onto the beach with a roar and much smoke from the calcium light, before it providentially shut off. The old Queen was delighted and patted it with her parasol. Such a good attack!

HMS *Vernon*, having no guns, was not to be outshone by Whale Island, the Gunnery School, on an occasion which called for a 21-gun salute. Accordingly, 21 mines were laid in a line somewhere off Lee-on-the-Solent, whence they could be controlled. Apparently the resulting 21 mine salute broke all the nearby windows.

Commander Walter had to defer the date of inspection until after my appointment to HMS *Scout* had arrived. Eventually, at one day's notice and at my request, the inspection was carried out. Thanks partly to the timely loan of 70 Ordinary Seamen, the ship was made presentable, despite rain squalls, and apart from the gun bores requiring more attention, all went well. The Commander-in-Chief, Lord Cork and Orrery wrote: 'I am pleased to receive such a favourable report.' After visiting Sheerness to see my new command refitting and subsequently calling at Admiralty, I took *Wrestler* to sea with the Senior Officer of the flotilla and my relief, Lieutenant R.L. Alexander. We mustered Confidential Books after dinner and I slept in the office. *Sea Wolf* discharge trials in a heavy swell that day had resulted in my first loss of a torpedo.

Pat collected me after dinner in the wardroom, and we stayed with her aunts in Weymouth, driving back to Sheerness on 2 December 1937.

NOTES

1. Later Commander Victor Clark, DSC*.
2. Lt-Commander Gerry Roope, VC (Posthumous) of HMS *Glow Worm* fame.
3. With my parents as guests.
4. With MPs on board, including my brother, and his wife.

The author as a naval cadet aged 14.

dmiral Sir John Kelly inspecting divisions in HMS *Nelson* – 1931.

The author as a member of the winning crew of the officer's gig HMS *Nelson* – 1931.

HRH the Duke of Gloucester boarding HMS *Venetia* at the 1935 Jubilee of King George V.

The author in HMS *Wrestler* – 1937.

Mr Maurice Henderson and Yew Ah Kow
the number one Compradore at Jardine's
rescued by HMS *Thracian*.

HMS *Venetia* – 1935.

Hong Kong harbour – 1939.

HMS *Vimy* – Long Range Escort Vessel – 1941.

Seventeen survivors from SS *West Lashaway* packed into a raft 19 days after
the ship was torpedoed.

The Japanese cruiser *Haguro* sunk after an action with British ships in 1945.

b-Lieutenant Raymond Venables RNVR and Carol, one of the survivors from *West Lashaway* rescued by HMS *Vimy*.

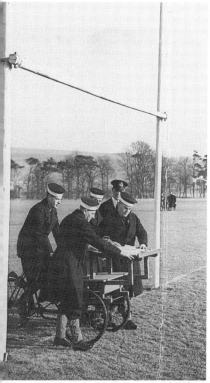

icer cadets learning navigation at 1S *Royal Arthur* – 1943.

The author with his parents at Teuchar Lodge in 1956.

HMS *Venus* – one of the ships involved in the action against the Japanese cruiser *Haguro*.

HMS *Venus* torpedo party at Trincomalee following the sinking of the Japanese cruiser *Haguro*.

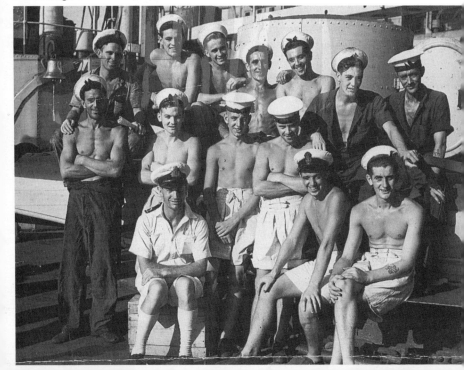

10

HMS *Scout* and Court Martial

My appointment for HMS *Scout* in command on commissioning for trials, and on commissioning as an independent command, directed me to repair on board at Sheerness on 2 December 1937.

Sadness to be leaving HMS *Wrestler* and the *Vernon* flotilla was tempered by the prospect of some excitement in China, and encouraging reports after a very satisfactory year carrying out the experimental torpedo trials for HMS *Vernon* at Portland.

On Tuesday 17 November, exactly a year since commissioning *Wrestler* from Reserve my boss the Senior officer *Vernon* Flotilla arrived onboard and said he would inspect the ship on Friday. However, he agreed to do it next day as I had arranged to meet the dock-yard officers at Sheerness on the 19th, during the forenoon. Having met them on board and seen my new command in typical dockyard deshabille, Pat and I drove to London where I called on Commander Halsey who told me Rear-Admiral Tovey had asked for me to go as Commanding Officer of an L-Class destroyer in the Mediterranean, but was told I was too young. He said that my appointment in command of HMS *Scout* would be for two years followed by a new destroyer if reports were good.

Completion date for the refit was deferred to 13 January 1938, the refit which should have ended in November being extended for six weeks, with much work to be done. Meanwhile HMS *Scout* commissioned with a special complement of 28 seamen and full peace engine room complement on 9 December and I took over as Senior Officer of Ships in Sheerness Dockyard, which really meant detailing them for guard duty by turns.

After much too-ing and fro-ing, Pat and I had packed ourselves out of our sweet little cottage at Hook, near Warsash, and had driven in two cars through snowstorms and fog to Sheerness.

My last visits to this yard had been when my sister and I as children twenty years previously, were allowed to accompany our Father to the landing stage and see him off to his flagshp, HMS *Dreadnought*. He told a story about two Midshipmen who had found an engine in the dockyard, during the dinner hour, and as it had steam up, and there was nobody about at the time, they thought it would be fun to try and drive it. All went well until they tried to stop it, before it disappeared in a cloud of steam into the basin. When the engine-driver returned from his mid-day meal, he was surprised that the engine was not where he left it, and searched all round the yard for it, finally having to report its disappearance, which no one believed. Years later it was discovered in a very sad state, by divers. Whether the Midshipman ever owned up is not recorded. They had managed to jump clear just in time.

The First Lieutenant and Sub arrived soon after us and a Royal Naval Reserve Lieutenant was appointed, but it was agreed that he was unfit for further service in a hot climate, and Sub Lieutenant John Stucley assumed the duties of Navigating Officer. Seamen were given Christmas leave and Engine Room personnel were promised theirs after sea trials due to start on 3 January.

HMS *Scout*'s guns had not been fired for over two years, and a representative of Whale Island Gunnery School was required to attend gun trials, for which Lieutenant Morgan-Singer was selected. He was still on Christmas leave at his home in Winchester, but agreed to return. Unfortunately the voice pipes for communication to the guns and telescopes did not materialise in time for the trials, which made things more than a little awkward as it turned out.

Anchor trials and adjustment of the steering compass were carried out on 3 January, followed by a very cold night at our buoy. The weather was fine and sea calm, the silence only broken by loud snoring from the cabin opposite mine. By two a.m. I could stand it no longer, and went on deck expecting to be met by the Quartermaster of the Middle Watch. Apparently feeling the cold, this worthy was warming himself in the ship's company galley for'ard. It seemed best for the First Lieutenant to investigate, so I called him and said, 'No 1, first you will find out why there is no quarter-master on watch, and then tell the Engineer Officer to stop snoring.' I then turned in and heard him knock on the cabin door oposite whence came a grunt, 'What do you want?' Answer, 'Chief, you're keeping everyone awake!' 'Keeping who awake?' says he. 'Well, the Captain and me.' After that silence reigned and the Engineer Officer remained awake all night, so he said. After colours at 0800 in the morning he was most apologetic, saluted smartly and said, 'I never realised before, Sir, how patient my wife must be.' (He and I being the only married Officers had not previously slept onboard.)

We then replenished with oil fuel and embarked the trials party and 30 boy seamen with their instructors from HMS *Wildfire* for a day at sea, a unique opportunity for them. My plan was to steam north as far as the Shipwash keeping about two miles east of Manks to check our speed over the ground and return to the sunk light vessel.

Visibility was patchy, but by 1330 I considered that it had improved sufficiently to the eastward for the gun trials, observing that no further opportunity was expected before sailing for China.

By the time we drew level with the Sunk light vessel speed had been reduced from 31 to about 24 knots, owing to a choked filter in the engine-room. The light-vessel was left five cables (half a mile) on our port beam, and I told the Officer of the Watch, Sub-Lieutenant Stucley, to alter course (from South 30 degrees West (magnetic) the course being steered) to South 15 East. He ordered 'port five', and I said 'use more wheel'. In his statement, Stucley stated: 'I gave the order to "port ten", and the ship answered slowly to her helm, while I watched the Jack staff for an indication of the rate of swinging; on looking back at the compass I observed that the lubber's line was three or four degrees from the mark "15". I gave the order, "Amidship" and subsequently "Steady" as the ship's head remained steady at the "15" mark. I reported to the Captain that the ship was steady on her course, (supposedly South 15 East, when in fact it was South 15 West, an error of 30 degrees)".

To be fair, without pushing the Quartermaster out of the way, and moving the azimuth mirror, by which he was steering, it would have been difficult to read off the course accurately.

I was anxious to train Stucley as my Navigating Officer and to encourage confidence and responsibility, so was not over-supervising him in the simple matter of steadying on a new course, as I had been doing during most of the forenoon. He was the only Commissioned Executive Officer, apart from the First Lieutenant who was also Gunnery Officer of the Ship, and I had complete confidence in his ability and integrity as Officer of the Watch.

At this crucial moment, the First Lieutenant reported '"A" gun ready to fire, Sir.' This was after repeated requests for relative bearings on which to fire, and to my horror I saw 'A' gun at full elevation pointing towards some merchant ships on the horizon. After showing the Officer of the Watch the new course South 15 East on the chart which would leave the Long Sand Buoy seven cables (just over half a mile) to starboard, I went down to 'A' gun with the First Lieutenant and took charge of the training myself! Being the only Officer there with binoculars, I gave the order to fire towards a patch of sunlight, clear of shipping to the Eastward, and after firing a second round with gun horizontal, returned to the Bridge. There the Officer of the Watch and everyone appeared to be alert and keeping a good lookout. 'B' gun was expected to fire shortly, and the Coxswain, who was not steering the ship, drew my attention to a ship bearing Red 60 (near the port beam), and I went down to 'B' gun and found it not ready.

My report to the Commander-in-Chief the Nore shows what happened next, but makes no mention of my being distracted by repeated requests for relative bearings on which to fire, culminating in the First Lieutenant's anxious report '"A" gun ready to fire, Sir', just as the Officer of the Watch had reported 'Ship steady on course South 15 East.

As I climbed the bridge ladder, I noticed a three-masted wreck in the mist some 20 degrees on the starboard bow. No one else had seen it, and looking at the compass I could see that the course being steered was S 15 E, as I expected it would be, and moved over to the chart to identify the wreck. As I did so, the ship brought up suddenly, with a grinding noise and a deafening roar of escaping steam which made speech inaudible. I immediately ordered 'Stop Both Engines' and wrote an order in blue pencil to the Engineer Officer to report any damage to the hull, and sent messages to close watertight doors, and take soundings round the ship.

The Trials Party and Engine Room Staff acted very promptly in shutting off steam and closing down boilers with relief valves blowing.

A more sickening feeling I never experienced and, but for the perseverance of Engineer Commander McLennan in charge of the Trials, we could well have remained on the Long Sand Bank on a falling tide. When asked for his opinion on the state of the engines, his words were 'The port shaft's buggered in 'eaps, but I might get the starboard one to move.' I asked him to do his best and rang down slow astern starboard. Nothing happened for about eight

94

minutes and then a trickle of water was seen to be passing up the starboard side and we started to move astern.

The ship was bumping heavily, with a breaking sea and strong wind from our starboard quarter, with an ebb-tide setting us onto the bank. Having identified the wreck, it was clear that we had grounded on the west side of the Long Sand Bank, and were caught by the propellors.

Evidently, worried at not sighting the Long Sand Buoy, the Officer of the Watch, on checking the compass, saw that the course being steered was South 15 West shortly before I returned to the Bridge for the second time.

It soon became obvious that we were in danger of being blown beam on to the bank, as wind and tide were pushing the stern round, even with the wheel hard to starboard. I ordered an anchor to be let go and veered two shackles of cable, then accepting the risk of driving the bows over the bank, with wheel hard a-port and starboard engine ahead, club-hauled the stern past the wind. The ship then 'lay to' until the wind was nearing the port beam, we then weighed anchor and came astern, with the wheel hard a-starboard. The stern came slowly round past the wind again, but an offing had been gained, and the Long Sand Buoy was sighted on the port quarter. Being now well clear of the bank, I went ahead using full starboard wheel to make a further offing and soon sighted the Sunk Lightship where all the trouble started. Returning to Sheerness by the Barrow Deep Channel, at five knots with the starboard engine, it was necessary to use 15 degrees of port wheel to keep the bows away from the wind.

It occurred to me that no adverse publicity by the press was desirable until the Admiralty had time to make a statement. Accordingly on our way back, I spoke to the Trials Party who had done so well in the sudden emergency, and then to the boys from HMS *Wildfire* who probably thought the events of the day had been specially arranged for their benefit! Finally I addressed my own Ship's Company on return to harbour, when I congratulated all hands on efficient drill, damage control, collision stations, sounding and good discipline. I swore them all to secrecy to prevent any leakage of news of the occurrence, and as far as I know they all played ball. Anyway, at the subsequent court-martial, the press appeared to be taken completely by surprise, and I think they showed some annoyance after the court-martial. The story was front page news for three days in the Daily Express, 'Destroyer Captain dismissed his ship'. My MP brother was not amused.

Being somewhat proud of my rather unorthodox method of club-hauling, I made the mistake of reporting the grounding to Commander-in-Chief The Nore, adding 'no underwater damage'. The words 'to the hull' should have been added. The truth was later revealed in a floating dock. I think the starboard propellor that got us back had about half of one blade left.

HMS *Scout* was placed in a floating dock in Sheerness Harbour. There was no electricity at night and I had to prepare my defence for the forthcoming court-martial by the light of oil lamps in the middle of a cold winter. The Captain Superintendent, Commodore H.R. Marrack, was most kind and Commander Ramsbotham, the Captain of the Dockyard at Sheerness, had my report typed in his office. A Board of Enquiry with Captain James Figgins as President was duly held in HMS *Wildfire* who provided Officers and men with lunch and shelter. It all seemed very fairly and well conducted, although the evidence of the ratings must have been very confusing. Their views of visibility varied from one to twenty miles!

Sub Lieutenant Stucley showed up very well and tried to take all the blame. My wife and I had seen a good deal of him over the weekend and tried to dissuade him from doing so.

A Commander I had met in Sydney invited me to come to Chatham and discuss the grounding, which struck me as a friendly gesture, and I hoped his advice might help me at the court-martial. This meant going up the River Medway on two occasions so that he could get his facts right. He entertained me with sherry, 'in accordance with the best traditions of the service', as he put it, and was most cordial and sympathetic. These visits occupied the best part of two whole days, and were hardly calculated to help in preparing my own defence. I should have realised that my host was to be the Prosecutor at my court-martial, as I was to discover later. I gather Sub-Lieutenant Stucley was similarly entertained.

Form CM386 sent by the Deputy Judge Advocate stated that, under King's Regulations, 'You are entitled, if you ask for it, to my opinion on any question of law relating to the charges or trial'. I met him just before the trial started and asked him whether the Prosecutor was justified in sending for me as he had done. He appeared to be most upset, and said it was highly irregular, but it was too late now for him to do anything about it.

My old shipmate St John Tyrwhitt agreed to act as my Prisoner's Friend, and was a great help with questions etc, likely to be asked. I should have let him act for me, but when I saw the President of the Court, the Captain of HMS *Liverpool*, a highly respected and genial Naval Officer, I decided that he and the Court would take a favourable view of a young Destroyer Captain conducting his own Defence from the witness box, instead of relying on his Prisoner's Friend. In the event the Prosecutor managed to tie me up in knots and got me to lose my wool. At least I did not blackguard my Navigator or the First Lieutenant for failing to get voice pipes for the guns as ordered. One question was 'If you were doing 24 knots in the mouth of the Thames (as we were at the time of the grounding) and saw a wreck fine on the starboard bow, what would you do?' I said, 'go on at 24 knots of course' which we did.

In his proposed council for the defence Tyrwhitt stated 'I may say that with six months' experience of these waters, I am not unduly perturbed by the sight of a wreck 20 degrees off my bow.'

The sight of my sword point directed at me as I entered the court room to hear the verdict and sentence of the Court, showed that I had been found guilty of Stranding. Hardly surprising, but still a nasty shock. Being dismissed the ship in her crippled state was doubtless inevitable, and I was reprimanded. The poor Sub was severely reprimanded, his offence being in not warning me as soon as he discovered his mistake in time to take the way off the ship.

After a promising Naval career and distinguished war service, Stucley studied Law and eventually became a Circuit Judge. The poem he sent me after the stranding is included at the appendix to this chapter, together with other documents relating to my court martial.

Returning home to Wentworth after the court-martial, I decided to leave the Navy and prepared ski-ing kit for Wengen, where Admiral Hall offered to lend us his chalet. Several very kind letters of sympathy from my old Captains and some Admirals, including the Commander-in-Chief Portsmouth started to arrive, and Admiral Evans, whose job it was to order the court-martial, send me a flimsy (Certificate of Service) written in his own hand, which read: 'Very much to my satisfaction.' This was a great encouragement, and when an appointment to HMS *Royal Sovereign* arrived, I took my father's advice and acknowledged it.

APPENDIX 1

Poem written by Sub-Lieutenant John Stucley.

My tale which here I put to verse
Might very easily be worse . . .

The Lightship's crew looked out with awe
On hearing racing turbines roar
With bone at teeth and bow wave high
The good ship *Scout* went thundering by.
Between each treacherous sunken ridge
Intrepid Stucley upon the bridge
She altered course, first East then West.
For reasons he alone knew best.

But look! . . . What distant object spied?

Upon yon mud-bank sits astride
A lovely Lady . . . teeth like pearls
With glass in hand, she combs her curls
Her skin like silk of milky texture
But pouting as if something'd vexed her.
Our hero . . . gallant, brave sea rover
Promptly ordered 'Helm hard over . . .!'
With spy glass glued to eye he stands
When
    Crash . . .
        the speeding vessel strands.

APPENDIX 2

Appointment to HMS *Royal Sovereign*.

C.W.

By Command of the Commissioners
for Executing the Office of Lord
High Admiral of the United
Kingdom, &c.

To *Lieutenant Commander H. G. de Chair R.N*

THE Lords Commissioners of the Admiralty hereby appoint you *Lieutenant Commander*
of His Majesty's Ship *Royal Sovereign*

and direct you to repair on board that Ship at *Devonport* on *8th February 1938*

Your appointment is to take effect from that date, *and on recommissioning*

You are to acknowledge the receipt of this Appointment *forthwith*, addressing your letter to the Commanding Officer,

H.M.S. *Royal Sovereign*

taking care to furnish your address.

Fodenhall
Wentworth
Virginia Water
Surrey
Admiralty, S.W.1.
2nd February 1938

By Command of their Lordships,

R. H. A. Carter

(30/1148) (1028) Wt. 12476/6903 5M 6/37 S.E.R. Ltd. Gp. 671.

99

APPENDIX 3

Letters of support.

FROM ADMIRAL SIR REGINALD HALL.

January 25th. 1938

My dear Graham,

It does not need my writing to tell you
how greatly I am feeling for you: and to beg you not to
despair; things so often work out better than one dares to
hope and if you remember the Psalms you will recollect
that never saw I the righteous beg his bread etc; and
thats just what I feel about you.
Now I dont know what your plans are; I HOPE you will just drive at
at them and get a job at once ; but if this be not possible
why not come out here with Pat for a time? We have a good
double room for you and her; live the simple life and
breathe good air. If this be not feasible, then perhaps my
cottage The Ropeway at Beaulieu may be of some service to you;
if so, please let me know; my old Nora can go down there at once
and open up; you will want a cook as I have Sherwood out here;
there will be nothing to pay of course except your food!
There is a small car there and Jim does the garden and
cars- also electric light.
Give my affectionate regards please to Pat
                    ever yours

100

Admiralty House,
Portsmouth.
Telephone 7068. 22 . 1 . 38

My dear de Chair

I am so sorry to see
you have had this stroke of
bad luck.

Don't let it discourage
you, I twice rec⁰ their Lordship's
displeasure when in command
of a destroyer & was court-
martialled as a Captain for
"hazarding".

Yours sincerely

Cork & Orrery.

H.M.S. "VERNON,"
PORTSMOUTH.

22nd Jan:

My dear De Chair.

I must send you
a line to condole with you
on recent happenings.
I am sorry about it &
trust that it will prove
no more than a temporary
set-back. You have an
excellent reputation.

Yours. v. Sincerely

A.U.Willis.

102

11

HMS *Royal Sovereign* – 1938

My appointment to HMS *Royal Sovereign* is shown in the previous chapter, and in accordance with custom, I reported onboard at 0900 on 18 February 1938 in frock coat and sword, and was greeted by the Commander with the words 'Will you take on gas and ventilation and sports?' My immediate reaction was to say 'I would rather not do sports until I know something about gas and ventilation.'

It appeared that there were no ventilation drawings in the ship, and both Devonport and Portsmouth Dockyards declined to prepare any, saying such an undertaking would be too big in view of the time limit and money available. Captain Dorling when I reported this to him said 'The only thing is for you to make the drawings yourself', which I completed in pencil, just before leaving the ship after only six months. We had a filtration unit designed to clear the ship of gas, but without considerable dock-yard work on the trunking it was obvious that the ship would never be gas-tight.

Other duties of a more congenial nature soon came my way, including Duty Commanding Officer by turns, keeping the morning watch in harbour, Divisional Officer of the Quarter Deck Division, Sailing, Regatta and Boat Officer, and responsible for control of the four-inch gun anti-aircraft armament inter alia. Responsibility for gas and anti-gas and ventilation involved marking fans and ventilation valves, watertight doors and hatches.

We recommissioned in February 1938 and carried out gun trials, followed a month later by searchlight trials and adjustment of compasses. Then we took part in a combined exercise in July, working war routine for 24 hours, which seemed endless. A film unit was onboard to take pictures of our air raid precaution arrangements and decontamination parties, which concerned me.

The Royal Marines in HMS *Royal Sovereign* never did anything by halves. They manned 'Y' turret on my quarterdeck, but without consulting me, painted the top of it with red oxide, shortly before it came on to rain. Result, red oxide all over the beautiful grey enamel sides to the turret. The Captain was not amused, and was even more concerned during remedial action. I got in touch with the makers of PARIPAN, who advised rubbing down with glass paper and polishing with Paripan Polish. The result was excellent, with the enamel as gleaming as ever, but not before the Captain had expressed displeasure at the rubbing down process.

The ceremony of Colours at 0800 was rigidly observed, with the Captain present. At the report 'Eight o'clock, Sir' he would say 'Make it so'. The Marines Guard presented arms and the bugle sounded the call for Colours, as the Ensign was hoisted. One day the Captain's corgi dog decided to do its business on the starboard side of the quarterdeck, just before the Marines Guard marched forward to disperse. They must have seen it, but took no avoiding action. With evident delight they all scraped their feet in it, leaving two long messy streaks on the immaculate teak deck, knowing full well that the quarterdeck men would have to re-scrub it.

Captain Dorling was a keen boat sailor and encouraged me as Boat Officer. We acquired six Royal Naval Sailing Association 14-foot dinghies, gunter lug rigged, and challenged HMS *Vernon* to a race against their sloop rig dinghies with tall masts. The results showed no appreciable difference in the performance of the two rigs, and gunter lugs became the standard rig for RNSA dinghies in HM ships, where the taller masts would make stowage difficult.

It came as a surprise to me when my appointment to HMS *Thracian* in Command arrived. Captain Dorling who had been my Captain (D) of the Third Destroyer Flotilla five years previously, may have thought I expected it, his only adverse comment on my report being 'He must cultivate forethought'.

I lent some brass fittings and wooden dolphins to the Commander for the boats, and got his receipt for them, as I hadn't the heart to take them with me. They came from my father's Flagship HMS *Dreadnought* in 1917 and I often wonder what the Russians made of them when they borrowed HMS *Royal Sovereign* during the Second World War. Possibly further evidence of Decadent Capitalism. Anyway I never saw them again.

12

HMS *Thracian*, Hong Kong Local Defence Flotilla. 1938-41

My appointment to HMS *Thracian* in Command was dated 14 August 1938. Passage to Hong Kong was arranged in the troop ship *Lancashire*, but the Sea Transport Officer informed me that there was regrettably no room for Senior Officers' wives, including mine. Accordingly, Pat drove with me to Southampton, intending to spend the weekend with her parents at the Botley Grange Hotel. On the way I asked her: 'If there is room would you come with me?' and she replied: 'Yes.' When I arrived on board, the Sea Transport Officer said: 'I am very sorry, de Chair, that we could not accommodate your wife, but if there is a passage, could she go?' I said: 'Yes', and he added: 'I'll let you know in ten minutes time.' Sure enough he later told me: 'You can have a double cabin on C deck, if you don't mind that.' Her fare was £10.17.0, instead of £160 in a P&O ship. So Pat went ashore to telephone. At Wentworth my mother got a taxi and brought our prepacked trunk and case luggage down to Southampton, 66 miles away, within the hour before the ship sailed, and Admiral and Mrs Ramsey also came from Botley.

The trip out was pleasantly relaxing, despite the heat of the cabin on C deck, and we shared a table with three Naval Lieutenants, including Alan Noble, and also a nice New Zealand couple. St John Tyrwhitt, Senior Naval Officer (SNO) Naval Draft, was also joining the Hong Kong Local Defence Flotilla in HMS *Thanet*.

We reached Singapore on the day of the Munich Crisis and all wives were landed there. Pat came on to Hong Kong as soon as she could and stayed with Lady Masterton-Smith while I was at Swatow. The *Lancashire* entered Hong Kong on 4 October and secured in heavy rain; there Bernard Tancock met me as I was to be his relief. He turned *Thracian* over to me the day after *Lancashire* arrived and gave me dinner at his house. He informed me that a typhoon was approaching the Colony and that the Japanese were expected to attack Swatow at any time. It was clearly important for me to sail as soon as possible to take over as Senior Naval Officer Swatow.

We slipped from number 10 buoy and proceeded at 12 knots by the Lei-mun Pass on Tuesday, 6 October, carrying out pom-pom firing and practising ship handling when clear of the island. The epicentre of the typhoon was reported as 300 miles to the south, approaching Hong Kong at 15 knots. I decided to maintain speed of 12 knots against wind East North East force seven and a heavy swell to clear the typhoon area, and made a weather report at 2200. I think the north-east monsoon drove the typhoon down into the Gulf of Tonking, but it was very reassuring at daylight to see the Breaker Point fishing fleet putting to sea – junks as far as the eye could see, a most impressive sight, all on the port tack and riding the sea very comfortably.

We entered Swatow harbour one hour after low water neaps with 23 feet of water on the bar in the Sugarloaf Channel, and secured alongside HMS *Duchess* (Lieutenant-Commander Robin White) at Messrs Jardine Matheson's number 10 buoy. He handed over the Senior Naval Officer's pack to me and sailed at 1400 after introducing the British Consul, Mr René Lee, with whom I dined in the evening. Calls were exchanged with USS *Tulsa* and the Commissioner of Customs.

The following morning, Saturday 8 October 1938, Mr Lee invited me to accompany him on board a British and a Norwegian ship, as he was mustering coolies. According to the Customs authorities, he received ten cents for each coolie mustered. This was quite lucrative, when there were 1,200 coolies at a time and gave him an income of about £800 a year.

The next day, Sunday, following Divisions and reading prayers, I spoke to the ship's company, this being my first real opportunity. They had had a perfectly miserable start to the commission, and had been sent out from Devonport with all scuttles leaking and so had been practically under water all the way to Hong Kong. I found their motto to be: 'Per Argua ad Ardua' (sailor's Latin). After two years, they were naturally looking forward to being relieved and sent home.

Meanwhile life was made relatively pleasant as Officers and men were invited to the canteen in the Consulate garden and made honorary members of the Customs Club, also patronised by the US Navy. USS *Tulsa* invited our Officers and men to attend their cinema every night and transported us in their large and up-to-date launch, which was a godsend. Their boat coxswains had a professional non-substantive rate which made them experts at the job.

During the next few days I exercised general drill and took the whaler away under sail. Apparently this was the first time in twelve months that the whaler had been used and several enthusiasts cottoned on to the idea for dog watch recreation.

There were some air raid alarms the following week and we managed to secure a copy of one of the Japanese leaflets dropped by a seaplane. The police were very quick to pick them up and any Chinese found with them were severely punished. The pamphlets would be accompanied by a couple of bombs by way of exhortation. The pamphlets which landed about twenty minutes later were to tell the people they had nothing to fear from peace-loving Japan if they behaved. One marvelled at the logic of the Japanese.

On 13 October I had an 'At Home' on board, attended by the Officers from USS *Tulsa* and most of the British community and their friends. Mr Webster of the Hong Kong and Shanghai Bank asked me to lunch afterwards. In the afternoon I bicycled 18 miles with Lieutenant Stevenson of the Hong Kong Naval Volunteer Force and saw primitive China in the raw – very attractive apart from the smell.

Gordon Campbell came on board on 17 October. He was expecting the Japanese to attack that night and was holding one of the Butterfield and Swire ships ready for evacuation.

Four of us attended an 'At Home' with Henderson of Jardine's and Indo China Steam Navigation Company Ltd on board their new steamer *Taisang* (Captain W.A. Balch), who was taking a record cargo of 2,400 tons up to Shanghai. We had supper in USS *Tulsa*, followed by cinema and animated conversation covering every possible subject.

A couple of days later, at dinner with Lawrence of the Asiatic Petroleum Company, I met Mr Chu Su Nan, the Mayor's Counsellor, who explained that the Chinese rapid retreat towards Canton had been to draw on the Japanese flying columns and cut them off, which they did.

HMS *Diana* arrived on Thursday 20th and I turned over SNO to Jimmy Machin, before returning to Hong Kong. There I was able to contact Pat and we booked rooms at the Repulse Bay Hotel, later moving to an attached house. After only a week in harbour, *Thracian* was sent to relieve HMS *Decoy* (Commander Robertson) at Urmiston Roads at the entrance to the Canton River to report Japanese movements. Lieutenant-Commander Clark, Senior Officer of the Second Torpedo Boat Flotilla joined me with Motor Torpedo Boat 10 and brought the Postman and Messman from HMS *Tamar*. He took me up river as far as our territorial limits and south to Lintin. I got him to impersonate the Commodore for a dummy inspection, which was just as well, after which I carried out my own inspection which left much to be desired. We also exercised night defence with the Motor Torpedo Boat and took some of the ratings for a run on a spying exercise.

HMS *Daring* relieved me on 2 November and I returned to Hong Kong, dining with the Commodore in the evening. Next day, the engine room, store rooms and gunnery department were inspected. Hands were paid and worked late, getting ready for the Commodore's inspection the following morning. In spite of what I considered a lamentable performance the Commodore gave us a good report.

We acted as target ship for submarines during the following week and returned to watch the Canton River in squally weather, with Motor Torpedo Boat number ten bumping alongside all night. The Commander-in-Chief passed in HMS *Seamew* on his way to Canton, coming straight towards us at full speed (very impressive), and we paraded a guard as he passed.

HMS *Scout* arrived in mid-January with Hugh Simms in command and we had more time for various joint exercises, such as gunnery, night encounter and towing. John Milner-Barry came as Senior Officer of the Local Defence Force. He had been passed over for promotion.

We were very sorry when the time came for Milner-Barry to leave and take his *Tenedos* to Singapore. Meanwhile, the Chinese New Year found me back at Swatow up the Han River at Kityang in a punt with the assistant manager of Reiss Bradley for three days (the best place for observing the dawn flight of geese).

There was a review of the Naval landing parties at Happy Valley, before the Fleet began to disperse to war stations. I led the three platoons from the Local Defence Force and gathered that the spectacle was most impressive to onlookers. The Commander-in-Chief, Admiral Sir Percy Noble, attended by his son and Pat Matheson, Flag Lieutenant, and all Brigade and Battalion Commanders, well mounted on horses. The Admiral's speech was clearly audible a mile away.

The following is an extract from a letter to my father, dated 10 February 1939:

'We have had a busy week. Night shadowing and Encounter exercises every night and two night shoots. Also a realistic night attack through the Hong Kong defences. I'm glad I have no nerves!'

On Wednesday night, *Tenedos* was leading me across the bows of the flagship, HMS *Kent*, which was returning from Wei Hai Wei. It was off the Ninepins near Bias Bay that this enormous haystack of a thing suddenly loomed up very close on our starboard bow. The idea had been for our division to attack from her starboard bow. Milner-Barry's First Lieutenant said: 'You can't do it, Sir.' 'Can't I?' says M-B, 'Full speed ahead both.' 'What about *Thracian*?' says the First Lieutenant. 'Oh, B-Thracian,' says M-B. He meant it kindly and obviously thought I could look after myself. The letter continues:

'I disobeyed the signal to turn to port and fire which would have entailed being rammed amidships, and turned to starboard. The result was most spectacular. *Tenedos* fired torpedoes from one cable on *Kent*'s starboard bow and lit her up before they saw him. Their eight-inch guns had not had time to train round onto him before we lit up the *Kent*'s lower scuttles with our ten-inch searchlight from less than a cable on her port beam and were out of it before the Major of Marines had time to shake his fist at me from the after control. The Commander-in-Chief signalled: "Attacks were well carried out" and terminated the exercise.'

On Tuesday, 21 March 1939 *Thracian* recommissioned with a new and very young but keen crew and things began to brighten up.

Shortly after this Pat and I were invited to dinner at Admiralty House. Milner-Barry with *Tenedos* had already left. Being the most junior guest, I was entering the dining room with the Admiral when he said: 'Now you have three ships, we will have to make you an Acting Commander.' I should have thanked him promptly and said: 'That would be a great help', but the moment passed. This was probably just as well as it was not long before I was to ask Commodore Peters to send me or the Captain of the *Scout* home to the war zone. Simms went and I was left ostensibly to train relief Commanding Officers.

SWATOW AGAIN

Admiral Noble came to Swatow in HMS *Falmouth* on 17 May 1939, and the Japanese celebrated his arrival with four air raids. These consisted of a poor exhibition of dive bombing in 45° glides and machine gunning ferries and sampans. The Commander-in-Chief was not impressed, but I was worried when he went ashore with his staff between raids, displaying a wholesome disregard for air raid warnings. He gave a lunch party on board HMS *Falmouth* and all the ladies came out to watch in their party dresses, while anti-aircraft gun crews stood by. He was entertained to dinner that night by the Consul and after making a very good speech, said: 'No reply is called for', whereupon Lee got up and said: 'Commander-in-Chief, a reply *is* called for: HIC' and then promptly collapsed!

The Gordon Campbells of Butterfield and Swire had very kindly invited Pat and me to stay with them, which was a great blessing as it turned out, for it was there that Pat received a telegram saying that her mother had died.

Most of the inhabitants of Swatow cleared out when air raids were expected. One Sunday in May about 4,000 Chinese were returning in their sampans across the harbour from Katchioh, when a line squall, an offshoot of a typhoon passing up the coast caught them halfway across. Thirty-five managed to reach *Thracian* and some got to a merchant ship, but about 200 were drowned. The Customs boat brought our libertymen back and landed our refugees after the storm had abated and after they had been comforted by our ship's company.

A week later, Stevenson, the Assistant Manager of Jardine's, brought Mr Tan Wui on board with the heads of all the local guilds and presented me with a silk joss flag in token of our rescue in the storm. It was eight feet long, hand-made, of deep blue silk with a red lining and a border of yellow tongues, and an inscription in

110

English and Chinese. We hoisted it at the main mast peak together with crackers which they let off, making a deafening row and burning holes in the quarterdeck deck corticene.

We also flew the joss flag while escorting Admiral Noble as he left Hong Kong for Singapore in the *Kent*. No other British warship had a joss flag to our knowledge. Sadly, it was stolen by my Chinese steward and never recovered.

Our daughter was born on 21 April 1939 at the Peak Hospital in Hong Kong. She was christened in the binnacle lid of HMS *Thracian*'s after compass, with Lady Masterton-Smith and Johnnie Henley as godparents, and the Chinese joss flag hoisted at the main.

HMS *THRACIAN* NEW COMMISSION. APRIL 1939

We had a fortnight in Hong Kong and ten days at Swatow to give the new crew a chance to shake down, before our working up programme. Finding Swatow in dense fog was a good exercise, running a line of soundings and plotting them, off Breaker Point where two big liners had collided two days earlier.

Mr Chu Su Nan, the Mayor's Cambridge-educated Counsellor, promised *inter alia* to keep me informed through our Consul on the state of mines and their moorings which were being examined after renewal in the harbour entrance. This entailed sighting each mine and working down the mooring to examine the sinker.

He expressed himself forcibly on the subject of Britain who he considered soft and easily taken in by Germany, Japan and Italy. I told him to assure His Honour the Mayor that if I saw a British ship or building being deliberately bombed or attacked by Japanese aircraft, I would have no hesitation in opening fire. The Chinese promptly painted Union Jacks on all their godowns, which we had to have removed.

HMS *THRACIAN* AND THE SEIZURE OF SS *SAGRES* BY THE JAPANESE NAVY

On 9 April 1939 I returned on board after tiffin with the coal merchant on Katchioh at about 1400 and received a signal from

Commodore Hong Kong to raise steam and report when ready, followed an hour later with orders to proceed with despatch to the assistance of SS *Sagres* in Chouan Bay. This was followed by some garbled signals to the effect that a British ship of the Moller Line was being interfered with and I was to investigate. Chouan Bay was about 50 miles up the coast to the north of Namoa Island, with its sheltered anchorage in clipper roads. We sailed at 1529, leaving two stokers and nearly all the Chinese stewards ashore, despite sirens, Blue Peter recall signal being hoisted and boat messages. We steamed with two boilers at 24 knots, passing the Japanese Fleet at anchor in clipper roads and giving their boats the benefit of our wash. The weather outside was rough, with a high sea, wind force five to seven and there was warning of a typhoon. The waves washed down steadily over the bridge and lower yard (quite exciting), and the wireless operator kept calling *Sagres* by wireless on 500Kcs, but could get no reply. Then soon after sunset we saw her wallowing along at about eight knots, escorted by a large Unagi class Japanese destroyer about two cables on her port beam and a trawler about a mile astern. The trawler was thought to have been operating with a submarine, whose periscope was sighted and later observed following the trawler, burning navigation lights.

We did not see the cruiser which was nearby in the gathering darkness, but the sight of the Japanese Naval ensign at *Sagres'* main masthead caused me to think seriously about carrying the *Sagres* by boarding. I don't think the Japanese would have opened fire. It was clear that they had a prize crew on board and my parting instruction from Commodore Dicken had been: 'You won't be thanked if you precipitate an incident.'

We eased down about 50 yards opposite *Sagres'* bridge, between her and the destroyer. No Europeans were visible and I could get no reply to signals made by flashing, flags and W/T, including 'L' international code flag, meaning: 'Stop. I have something important to communicate', and 'Please stop'. It transpired that the Captain of *Sagres* was being restrained with a pistol at his back. As neither signal had any effect, I piped: 'Hands to action stations' and uncovered guns which had not been possible during our approach owing to the sea and spray. As a mine-layer we only had one four-inch gun and a two-pounder pom-pom. The Japanese destroyer was also at action stations with four guns and torpedo tubes.

I decided to force the issue by making the destroyer go astern and stop, to avoid hitting me, by converging on him from his starboard bow. He stopped about 20 yards short of my fo'c'sle; being a good seaman he knew that collision under these conditions would put him in the wrong. The convoy then came to a halt and I signalled: 'What is the matter?' He replied: 'Never mind.' I made: 'Am sending boat', and received the reply: 'Wave so big, so very dangerous.'

The Japanese threw a rope ladder over the side, which, being badly secured, gave way. Lieutenant Easy, our First Lieutenant in charge of the boarding party, fell back into the whaler, doubtless as intended (Japanese joke, loss of 'face'), but he managed to catch hold of the guardrails at the next roll and haul himself on board. He was conducted to the bridge to see Commander Sato IJN who took him down to their wardroom, where he repeated my protest that by international maritime law we had prior right of visit and search of a British ship, and as we were not at war with Japan, we must protest at their seizure of the *Sagres* and that we would now take her over. The Japanese Captain was very firm and polite, and kept saying: 'Very sorry, cannot allow it', although it was explained to him that we were there to help and clear up any misunderstanding or difficulty. I had some problems in keeping to leeward of the Japanese destroyer and after half an hour on board, Lieutenant Easy was asked to hurry back to *Thracian*, in view of worsening weather.

It appeared later that the Japanese Commander-in-Chief had ordered Sato to capture the *Sagres*, which was known to have been loading salt for the Chinese Government and suspected of carrying their troops. The Moller Line were generally suspect and when caught like this, shouted for help. We were told that *Sagres* would be taken to an examination anchorage at Baku, in the Pescadores, and I signalled that I would follow and be present at the examination, as I wished to see *Sagres*' manifest. His answer to that was: 'I cannot permit you to board *Sagres* and am sorry.' I continued to protest and pointed out that their action was quite illegal, Japan not having declared war on China, and argued that they should have asked me to verify any breach of flag neutrality agreements.

The whaler nearly got swamped and smashed, owing to indifferent seamanship when being hoisted in the heavy roll. Half our seamen were short service ordinary seaman, the best hands being take for action stations. The destroyer went ahead, fully darkened except for navigation lights, and signalled 'Good day'. I replied: 'Thank you, I will follow'. At 0200 I received orders from Commodore Hong Kong to return to Swatow.

The British Ambassador, Sir Archibald Clark-Kerr, came down from Shanghai. While walking with me on the bund at Katchioh, he commented: 'Thank God you didn't do any more.' I had certainly investigated the situation and both he and the Commodore said I had done everything possible. The *Sagres* was kept under examination for three weeks before being released, and when Captain Morren brought his wife to dinner at our house, we heard the full story. The delay cost Mr Williamson of the Douglas Shipping Company HK$1,000 a day, but he was nevertheless very grateful for what we had found out.

LOCAL DEFENCE FORCE AND THE JAPANESE
CAPTURE OF SWATOW

The Japanese captured Swatow on 21 June 1939. HMS *Thanet* (Lieutenant-Commander John Mowlem) was in harbour as Senior Naval Officer. His first intimation of attack was a flying boat landing nearby, followed by four or five destroyers steaming up the harbour. The Chinese had offered no resistance after the two posts and mine hut at the entrance to Sugarloaf Channel had been captured, and there was very little panic. The Chinese Army, with characteristic philosophy, had reported to Chow Chow Fu some 20 miles inland, leaving two militia to guard the fort.

The Japanese ordered all foreigners to clear out. However, they remained!

Off Swatow, HMS *Scout* discovered a Japanese squadron at anchor, and four British merchant ships waiting to get in. The flagship signalled him to stop, but *Scout* (Lieutenant-Commander Hugh Simms) hoisted the international code signal: 'Follow me' and proceeded into harbour, followed by SS *Tsinan* at full speed. The Japanese blared their sirens and hoisted signals, but he took no notice. Guns on the mainland started firing at the island opposite as *Scout* passed through the Channel, and shells whizzed over him. They were furious, having said it was not safe to enter

114

Swatow harbour, and seeing that we had openly defied them. When *Tsinan* berthed there was no one to take her lines, the piers were all barricaded with barbed wire and machine guns and she had to sail without discharging her cargo. After conferring with *Thanet*, *Scout* sailed, held a conference on board the Japanese flagship *Myoko* in the entrance, and then sailed to Hong Kong at full speed to report. The Commodore sent him straight back to Swatow. There the Japanese had taken his forcing the entrance very much to heart, considering they had lost much face, and refused to meet him or the Commanding Officer of HMS *Thanet*.

HMS *Thracian* at Hong Kong was engaged in an interesting mine-laying exercise in Port Shelter, when ordered to relieve *Thanet*, arriving at Swatow on 8 July. Capatin Hayakawa received me on arrival in the flotilla leader *Unagi* quite pleasantly, but insisted on three postulates:

1. Only one foreign ship a week to visit the port.
2. No foreigners to enter or leave the port without prior permission.
3. No leave to be granted in Swatow without a special pass.

I managed to increase the calling of ships to one each way per week and was eventually allowed to go out and meet ships on the bar.

The post office was closed, and the Postmaster General from Hong Kong had to return to HMS *Thanet*, after several unsuccessful attempts at getting it opened. No merchants ships had been allowed in for about a fortnight, but Captain Haikawa agreed to let SS *Yatshing* in with fourteen bags of mail. These were landed without any trouble and were efficiently dealt with by the Japanese Postmaster, who appeared cultivated and well disposed towards us. I said there would be a large mail, with some passengers arriving next day in SS *Kayang*. She had 168 bags of mail and the passengers were returning to their homes on Katchioh. I was told: 'You have had your ship this week. All mails and passengers will have to be brought on board *Unagi*, and no passengers can land without Japanese Consular permits from Hong Kong'. The question of consular permits had not previously arisen and was one which we did not recognise, as was also the limit on entry of British ships. In any case the passengers had already left Hong Kong and could not obtain permits.

We sailed the following morning and met SS *Kayang* on the bar; after embarking the passengers and mail, HMS *Thracian* anchored near *Unagi*, but declined to transfer the mail. After about an hour I took the passengers on board, preceding them in frock coat and sword. We were cordially received by Officers and sat down on deck drinking fizzy lemonade, but Captain Hayakawa did not appear for another hour. When he did, he refused to let the passengers land without consular permits, so after protesting that they were returning to their homes and businesses, I took them back on board *Thracian* for lunch. Commodore Stapler USN arrived in the afternoon, and called on the Japanese Consul, but to no purpose, and at my request took the passengers back to Hong Kong in USS *Pillsbury*, which saved us a lot of face. He and the USN were a great support and help to us.

No one was allowed to do anything without permission of the Senior Japanese Officer and if any of our taipans wanted to see him, I had to accompany them wearing sword and medal. All for 'face'.

Japanese soldiers were accused of raping in Swatow and I went on board to protest to the Senior Japanese Naval Officer. His only comment was: 'Ah well, you can't stop rape, but plenty soon Japanese get 200 girl and you can get own back'. They imported hundreds of Geisha girls in blue uniforms and started their headquarters behind the American Consulate (to keep the soldiers quiet).

The Japanese wanted Jardine's number one Compradore to be their puppet mayor and Mr Henderson asked me to give him a passage to Hong Kong. I said I could not agree to do this as the Japanese would regard it as a *casus belli*. However, I accepted his invitation to tiffin and sure enough, Mr Yew Ah Kow was there. They were both terrified of his being discovered by the Japanese, who would then have had a first class case against us, and I realised how awkward it would be for the British community if they knew he was taking refuge in the agent's house across the harbour in Katchioh.

I invited Henderson to bring Yew Ah Kow to tea on board at 1600 and told him to bring a suitcase and embark on the blind side from the Japanese destroyer, which he did, happily during a rain squall. We took him down to the wardroom where he remained for the next four days. When off the Ninepins, within thirteen miles

116

of Hong Kong, I received a signal for *Thracian* or *Thanet* to proceed to the vicinity of Amoy to escort HMS *Duncan* back to Hong Kong. *Thanet* being in harbour, I turned round and met the *Duncan* by sunset.

With tears of gratitude for his life, Yew Ah Kow went ashore in Hong Kong and wanted to give us all presents, and on finding that useless, wanted to give the sailors beer. I told him the best present he could give was to keep his mouth shut, and tell no one. However, Newbeggin, Jardine's number three persuaded me that he would lose too much face if we would not accept a present and we opted for a water polo cup. A fine silver cup arrived, which, thanks to Lieutenant Frank Carter, the new First Lieutenant, we won easily, as we did the football.

When Pat and I eventually left Hong Kong, Mr Yew Ah Kow invited us to dinner at the Kamloong restaurant, with Newbeggin and any friends we liked to bring. We were honoured during the course of the evening by a huge display of firecrackers in the street, which attracted large crowds. He was a rich man, having spent 40 years in the company and had much influence with the Chinese. (The photograph shows him with Henderson at Swatow.)

HMS *THRACIAN* AT SWATOW

All communications, and these were frequent, were conducted by an Officer of the Guard or me, with Guard pendant flying. When *Thanet* was Senior Naval Officer, it was often Lieutenant John Stucley's doubtful privilege. He was an impressive figure, standing six feet seven inches tall, and when he stood on the *Unagi*'s gangway his head was above their awning. The Japanese refused to speak to him unless he sat down, no doubt to save face. Both he and Kenny, the first Lieutenant, had been appointed to *Thanet* from the *Scout* after we had been court martialled for grounding, and the addition of *Scout* to the flotilla did not let us forget it.

Our relations with the Japanese were improving gradually, but they were obviously determined to oust us as soon as possible.

Much of our time was spent cyphering and deciphering signals, and the Japanese cyphers probably caused them more irritation than ours. They used to work at them on deck and sometimes only just had time to hide them behind their backs as we went on board.

I felt quite sorry for them, but one never knew what the morning might bring forth. Lieutenant Ito would arrive at 0800 and say: 'This morning I am very displease. You are very discourteous. Why do you land British Consul without telling me, a week ago?' René Lee's sins had found him out, we had brought Bryant up from Hong Kong to relieve him, and I was virtually Acting Consul as far as the Japanese were concerned. Another day he arrived very punctiliously to thank us for putting a fire out in one of the Japanese barges.

On the whole the Japanese Navy were better behaved than the military or civilians ashore, and gave me a pass to the Doctor which worked like a charm at all the barriers for anyone landing.

After nearly three weeks I was beginning to despair of much further improvement in British trade and living conditions in Swatow. The value of Swatow drawn work alone had been worth two million pounds a year. Hearing that Captain Hayakawa liked beer, I sent him two pewter beer mugs with an invitation to an 'At Home', which he declined, but not to be outdone in politeness, sent me three bottles of the best saki, one of which I later gave to a Japanese Major on the Hong-Kong border with China, at Shateau Kok.

I had a private arrangement with our Army at Shateau Kok off Bias Bay. After they signalled 'Nips', I was to give them fourteen minutes to leg it for Hong Kong before opening fire on the advancing Japanese troops with my four-inch guns.

The duty of Senior Naval Officer Swatow was shared by various destroyer commanding officers and I must have done it about ten times by 1939, when Britain declared war on Germany and relations with Japan became progressively strained.

Working on board during the summer with no air conditioning was not made easier by living in a tin oven. My cabin temperature was sometimes 110°F and one could not write without wetting the paper with sweat if you inadvertently touched it.

HMS *THRACIAN* AT HOI HOW. JULY 1939

Mobilisation of the Fleet took place in July 1939, and war seemed more likely than ever. Eleven large Japanese warships having evaded the vigilance of our Intelligence Department, HMS

Thracian was sent off to look for them, since they were possibly in the Hainan area. Accordingly, we proceeded to Hoi How where HIJMS *Chioda* a seaplane tender and four transports were at anchor, the latter landing troops. At about mid-day as we anchored a sudden storm got up which caused them considerable trouble with their motor landing craft, particularly in embarking horses. I guessed these were destined for attack on Pak Hoi, but heard later that they were for an attack on Hong Kong organised to coincide with a German attack on Britain. *Chioda* sent his Officer of the Guard, but I was unable to return the call as our motorboat had broken down.

The harbour master took me ashore, and I spent an interesting afternoon with the British and other foreign residents who had seen no Britons since the capture of the island some six months earlier. HMS *Scout* had arrived, but her Commanding Officer only succeeded in reaching the pier where he was locked up in the guard-house after a neck and neck race with a Japanese escort vessel.

USS *John D. Edwards* had visited Hoi How during the original Japanese occupation, despite Japanese protests with signals to stop, zigzagging ahead as she entered Hainan Strait. Commodore Stapler flying his broad pendant, got fed up and hoisted what he called his 'What the hell pendant', a white flag with a red question mark and various hieroglyphics all over it. After feverish efforts to look it up, they sent over in desperation to ask what it meant, and were told it was a new international signal. They said: 'It's not in our book', at which the Commodore is reputed to have said: 'Well, I guess your book is out of date!'

Chioda sailed at 1900 and, guessing she was bound for the Pak Hoi area, we followed at midnight, finding her at dawn anchored off Gewichau Island, where the area was very badly charted. I then proceeded to Pak Hoi to see what was afoot. All the navigational marks had been removed by the Japanese, but we eventually anchored above the fishing stakes and I landed with the Gunner in the Customs sampan. The only British resident was a missionary, a Miss Bradley, who was assisting an Austrian doctor to look after a leper settlement and hospital. After inspecting the lepers with her, she took me to call on the Mayor, with whom she spoke fluent Chinese, and said that my visit had given them all renewed courage and was much appreciated.

I persuaded the Commissioner of Customs to lend me his

sampan again, although the Japanese were still machine gunning sampans, because I was anxious to leave in time to reach Gweichau by sunset. We had heavy rain and lightning, with corposants at the masthead and yard-arms, an eerie sight.

HMS *THRACIAN*. HONG KONG LOCAL DEFENCE FORCE. 1940

A Russian ship with a cargo of wolfram was expected to leave Manila during the first week of January 1940, northbound, and *Thracian* was detailed to try and intercept her and bring her into Hong Kong for examination. We knew the course she would take and her expected time of departure. I decided to make sure of reaching her track by aiming well astern of her expected position, which meant running towards Manila with the monsoon on my quarter. With hindsight, I would have done better to aim well ahead with wind abeam and run down the line with wind and sea astern, when I got there. One of our cruisers may have done so and caught the ship.

In 1940, war with Japan appeared imminent and all the young wives were evacuated to Australia and Manila. Brigadier Reeve and I had previously written separately to Brigadier MacArthur, asking if he could arrange for them to be accommodated in Camp John Hay at Baguio if this happened, and after three miserable days in a leaky Red Cross bungalow, Pat and some other wives and children, including my daughter Anita, were taken there and looked after by a Colonel Love.

The British Consul in Manila was no help and kept apologising to his American friends for the British refugees who only had summer dresses and what they could carry. After three hours in a train, they arrived in Baguio feeling very cold. Pat had to carry Anita, then one year old, and when she asked a porter to carry her suitcase, he said: 'How much will you give me?' By this time, being thoroughly distraught, she hit him over the head with it, and he then carried it!

I was able to send the amah to join them with a packing case full of clothes soon afterwards. I spent the first week on board after Pat left and decided to keep our home on in case she was able to return.

After one night alone with a big house and staff, I invited Lieutenant-Commander Melrose, the first lieutenant of an armed

120

merchant carrier, and an Australian squatter of some substance, to dinner. My instructions to Ching, the number one boy, were 'Ching: one master come dinner tonight. You catchee good dinner, lamb chops and lemon sponge.' My guest arrived and after a few drinks we sat down. In front of us were two plates, each with a very small chop, no vegetables or gravy. Then came two plates with a very small round thing in the middle – lemon sponge. We left the table and proceeded to dinner in the town. On my return I expostulated with Ching: 'You catchee very bad dinner. Tomorrow four master come dinner and you catchee good dinner.' I realised how patient Pat had been in writing out every little detail of menus, and I then followed her example.

Since we were officially at war with Germany and unofficially so with Japan, the work of the Local Defence Force became exacting, involving peace routine by day and war routine with patrols round Hong Kong at night.

Before shipping our two guns which had been landed for peace-time duties, HMS *Thracian* laid six lines of mines in the West Lamma Channel, and a large Chinese junk a month out of Singapore tacked through them all without blowing up. Chinese joss!

Patrolling round Hong Kong at night was religiously carried out for appearances, and a ship of the Defence Force could be seen leaving harbour at sunset past Green Island and out through the East Lamma Channel. We never saw any ships and contented ourselves with communicating by voice on TBS (Talk Between Ships), or the equivalent, with a gentleman in Hong Kong who prided himself on being the first and only person capable of operating the new language. Under the circumstances it seemed to me that one boiler was quite adequate and allowed for economy in fuel, once on patrol – at very slow speed, clear of the Channel. Apart from the First Lieutenant, Gunner and myself, the newly appointed executive Officers were an RNVR Sub-Lieutenant and a midshipman, both of whom were expected to keep watch.

Midshipman Dobson was a very promising young Officer under my instruction. On one occasion I was in the charthouse on a very dark night, when he called me to the bridge because a ship, fully darkened, had loomed up very close on our starboard bow, obviously making for the eastern entrance to Hong Kong harbour. We were all tired after long days of high speed exercises and were cruising along at four knots. I ordered 'hard a-port and full astern'

121

and to switch on navigation lights and illuminate the object by the ten-inch signal projector. My night glasses got knocked so that the ship was not clearly seen before there were sickening sparks as our stem touched the iron-sided vessel, still showing no lights. Unfortunately it was the Signalman of the Watch's first day in the ship and he could not find the switch for the signal projector in the dark and neither he nor Midshipman Dobson knew where the navigation light switches were, not having been properly briefed on taking over the watch. An unfortunate comedy of errors.

Any damage was superficial, but by the rule of the road we were at fault, and I would have apologised had not the Captain of the ship, which turned out to be the *Van Heutz* from Batavia, reported the collision. In my opinion he had no business to be approaching Hong Kong with no lights, but there happened to be a British Army Officer on board who persuaded the Dutchman to complain to the Commodore. The result was the attached letter from the Commodore Hong Kong, copies to Admiralty and Commander-in-Chief, which effectively put paid to my appointment to a new destroyer, 'if reports are good'. I offered no excuses.

After two and a half years in *Thracian*, I reported sick with a carbuncle on my neck and was sent to the RN Hospital (RNH), where a friend, Bonzo Bousefield, Head of the Asiatic Petroleum Company, visited me and invited me to stay and convalesce in his lovely home on the Peak. Pat managed to get back from Baguio with Anita, where she had made friends with his wife Pooh Bousefield, and we stayed with Bonzo until it was time to return to the UK in SS *Narkunda* early in January 1941.

The trip home took ten weeks and we were not allowed ashore in Mombasa because some Poles who had walked to Bombay had smallpox and some on board were suspect. However, thanks to judicious entertaining of the port health officer at Capetown we had a weekend ashore at Ida's Valley. From Freetown we sailed west to avoid U-boats and on returning inadvertently grounded off the Gambia, thence back to Freetown, where I called on the Staff Officer Operations (SOO) and told him we could do 17 knots. So after calling at Gibraltar we were put in an aircraft carrier convoy with four aircraft carriers, two battle cruisers, some cruisers and destroyers. *Narkunda* was the last P&O ship to leave the Far East until after the war with Japan.

Pat and I were lucky in having a cabin on deck with two chaises-longues. Anita, aged 18 months, was a great favourite on board and she was delighted when our six-inch gun was fired for practice, saying: 'Bang, bang, lovely bang, more bang!'

We eventually arrived at Greenock in April, much to the consternation of the local authority who said we should have gone to Liverpool. We were told: 'However, now you are here you can land, but passengers' luggage must go to Liverpool'. Pat's father, Admiral Ramsey, was Commander-in-Chief at Rosyth and so Vice-Admiral Watson sent his barge to remove the de Chair family and luggage from the ship. All passengers' luggage had been got up on to the fo'c'sle and I had a hard job finding our 23 pieces, three of which were missing, so I had to return from Rosyth to Greenock the following day to retrieve them.

13

HMS *Vimy*, South Atlantic Escort Vessel 1941-42

During a short course at the Staff College, Camberley, I received my appointment at HMS *Vimy* in Command, to join at Portsmouth on 20 May 1941. I had hoped for a Fleet Destroyer, and was rather disappointed to find this World War I ship being converted for long range escort work as a 'Converted Vee Type Escort vessel', one of the first to be so treated.

In place of the forward boiler room she had an 80 ton oil fuel tank, which was surmounted by two messdecks. This was supposed to give an extra four days steaming. In the event, it entailed a lot of fuelling at sea. The torpedo tubes had been removed, and depth charges, high-angle guns, bridge oerlikons and pom-pom were added. Conversion and refit occupied at least three months, and the ship also needed new boilers and a new motor boat, which, as it happened we never received.

HMS *Vimy* had been at Dunkirk, during which operation she had four Commanding Officers in six days. The chain of events as recorded in the official records would have made us proud to serve in her. The following account from these records has been slightly amended:

HMS *VIMY*. MAY 1940

The *Vimy* made two sorties to Boulogne on 23 May 1940; first to land a demolitions team and a RM/RN covering party (235 men in all) under artillery, mortar and machine-gun fire. She returned to Dover and was sent across again during the afternoon to bombard German tanks and vehicles, and then into the harbour to assist in evacuation. It was then that Lieutenant Commander C.G.W. Donald was mortally wounded on the *Vimy*'s bridge by machine-gun fire; another officer was also killed. HMS *Keith*, inboard, also lost her Commanding Officer. Both ships returned to Dover under the command of their First Lieutenants.

124

Lieutenant Commander R.G.K. Knowling assumed command of the *Vimy* on 24 May and late on the evening of 27 May was ordered to proceed with utmost despatch to the beaches to the east of Dunkirk. Lieutenant Commander Knowling left the bridge at 2355 and was not seen again; he was officially reported as presumed lost overboard. His place was taken at 0300 on 28 May by the First Lieutenant, Lieutenant A.P.W. Northey, who completed this evacuation sortie, as well as another later on the same day, before handing over to Lieutenant Commander M.W.E. Wentworth at 1545 on 29 May.

The *Vimy* thus had four Commanding Officers in six days. Between them, these Commanding Officers undertook at least ten cross-Channel operations between 22 May and 1 June and brought off over 3,000 troops from France. Northey eventually retired as a Captain, with the CBE and a DSC and two Bars, the latter awarded for his conduct at Dunkirk and Boulogne.

I arrived on board a few days ahead of time and seeing the mess the ship was in, took another week's leave. Bombing and shortage of skilled labour had so delayed the refit that I declined to take her to sea when supposed to be ready, and was granted an extra week to complete. Refitting at Portsmouth in 1941 was a severe problem with the constant air raids.

Eventually, after preliminary trials, it was agreed to carry out a full power trial on passage to Devonport. Our sailing orders stated that one of our submarines would leave The Needles at 2000, and we were to give her a three hour start, to avoid confusion.

We cleared the Needles with our untrained crew at 2300, as ordered. A new toy had been fitted called RDF, (Range and Direction Finding), a primitive radar device with a fixed aerial, which to our delight detected each of the four unlit Channel buoys off The Needles. However, not content with that, it also detected an extra one! Could this be our submarine three hours late? Very probably, but possibly not. We could not afford to take risks. The entrance to a searched channel seemed an ideal place for a U-boat to lie in wait.

The action alarm was sounded and very soon the object could be seen as a submarine ahead of us on the surface, on the same course. We challenged and received no reply. We then increased speed and challenged again. Still no reply. Then, as we passed about three cables off at full speed, we challenged again. Still no reply. I ordered: 'Open fire'. Almost immediately a winking light from the conning tower signalled: 'Sorry, my light jammed'. Fortunately the salvo fell well ahead or over. The incident was not reported officially as it was the submarine's first patrol and also our first night at sea. A salutary lesson to both of us.

We then carried out a full power trial in fog using our RDF, which detected aircraft raiding Portland as we passed. We had to stop the trial in Lyme Bay, where the engines broke down. The RDF had been playing tricks and we couldn't find the Eddystone lighthouse in the fog, and so closed Start Point. Luckily the First Lieutenant, a native of Devon, recognised the Thurlestone Hotel above the morning mist, so we knew where we were!

Devonport dockyard welcomed us with open arms, delighted when we had to admit to forty defects after refitting at Portsmouth. Repairs delayed completion and there was considerable doubt as to which station we should join. We were actually accredited to thirteen Flag Officers and five Captains (D) within three months, before finding our pay accounts at Freetown. One thing was abundantly clear: we could not be allowed sufficient time to do the normal work-up on commissioning, and, after several requests, we were detailed to carry out trials towing Motor Launches for passage to Gibraltar. When I remonstrated about the need for a work-up, I was told in the nicest way: 'You are nothing but a bloody tug'.

The fact was that we were very short of destroyers. An Officer in Operations Division wrote: 'Don't be too hard on us. In the last war we had 400 destroyers, plus Italians and Japs. Now we only have 240 minus both, and a lot more work to do.

TOWING MOTOR LAUNCHES

The meterologists promised us lovely weather for at least two days, and we gaily set off for Gibraltar with the firm intention of averaging 18 knots. Four destroyers (including *Vimy*), each towing two Motor Launches, seemed easy enough, as we had towed five at a time at a speed of up to 22 knots on the trials; two in tandem on either quarter and one on the towing slip.

The weather turned nasty on our first day out and tows began parting. It was soon apparent that eight knots was as much as we

126

could hope for, and we went out to 18° west to avoid enemy aircraft.

After two days, our Engineer Officer reported: 'Evaporator broken down', with only four tons of fresh water remaining.

We were under command of Lieutenant-Commander Steven Norris, DSO, DSC, RN, in HMS *Firedrake*, with HMS *Beverley*, HMS *Vidette* and *Vimy*. The tows were each 500 fathoms of three and a half inch wire and eight inch manilla, but most of them parted about five times in two days. *Vidette* made seven new girdles before we had gone half-way. In *Vimy*, we freshened the nips every four hours and had no trouble until a tow parted after five days in heavy weather off Lisbon.

By then we were in company with *Beverley* only, *Firedrake* having waited for *Vidette*. Our turn came at dusk when the starboard tow parted at our end, leaving the Motor Launch virtually anchored with 300 fathoms of heavy wire and an eight inch manilla, wallowing in an uncomfortable sea.

We turned round head to wind with the other Motor Launch still in tow, endeavouring to keep it clear astern and at long stay. There was every likelihood of her tow fouling our port propeller so we had to get it in – this took half an hour, with all hands sweating swearing and slipping in the heavy roll.

We obtained an asdic contact 'probably submarine' at the same time, but could not attack until we had weighed both tows. It was getting dark and the Motor Launches decided to proceed under their own power for the rest of the trip. We had told them to wait for us off Cape St Vincent and I received the signal from *Beverley*: 'Suggest you put a little salt on their tails'. In the event, we all managed to reach Gibraltar together – an imposing fleet of twelve ships! (The eight Fairmile MLs were desperately needed to operate defensive patrols off Gibraltar).

Being short of escorts, Flag Officer Commanding North Atlantic (FOCNA) postponed *Vimy*'s departure, though our pay accounts had already gone to Freetown. We did not connect with them until nine months after commissioning.

HMS *Firedrake* was hit in the boiler room soon after arrival, and I remember seeing an enormous gap in her side. The Flag Officer, Force H, diverted his morning pull in the skiff into this inviting cave, to row round the now flooded boiler room. As he emerged, a stoker leaning over the guard rail above, called out: "'Ere, haven't you got a hole of your own to go go?'

127

We were starting to exercise with a submarine and *Vidette* when ordered towards Malta to escort HMS *Manchester* who was returning to Gibraltar after having been torpedoed.

After that, most of our time was spent escorting homeward and outward bound convoys, which often meant ten days at sea, with only two or three days spent on actual escort duties, during which time we were constantly shadowed by Focke-wolfes and U-boats. The convoys varied in size, generally averaging about 50 ships with, say, two destroyers, a sloop and as many as twelve corvettes as escort.

About the middle of September we formed part of the escort convoy HG 73, a homeward bound convoy. Admiral Creighton was Commodore of the convoy, with Commander Carlisle as Senior Officer of escort in HMS *Farndale*, a hunt class destroyer, for the first three days.

We realised that German agents at Algeciras were reporting arrivals and departures in Gibraltar Bay and so were not greatly surprised when towards sunset off the Moroccan shore, a Spanish aircraft flew round and had a good look at us. The next day a Focke-wolfe appeared, probably from near Cadiz. HMS *Maplin*, one of the new Carrier Armed Merchant Ships carrying eight four inch anti-aircraft guns, and a Hurricane fighter aircraft had been included in the convoy. The Hurricane was duly catapulted into the sky and attacked the Focke-wolfe. Unfortunately, three out of four of the Hurricane's guns jammed and the Focke-wolfe escaped. On the following day, our third since leaving Gibraltar, two Focke-wolfes circled round us for most of the day and there was also a U-boat scare. We carried out anti-submarine sweeps but found nothing and at dusk *Farndale* left to refuel, leaving me as Senior Officer of the escort, having received many signals from Admiralty telling us that we had been sighted by a U-boat.

Three days later on 21 September 1941 we were being shadowed by three U-boats, whose number was later increased to eight or nine. Some seven ships in this convoy, including HMS *Maplin*, were sunk on the way to the UK.

Meanwhile, in *Farndale*'s absence, I extended the sweep by our two destroyers to ten miles ahead of the convoy, then doubling back at visibility distance, either side of it to ten miles astern, with the idea of rejoining the convoy after dark. *Vimy* was out of sight, astern of the convoy and was about to turn back when we sighted brown smoke ahead, and then what looked like a funnel; having no masts, we knew what it was, and closed at full speed. After nearly two hours of chasing the U-boat, we opened fire from 'A' gun at about 8,000 yards range, closing to within half a mile as darkness set in, when the U-boat dived. The Gunner's Mate claimed a hit on the conning tower.

We passed through the swirl of water where the U-boat had dived, having reduced speed to 18 knots and lowered the asdic dome for an attack. With hindsight, I wish we had not done so, but had instead initially fired a shallow pattern of depth charges at full speed in the old World War I fashion. However, it was getting dark and we did not expect to see the swirl of water. Whenever we fired a pattern of depth charges, all our electrics failed and it took a couple of minutes to put matters right; I then turned the ship away from the afterglow of sunset, and obtained asdic contact, attacking with a 14 charge pattern from about 700 yards. We regained contact and attacked again with a five charge pattern, which was as much as the crew could do to reload in the time and with sea state four (rather rough).

After running on for some time, we regained contact and delivered a further 14 charge pattern from close range set deep and waited, then stopped. After several minutes there were three loud booms, a most erie sound, and we then found an oil slick about a mile long. A sample of the oil was recovered in a bucket and placed in the wheel-house, after which we searched for more tangible evidence of a kill. One of our Stoker Petty Officers in the boiler room reported hearing a loud hissing sound and rending noises just before the booms.

I felt fairly certain that the three booms we had heard meant the end of the U-boat, probably due to her tanks collapsing, and that the likelihood of anything surfacing after a good attack with 14 charge pattern was remote. We continued search until midnight and returned towards Gibraltar, being relieved by *Farndale* (Commander Carlisle) as Escort Commander.

Returning to Gibraltar, the night was dark and the Officer of the Watch of the morning watch reported: 'Darkened ship on the starboard bow.' Turning away, he called me and rang the alarm bells, so as to be at full action stations before engaging, in accordance with standing orders. No one else had seen anything. We closed the position but found nothing. It was probably another

U-boat charging batteries on the surface and a golden opportunity of ramming was missed, but we obtained asdic contact three hours later, some ten miles nearer Gibraltar and made a promising attack, but again found nothing. Our motto from then on was 'NO REMAINS'.

As *Vimy* was supposed to be part of the Freetown Escort Force, Flag Officer Commanding North Atlantic was obliged to report our attack and send *Vimy* to her proper station.

According to the Naval Historical Branch the submarine we attacked on 21/22 September 1941 to the west of Portugal was in fact the Italian vessel *Luigi Torelli*. This boat sustained very serious damage, but survived and managed to regain her base at Bordeaux.

Post-war evidence from the Italian Foreign Office confirmed that the *Alessandro Malaspina* was sunk by HMS *Vimy* in her later attack at about 0800 on Monday, 22 September 1941. This attack was not reported for lack of evidence, but evidently the asdic trace was forwarded.

SOUTH ATLANTIC ESCORT VESSEL

We left Gibraltar after a hurried boiler clean on 27 September 1941 and with HMS *Wild Swan* escorted four assault ships to the latitude of Bathurst, where we spent two pleasant days.

On the following Sunday there was a church parade and service in the cathedral lasting two and a half hours. The Wing Commander and I read the lessons.

It was very hot and so after church we bathed from the beach, where the men undressed, some of them naked, there being no one else about and only one house a long way off, which turned out to be Government House. Evidently the Governor's wife's native maid was highly indignant, and kept a close watch through a telescope, reporting the while to her mistress, so that a complaint was made to the Naval Officer in Charge. The Governor and his wife lunched on board later and we took them up the Gambia River, and were forgiven.

We were on our way to Bathurst for fuel when we were ordered to assist a Sunderland near Dakar in Vichy waters. The weather being fine and sea calm, we towed it with our fog buoy wire, working up to 12 knots, at which their towing link parted. We

130

subsequently got them in tow again until another Sunderland appeared with 110 gallons of fuel. Our little skiff motorboat took over an hour to transfer the fuel, as the relieving Sunderland had stopped three miles away. However, a good liaison was established with RAF at Bathurst, where we were always welcome.

There we fuelled from the Norwegian tanker *Liss* and I then called the Naval Officer in Charge, giving him the position where we were to meet a WS convoy in the morning. This was fortunate, as a Hudson aircraft returning from patrol over the Cape Verde Islands had just been reported as having crashed right on our route. We left harbour about midnight and I reckoned to reach the position of the crashed Hudson at 0800, steaming at 20 knots. A good look-out was kept, but by then nothing could be seen. The aircraft had been down for two days and reluctantly we continued our course and speed to join the convoy, feeling very sad for the crew of the lost Hudson.

Forty minutes later we passed pages from a book floating in the water, so 'made smoke' and started to turn round and pick some up as a possible clue. As we did so, the signalman of the watch reported 'object bearing Red 45'. It was only a speck on the horizon, barely visible through glasses, but it turned out to be Flying Officer Henry standing up in a rubber dinghy holding his lifebelt above his head, whilst his three companions held him up. They had seen our smoke and had fortunately made themselves look as large as possible.

We soon had them on board – two officers and two Sergeants – who were none the worse for having spent two days in the tiny rubber dinghy surrounded by sharks and having weathered a tornado. Apparently their engine had been running rough for some time on previous trips, but in view of the shortage of spare parts out at Jeshwing aerodrome, they had not wanted to make a fuss for fear of being thought 'yellow'. They 'force landed' after a brief SOS and in 15 seconds the Hudson had disappeared, leaving them swimming about in the water. No one had thought of the rubber dinghy until one of them saw a yellow piece of rubber floating about. After some time they tried blowing it up and were able to get inside. Six aircraft passed without seeing them. Nevertheless, it was an aircraft which had spotted them the day before we found them and which had dropped half empty bottles of water nearby. Anyway, they were safe and wanted to give us their dinghy, but we accepted their lifebelts instead. Rubber was too valuable in those days. We landed them in Freetown, where we arrived for the first time after six weeks of being nominally on the station, and after covering 12,144 nautical miles.

We followed a convoy and two cruisers into harbour in the late afternoon and had difficulty in finding an oiler. Finally, we got permission to berth on an oiler which was fuelling the cruiser HMS *Devonshire*. One of our Officers had just spent three years in her and asked if he might stay on board for dinner. Her Officers were in merry mood, having just come from the frozen north, but time and tide waits for no man. Neither do Freetown tornadoes. At about 2230 the weather threatened with black clouds and flashes of lightning, the usual precursors of a tornado at that time of year. I sent word over to the wardroom of the cruiser three times, warning my Officers that we might have to shove off. After over half an hour I could wait no longer. The rain had started and I let go headropes to swing the bows out on the tide. Then I ordered: 'Let go aft', to get clear before the weather became too thick to see anything in the tropical downpour. Evidently my young friends managed to return on board onto the quarter deck as the bows were paying off.

A few days later we were ordered to escort this cruiser on a hunt for U-boat supply ships. We possessed what was probably the best Medium Frequency Direction Finding set on the station and had good, enthusiastic operators, so generally had it manned. One night we picked up what we thought were U-boat homing signals and got permission to follow them, which we did for about eight hours until the signals seemed to be all round us 'no zero'. The leading telegraphist said that we must be over a U-boat transmitting from less than 30 feet deep, but after searching round we could find nothing. Meanwhile the cruiser's Walrus aircraft had flown off at first light to assist in our search. Unfortunately for her and perhaps our enterprise, her engine conked and she was forced to make an emergency landing in the sea. By a curious plotting error we returned too far to rendezvous with our cruiser, so sighted the aircraft whose crew had resigned themselves to many hours, if not days, in their uncomfortable predicament. We were thus instrumental in rescuing the crews of three aircraft within one week. Incidentally, we received a bag of nuts from the Commander-

132

in-Chief for our D/F chase which helped to catch a supply ship, though we never knew how.

After this we had a few days at Freetown for a much needed boiler clean. There was a strike among the natives, as an agitator from Clyne Point had been allowed to stir them up. He may have been paid by enemy agents, but the Government was weak and let him get away with it. Several corvettes and ourselves were waiting for native boiler cleaning parties and so I ordered our boilers to be cleaned by Stokers, Midshipmen and Seamen in relays. The word went round, other ships followed suit and the strike soon ended, which was just as well, as the heat was intense.

Our next trip was to Bathurst with HMS *Brilliant*. SS *Nurkunda* of the P&O Line had sailed for the UK ahead of us and we were overtaking her at 20 knots, when at about 2100 the Officer of the Watch reported a flare on the starboard beam. We turned to investigate and prepared to attack a U-boat. Then green flashes close together appeared and it was some time before we made out that the word spelt 'survivors'. We closed at speed and found two lifeboats under sail from the American freighter SS *Lehigh* which had been torpedoed early that morning. The two other boats were found by walrus aircraft from HMS *Albatross* and rescued by motor launches the next day. We took our survivors to Bathurst and they enjoyed their trip in a destroyer at 20 knots but were highly incensed that they, a neutral American freighter clearly marked, should have been sunk by the Germans. Apparently they only had one flare remaining and on hearing engines in the dark, fired it. We fortunately saw this flare from a distance of about five miles. They must have heard the *Nurkunda* at 16 knots as well as ourselves.

EGGS

The orders at Freetown in 1942 were quite clear: 'No black market eggs'. In other words, all eggs had to be bought from the Navy, Army and Air Force Institute (NAAFI), who stipulated that at least 48 hours' notice was required before any order for eggs could be filled. After nine months in the Freetown Escort Force, which seldom necessitated spending more than 24 hours in harbour for fuel, we consequently never got any eggs, and the desire for them became an obsession.

Our wardroom Steward and canteen manager were accordingly sent ashore to buy eggs. 'Never mind how you get them, but get eggs', was the parting injunction. This they did, as we knew they would, in the black market. Unfortunately, they also got some palm wine, the local alcoholic wine, which has a depressing effect.

At about 1400 when the Officer of the Watch was investigating a defaulter on the quarterdeck, there was a disturbance alongside and our friends returned on board with the eggs, but drunk. The eggs were duly removed from them, and the Petty Officer placed under restraint in the tiller flat. There he remained peacefully until 1700 when he awoke with a sickening headache. With a vague feeling of resentment against the Officers, he crept up the ladder and succeeded in reaching the wardroom galley inside the after screen, unobserved. It was empty, and on opening the oven door, he found a fine joint roasting. He had it overboard in a trice and was back before anyone saw him. The wardroom cook reappeared after a brief absence and to his dismay found no joint roasting when he opened the oven door. Distracted, he ran forward to see if by some fluke it had made its way to the ship's company galley; it wasn't there, but when he got back all the bread had gone. So it befell that the officers had nothing but eggs for dinner that night and the Petty Officer Steward lost his rate. Moreover, the ship went home without him.

We spent very little time in harbour and had barely sufficient time to clean boilers about once a month, but preferred being at sea where the weather was generally very good and men could sleep on deck at their guns. One trip in November 1941 sticks in my mind, as I had a row with the Naval Officer in Charge (NOIC) at Takoradi and reported him for inefficiency.

Apparently the US steamer *Arcadia* had been diverted from her run to the West Indies and instead was escorted to Lagos by an American cruiser and with two destroyers, for fuel. She had on board a large number of Pan-American Airways personnel in order to relieve our RAF at Takoradi and Accra, but refused to sail without a British escort. Her Captain and the American Consul arrived and we had a conference, the Consul's parting words being to remind everyone that I was in command. The skipper said he could do 20 knots which would get us to Takoradi by 0900 the following morning. The local army insisted that I disembark both stores and personnel in one day. This was necessary, but they had failed to impress the fact on the harbour master at Takoradi. We watered and fuelled with 100 tons short and finally got away just as a canoe arrived alongside with fresh provisions. We shoved off, I regret to say without paying for these, as the man seemed very vague about what he had. However, all was amicably settled by letter later, through the base accountants' officer.

When put to the test, the *Arcadia* could barely make 18 knots and we only just reached the entrance to the Takoradi searched channel by 0900, instead of being berthed alongside by that time, as requested. We were met six miles from the breakwater by HM trawler *Skudd VI*, who insisted on carrying out his orders to sweep us in at six knots – presumably NOIC's idea of creating a good impression. *Arcadia* arrived in the bay about 1000 and we waited for a pilot to take her in. After some time the pilot appeared, but he proceeded to board a Dutch ship anchored there, instead. The Americans were furious and then anchored, being piloted into harbour at about 1130 after three other ships, which to anyone not knowing the facts appeared reasonable.

We patrolled to seaward meanwhile and awaited orders to fuel. At 1400 we were told to send for provisions and as there were no ships left in the bay I sent the First Lieutenant to protest at the delay. At 1430 we received an SOS from a ship being attacked by a U-boat 100 miles away and being the only destroyer on the coast, I considered that we should take action, but lacked sufficient fuel. There were still no orders for fuel or berth, the outer fuelling berth being occupied by a very small coaster. Accordingly, I entered the harbour, the boom being inadvertently left open and had a look round for a berth, but found all the quays occupied by American and Dutch ships. The boom-carrying vessel HMS *Ethiopia* seemed our only hope and her Captain and Officers were keen to help, but had no oil hoses.

It appeared that the harbour master had no use for NOIC and refused to allow him any say in the berthing of HM ships. However, he reported our presence in the harbour and we were ordered to anchor outside and to commence fuelling after the coaster, at 1900. On anchoring, we received a signal from NOIC: ' Who gave you permission to enter harbour?' By this time I was annoyed! We were short of fuel and provisions, a U-boat in the offing and unable to get a move on. I replied to NOIC: 'In view of U-boat report, submit no one. I was trying to get fuel and a full report will be forwarded to the Commander-in-Chief.' This reply had an instant-aneous effect: I was sent for by the NOIC who complained to me that he had no control. Finally, the coaster sailed and we berthed stern to the pontoon with two anchors down, well spread ahead, and after much argument got a huge hose floated out on rafts and passed over the quarterdeck and down through my cabin hatch into an open tank. In consequence I was an hour late for dinner in *Arcadia* with the American Captain, and the waiters had to be paid overtime. My delayed arrival was very disappointing as the dining room was decorated with the Union Jack and the Stars and Stripes – quite a feature, since the US was still neutral.

Fuelling commenced at 30 tons per hour, but soon tailed off to five and at 0400 I ordered the Chief to stop the pumps and we sailed for an offensive sweep before and after dawn. The ship had been lying in an open anchorage stern to the wall, two anchors down, with a full moon and within range of a U-boat known to be in the vicinity. We returned to harbour for provisions and some wine we had ordered, but were unable to embark it, £78 worth, so left at 0900 for Freetown, escorting our Americans and calling at Monrovia in Liberia en route, most of the way perforce on one engine.

Two motor launches met us off Monrovia and we spent the day on an anti-submarine patrol off the anchorage, while the Americans lunched and saw the sights ashore.

My report on Takoradi raised quite a furore, but when asked for reasons, the NOIC had quite another version, much of which I am sorry to say was wholly inaccurate; I later returned there and was able to verify this. Perhaps it was a lesson in 'live and let live' and little improvement resulted under the existing regime. Running my Senior Officer in for inefficiency was certainly of no personal benefit to me, though I had felt it my duty.

On our next visit to Takoradi, we embarked (voluntarily) £20,000 worth of gold bullion and on our arrival at Freetown, a bank clerk came to collect it. We had armed sentries posted, but he refused to give me any form of receipt, so I sent Midshipman Morrison (ex-*Dunedin*) with him to the bank for it.

FOG AND SAWDUST

Our condenser tubes being 25 years old were due for renewal at the end of 1941, but this fact had been overlooked during the

136

conversion to escort vessel and refit. Consequently, leaks began to develop as early as November and we spent the next three months running about on one engine. Leaks appeared first in one side and then in the other, but fortunately never in both together. Our Engineer Officer and his staff became experts at Canterbury Test, but it was an uncertain and trying time for all. They called it 'running on luck'.

Our Engine Room Artifices became expert at shifting bubbling tubes (the Canterbury Test), but as this meant stopping the ship and then only in calm weather, we took to carrying bags of sawdust. Sawdust was poured into the circulating water inlet until a piece got sucked into the hole in the condenser tube.

On 22 February 1942 we sailed for the UK to refit our condensers, escorting Convoy SL 101 with Vice-Admiral F.A. Marten, my old Captain at Dartmouth, as Commodore, and 44 ships with five corvettes. I was Senior Officer of the Escort, until Commander Allen in HMS *Rochester* with 43rd Escort Group joined us in the latitude of Cape Verde.

After three weeks, the port condenser gave out. It was too rough for the old Canterbury Test, but by this time our sea water inlets had been specially adapted. Two bags of sawdust sufficed to stop the leaks for a week and we had only two days to go on one engine. After 28 tedious days we finally reached Movile (Londonderry) with five leaky tubes in one condenser and none in the other.

During the trip we fuelled in convoy from the tanker *British Hussar* four times, the last two in very rough weather, rather rashly, as the tanker was yawing wildly. Thanks to Commander Allen's complimentary remarks, we received a pat on the back from the Commander-in-Chief Western Approaches. Little did he know of the battle we were having with sawdust and our port condenser.

The following extract from a report of proceedings from Senior Officer 43rd Escort Group is forwarded with pleasure:-

"I consider great credit is due to the Commanding Officer of H.M.S."Vimy" for fuelling his ship successfully on several occasions when weather conditions were far from suitable, as for instance on March 5th when I logged the wind as Force 6 and sea and swell as 44. By fuelling on this occasion he avoided the necessity of having to go to Ponta Delgada and leaving the convoy of 44 ships with only three escorts."

ADMIRAL.

We only had enough fresh meat for three days, but the tanker gave us what she could. Her trough method of transferring oil and stores with whip and outhaul, long hoses held up high and with good winchmen, was very efficient. As the only destroyer, we generally acted as canteen boat, by taking any messages around the convoy, which often meant passing through the lines.

We were about to pass ahead of a tanker on one occasion, when I realised that we were losing speed. I immediately ordered 'Hard a-port' and just as well, for the engines stopped, owing to the air pump being on dead centre. But for the turn, we would have been cut in half.

Stragglers in convoy were always a nuisance and we sent one back to Freetown within 24 hours of leaving, but allowed the Greek SS *Rhino* to remain, emitting much black smoke. She could not make our seven knots, and somewhere near the Canaries her engine packed up. Our Engineer Officer boarded and advised her on patching the cylinder head, gave her an Aldis lamp, and we rerouted her to cut off corners. She rejoined us a week later, still emitting volumes of black smoke!

After fuelling at Movile and removing our leaky condenser tubes, we sailed for Greenock as escort for a tanker, RFA *Eagle Dale*, but fog shut down off Rathlin Island and we had difficulty in keeping to the searched channel. Our charge lost it altogether and we never saw her again. We anchored in Holy Loch on the Clyde and I reported on board HMS *Forth*, submarine depot ship for orders. These were to escort submarines HMS *Sturgeon* (damaged, with a maximum speed of 11 knots) and the Dutch submarine *023* south to Plymouth and the Wolfe Rock, respectively. I explained to Staff Officer Operations that there was dense fog south of Ailsa Craig, but he insisted that we must go regardless, as the submarines were urgently required for operations. My instructions were to interpose my ship between the submarines and any ships we encountered which might cause danger to the two submarines.

At about 0500 the following morning, the fo'c'sle lookout reported red light on the starboard bow. We had been doing eight knots and were now reduced to four, having obtained an RDF warning echo ahead (our type 986M radar set was most unreliable). I sounded two short blasts on the siren, went hard a-port and switched on a ten-inch searchlight which we kept burning for some hours. Then we stopped engines and wallowed, while the submarines came up on either side. We got the name of one ship as she passed and reported to Commander-in-Chief Western Approaches, in view of invasion scares, but it turned out that she was part of a convoy lost in fog and making for Liverpool.

By 0800 visibility had cleared to about five miles and we sighted an inshore convoy on opposite course who gave me a bearing and distance of Bardsey Island. Thick fog then descended once more and I decided to disregard my route orders and make straight for the Smalls, the light marking the most western point of Wales. We heard its fog gun bearing due east at 1600, as planned, also an increasing number of ships' sirens from several convoys rounding the Smalls all round us. The fog was dense, clammy and cold and my teeth were chattering. Meanwhile, the submarines were feeling the strain of keeping station on our searchlight and asked if they could anchor. On reflection, we might have turned back and felt our way into St Bride's Bay, but instead I looked for an anchorage ahead. Milford Haven would have been too difficult in the fog and tideway and ahead of us was a mine barrage extending to the Cornish coast. The only hope seemed to be a bay between two sound signals on St Anne's Head and Skokholme Island. This seemed better than getting lost in the Bristol Channel, with its minefield and strong tides. We anchored on the 20 fathom line after seeing breakers off what we hoped was St Anne's Head, but were not prepared for a tidal stream of anything up to 12 knots, over foul ground. The Dutchman lost his special type anchor almost immediately, but by good seamanship kept close alongside Skokholme Island Cliff for the next three hours. *Sturgeon* anchored three times with two anchors down and dragged, so he upped hook and somehow found his way into St Bride's Bay, probably over a minefield up the Sound. *Vimy* spun round like a top and veered cable rapidly until she was brought up facing the entrance in 18 fathoms. There was a heavy swell and we rolled at anchor cold and wet, with the sounding machine going, steam on the engines, and the blanket of fog thicker than ever. What a homecoming!

Towards midnight there was a shout from the fo'c'sle: 'Cable growing broad on the port beam and coming aft rapidly.' We had run up on the cable with the turn of the tide. I ordered engines 'slow ahead starboard' and 'slow astern port', to ease the strain. Then we felt a couple of tugs as the cable parted.

Soundings dropped from 18 fathoms to 15, 12 and then five, at which point we could hear the breakers. Then the miracle happened. The fog lifted and we could just see the coastguard cottages silhouetted on our port bow. I signalled: 'Where am I?' and received the reply: 'You are three point three cables 313° from St Anne's Head'. We were just in time and could see the breakers round and astern of us, and shot out of the Sound at 20 knots, joining our Dutch friend at the entrance. There the fog enveloped us once more, and we kept our searchlight on for the submarine's benefit. Together we stemmed the tide on the 20 fathom line between the two sound signals for the rest of the night.

At daylight the fog cleared slightly, so we parked the Dutchman in Milford Haven and collected *Sturgeon* happily returning through his minefield after a comfortable night in St Bride's Bay. The rest of the trip was relatively uneventful, except that we suspected ourselves of digressing into the mine barrage off Hartland Point.

By March 1942 we had been abroad for nine months and our men had hardly ever seen a Wren. Their surprise, therefore, when a harbour launch came alongside with our mail at Devonport, was comic. The girl in the stern sheets (probably an Admiral's daughter) threw a heaving line, but the quarterdeck men were too overcome with emotion to catch it. They could only stand and gape, but made up for their lapse later. Three of them handed it back on a silver salver when the boat shoved off, 'With our love, Miss!'

We de-ammunitioned and de-oiled, only keeping enough for passage to Falmouth the next day. After a speedy passage, we were immediately besieged by the local parson, closely followed by the representatives of Silley Cox Ltd, the firm due to refit us. Silley Cox said they'd never seen a ship in such a bad state. We did not want to pay off, so they told Admiralty (and us) that we'd be finished in six weeks. This was extended to ten, as I'm sure they knew it would be. The engines were well refitted, but some of the other work turned out to be poor compared to standards in royal dockyards.

Soon after we arrived, the First Lieutenant was appointed as the First Lieutenant to build HMS *Opportune* and I was asked if the Second Lieutenant would do as his relief. I said 'yes' and wrote to Butch Butchard accordingly, but he felt it would be too much for him. Later on, he changed his mind. I was staying at Yelverton with my wife, refreshing my memory on gunnery and torpedo at Devonport, when he rang me up from London to ask if I would have him as First Lieutenant and could he get married and have a week's leave! I was delighted and never regretted my favourable answer. We turned out to be a very happy party, but were sorry to lose our doctor. He was a gynaecologist and felt that his talents had been rather wasted in a destroyer on the west coast of Africa, where his sole duty was to administer quinine and various other perquisites of a tropical nature. When crossing the line, the sailors lashed him up with adhesive tape, squirted red ink down his back and made him drink a double dose of quinine. He had a fearsome beard. My wife and daughter Anita had come down to stay at the Falmouth Hotel and he and I had to sit at another table to avoid frightening Anita at lunch.

As our refit became extended and we were not paid off, it became necessary to accommodate the ship's company. We appealed to RN Barracks Portsmouth, whose Training Division were most helpful and who agreed to give the men a three week

141

course which included assault training, boatwork and discipline.

Eventually we left Falmouth for full power trials and proceeded to Plymouth for ammunition and fuel. No sooner had we cleared Falmouth Harbour than we received a double red air raid warning and were promptly 'beaten up' by two British aircraft, one coming down out of the sun and the other a Whirlwind, carrying out a dummy run torpedo attack from the beam. He shot up in the sky, revealing the RAF roundels, when he saw our tracer coming at him.

After anchoring in Plymouth Sound, the nut securing the ship's wheel was found to be missing and as sabotage was suspected, I had another riveted in its place. Whoever was responsible then thought of a better way of delaying our return to Freetown and removed all the semi-automatic gun locks from our four-inch guns, of which we had no spares on board. When these were reported missing I cleared lower deck and told all hands to search for the missing gun locks until they were found. By midnight the Leading Signalman had confessed that he had thrown them over the side, and the matter was reported to the Commander-in-Chief. New locks were provided and our friend was left to languish in his home port under restraint: not quite what he had anticipated.

After two days in Devonport we sailed with HMS *Dragon* (Captain Alan Peachey) and HMS *Phoebe* (Peter Friend) for Greenock. We did 22 knots into a head sea round the Land's End and flooded our messdecks and asdic compartment, so were not much use for screening. When we left Falmouth, I had called for three cheers for Silley Cox: now as every green sea flooded the messdecks, the cry went up: 'Three cheers for Silley Cox'.

My wife and daughter stayed at the Bay Hotel in Greenock while we were working up from there and at Londonderry with HMS *Brilliant*. The work-up, particularly at Londonderry, was very good value and hard work, which was useful for the new commission. We had 35 new youngsters and had lost most of our old hands.

Operations Division agreed to let us have a work-up, and to call at Ponta Delgada for fuel en route for Freetown. HMS *Brilliant* went there first and I asked him to order a variety of things for us, including Madeira and 60 pairs of silk stockings. We had a bit of difficulty finding the island, owing to bad weather and poor visibility. As a result, we overshot it, before turning back and passing *Brilliant* and a 'hunt' class destroyer making heavy weather at high speed on opposite course. They shot out of the fog, mostly consisting of spray, which made a fine sight.

PONTA DELGADA

The Portuguese pilot boarded us off the breakwater and indicated that he wanted to handle the ship. A friend had warned me that his orders were roughly: 'All right, Captain, full speed ahead; no, full speed astern; no, let go both anchors.' He spoke fairly good English and our relations were cordial, but it was almost impossible to discover where our berth was and what his intentions were.

Our next visitor was the Resident Naval Officer (RNO), an impressive figure in civilian clothes. He was accompanied by a harbour official who required me to fill in our particulars on a form, beginning with the name of the Commanding Officer. The RNO intervened and said: 'Don't give your own name.' I thought for a moment and wrote 'Gordon' and signed it 'R.C. Gordon Lt. Comdr. R.N.', with subsequent apologies to the Operations Commander at the Admiralty bearing that name. The theory was that the Germans were told names of the Commanding Officers and were thus able to get names of ships visiting Ponta Delgada. We were only allowed there once every three months, a rule that was strictly observed.

Returning to Freetown held no thrills for me or the old crew, particularly in the rainy season. I tried to disguise it, only going ashore twice and in August asked Captain (D) to get me relieved. We had no mail for about two months and were hard put to it to keep up our interest. The ship's company, assisted by two Sub Lieutenants, produced an amusing concert which was supposed to be a secret from me until the great day. They rehearsed in odd corners of the ship at sea, away from prying eyes.

HMS *Queen Elizabeth*, which had been mined at Alexandria and patched up with a false bottom for the passage, arrived via the Cape. Three destroyers were required to escort her to Norfolk, Virginia; the escort comprised HMS *Quentin*[1], HMS *Pathfinder*[2] and *Vimy*. The unit proceeded to zigzag at 16 knots most of the way to hamper submarine attacks.

The normal method of transferring stores and mail under way is to haul them over on a wire jackstay, or by heaving line if light, when the two ships are steering the same course and speed, about fifty feet apart.

Vimy, being the oldest destroyer, did the greater share of this, but on the last occasion became over-matey with *QE*. The suction of a battleship's propellers at 16 knots is very considerable and it is customary to approach from near amidships and if necessary, drop astern to avoid it.

Fresh provisions were all ready on the *QE*'s quarterdeck and *Vimy* came up from astern at 21 knots, reducing so as to drop nicely into station and edge in between zigs. Looking back at the compass which was inconveniently placed too far aft, I noticed at the crucial moment that the coxwain was four degrees off course and closing *QE*. So I ordered 'hard a-port', but it was too late! *Vimy*'s bow was already being sucked across. The ship heeled over onto the battleship's glacis, with her fo'c'sle level with the quarter-deck. With great presence of mind, the Commander picked up a bag of bread and plonked it on our fo'c'sle. The idea caught on. Beef and spuds followed. You never saw such a quick transfer!

Vimy reduced speed to 12 knots so as to keep steerage way on, but the Captain of the *QE*, seeing our plight, swung his stern away under full helm in an attempt to clear her. This had the effect of sucking our bows further in and caused us to ram *QE* repeatedly in the Admiral's stern walk at progressively broader angles.

We were left spinning in a swirl of water with our fo'c'sle split level with the upper deck for some twenty feet. We were in an undignified but not dangerous state, and fortunately the weather was fine for mid-Atlantic. Hammocks and shores made passable repairs, but a visit to a dockyard was desirable and we thought a sojourn in Bermuda would be a pleasant change. A signal was accordingly addressed to *QE* from *Vimy*: 'Request permission to accompany you as far as Bermuda', to which we received the disarming reply: 'Suggest you await a more favourable opportunity', a polite way of saying 'no'.

An American relief escort was due to meet us in 40° west at 0900 on 3 September, but was ahead of time and met us at 0400, fortunately in bright moonlight. We spotted them ten miles off, but the destroyer taking our place ahead of the *QE* evidently did not see us. We were proud of our camouflage but never dreamed he would not see us, until he sounded a fearsome blast on his siren and made an unprovoked attack from our starboard beam.

Having handed the *QE* over to the Americans, we were steaming at 17 knots in line abreast about one and a half miles apart and were looking forward to reaching Trinidad the following morning. The more suitable opportunity was not long in coming.

THE SINKING OF U-162

At about 1800 we observed what looked like a whale blowing on the surface astern of HMS *Quentin*, but as the spray persisted and overtook her we realised it must be a torpedo running on the surface. *Quentin* had managed to avoid it and HMS *Pathfinder* had already made contact with a U-boat.

Now the hunt was on and we each got contact and attacked with a full pattern of depth charges. *Pathfinder* organised a good search and decided to take *Quentin* eastward with the intention of returning at 30 knots after moonrise at 2300.

The night was pitch dark and *Vimy*, being short of fuel, was left near the estimated position of her last attack and to fill in a possible gap in the search. The U-boat apparently saw us all turn and tried to get away on her motors steering west. *Vimy* was zigzagging at 12 knots with staggered revs on a mean course of north-west, when our type 271 radar set picked her up at 2800 yards on the port beam. Sub Lieutenant Griffiths SANVR[3] who was Officer of the Watch with the Gunner (T), increased to 18 knots, turned towards and rang the alarm bell for action.

I was in the chart house looking at the plot and increased to full speed on reaching the bridge and opened fire from 'A' gun, hitting with the second round. Star shell would have been more useful but the guns had already been loaded. RDF reported that we might be chasing a large surface vessel and flashes from 'A' gun were blinding us on the bridge, so I ordered 'cease fire' to see more clearly for ramming. The U-boat could be seen stern on and I hauled out ten degrees, intending to ram her from her quarter.

The sea was rough and the submarine fired two blinding red flares in succession at our bridge. A red flare happened to be the current recognition signal for a British submarine and when our searchlight was switched on, a US flag was reported as painted on the conning tower – which did not deceive us. We were doing 23 knots and estimated the enemy's speed at 19. In fact, he couldn't have been doing more than 14, and turning in from his starboard beam it was obvious that he would shortly ram us near the stern. I ordered: 'hard a-starboard, full astern, both', but the rolling of the ship threw both telegraphmen over and they only succeeded in ringing down 'half astern'.

The U-boat hit *Vimy* in the forward boiler room at a fine angle, striking her on the fan bracket, the strongest part of the ship. Her hydroplane cut us open above the waterline, there was a flash-back in the boiler room and black smoke poured out of the ship's side. We were then left wallowing alongside the U-boat, whose crew were on deck wearing lifebelts, but it was far too rough to board her.

No textbook or anti-submarine course catered for a situation like this, but something had to be done quickly to prevent the U-boat escaping once more or doing us further damage. The normal minimum speed recommended for dropping depth charges was 18 knots, but here we were wallowing and stopped, bumping alongside our victim who was still very much alive. With hindsight, I believe the crew intended to surrender.

I ordered a snowflake to be fired from X gun and for the port depth charge thrower to get set to 50 feet and fired over the U-boat, whereupon she heeled over and sank, leaving her crew in the water. *Vimy* went ahead at the same time and although nearly stopped, suffered no ill effects from her depth charge as the U-boat provided the necessary cushioning effect. However, she seriously damaged our port propeller when grinding alongside us.

After an all-round anti-submarine sweep we fired more snow-flakes and subsequently rescued 32 Germans, including the First Lieutenant, Barntd von Walther und Croneck, an ocean racer of no mean repute.

Both *Pathfinder* and *Quentin* closed as soon as they received my report and together we picked up 49 survivors from the U-boat, all except the Engineer Officer and one rating who may have stayed below to scuttle.

My black cat was sleeping in the scramble net when it was let down to rescue the survivors from the U-boat. One of our men went in after it and was mistaken for a German when he re-appeared on deck.

The doctor spent all night medically examining the prisoners, another Officer being present for interrogation. The following morning we gave them all a good scrub with soap and water on the fo'c'sle, as they hadn't had a bath for months.

United States Navy motor torpedo boats met us in the entrance to the Gulf of Paria and we transferred the prisoners, blindfolded.

It was a weird sight watching them feeling their way with our able seamen escorting and pushing them down the hatch. The roar of engines must have been frightening as they left, but they were grateful to us for good treatment and said so. I gather their subsequent treatment was relatively harsh.

HMS *Vimy* was berthed on the repair ship USS *Altair* at Five Islands. Her officers were very kind and helpful, putting all their facilities at our disposal, including cinemas, buses, ice creams, hairdresser, dentist and a laundry with the latest and best equipment. They had three gangs of 60 working in straight shifts on our splits and did their best go get our port propeller off and to cut down the blades evenly. After listing us over to 25° and down by the head, this proved unsuccessful and I had to call a halt for fear of capsizing if we went much further. Our 14 foot draft surprised the Americans who were used to dealing with four-stackers with inturning screws only eight foot below the water line.

The American Admiral commanding the base was a Vice-Admiral and my former Commander-in-Chief, Admiral Sir Michael Hodges, the Senior British Naval Officer, was serving in the rank of Rear-Admiral. He was relieved by Rear Admiral Phillips two days after we arrived.

Our Officers received many invitations of hospitality and were made honorary members of the Officers' Club, but the RNVR Liaison Officer further insisted that our men should be the guests of the 'Win the War Association' on a visit to the Pitch Lakes. It was a very hot drive and the men wished they had not gone, despite being given two bottles of beer each!

Pathfinder and *Quentin* left after four days to escort a convoy back to Freetown, and I had HMS *Burdock* (Lieutenant-Commander Lynes RNR) to keep me company. After fruitless efforts to get at our propeller, we were ordered to escort a tanker convoy to Gibraltar with *Burdock*, the only other escort.

Survivors from torpedoed ships arrived in Port of Spain nearly every day, and there was much U-boat activity in the Caribbean.

The convoy conference took place in a busy office at US Navy HQ. Unfortunately the Base Commander was ill and the chair was taken by an RNR Lieutenant who gave out papers and left me to do all the talking, being Senior Officer of the Escort.

No arrangements had been made for returning the Masters to their ships, so I invited them all on board *Vimy* to await developments and meet informally. They all gave me their names and addresses, no doubt feeling as we did, that we were about to take part in a momentous voyage, with about one hundred U-boats in the Atlantic, to say nothing of surface raiders.

They vowed never to leave another conference until they knew how they were getting back to their ships. Eventually they all embarked in HMS *Burdock* who took them alongside each ship in turn, as they were all lying some miles out in the bay.

In view of considerable U-boat activity, I had refused to sail without some additional escort, such as motorboats or aircraft, at least while in the Caribbean. 'O.K., Captain, we'll give you Air', said the Lieutenant, and we duly set sail for an offensive anti-submarine sweep, meeting the convoy as it emerged from Boca di Navious about sunset.

The first sign of air cover was a bomb dropped on our port beam near the horizon at about 0900 the following morning, at which point *Burdock* went off to investigate. No sooner was she hull down than a conning tower appeared on the same bearing but much closer. *Vimy* sounded six blasts and turned to attack, whilst the convoy went off smartly in the other direction, unescorted. We could not exceed 15 knots without excessive vibration from the port propeller and now we were doing about 19, with stern steam on the port engine. We opened fire. The radar was out of action and control was difficult owing to vibration, but some of the U-boat's upper works disappeared and she seemed to be stopped. Then a dirty white flag was seen waving; we ceased fire and reduced speed. Somehow the object looked rather too small for a conning tower and when within a mile, definitely odd. Not until we had slowed down did we realise that our 'conning tower' consisted of people packed tight together, standing on a raft whose sail we had shot away.

As we drew alongside, this ragged party made a brave but pathetic sight. They were 17 Americans, including two women and three children, with barely standing room only on their raft. Their clothes were tattered and faded but they looked fit and tough. Their ship the SS *West Lashaway* had been torpedoed nineteen days earlier over 500 miles to the southeast, whence the Bosun had sailed the raft.

Apart from severe swelling of the feet and ankles, known as 'immersion foot', caused by standing so long on the grating in salt water, the survivors were in remarkably good shape and bore us no malice for firing at them. According to the Bosun, they were relieved and delighted that we had done so. He said they knew they would be mistaken for a U-boat because two four-stackers had already passed them. On being lifted on board, a little girl[4] exclaimed: 'When I heard the cannons roar, I prayed to Jesus that I might live.' Her little brother's comment was more objective: 'When you started shooting, I thought they were "baam sharts!"' (bum shots).

A missionary lady in the party later wrote a book[5] which rightly thanked the Almighty for a wonderful deliverance and which described her feelings about the destroyer which fired at her.

We gave the ladies our concert party dresses and rigged the survivors up somehow before transferring them all to a Dutch ship bound for Barbados, the only ship in the convoy not a tanker. The actual transfer at sea in rough weather without using boats was rendered somewhat tricky by the language difficulty.

We now headed for Gibraltar, with good weather for the first ten days and were fuelled from the *Abbeydale* before bad weather set in. Waves of west bound U-boats and two other groups following about 100 miles astern were reported. Then for over a week a northerly gale near the beam produced a heavy sea and swell which made us roll never less than 25° either way, and for two days like *Burdock*, up to 45°. Life was becoming tedious, with not much to look forward to, so I suggested to the Commodore that a daily joke should be signalled round the convoy at 1600 every day, being produced by each ship in turn, beginning with the two escorts. The results obviously gave Officers something to think about and produced some very salty yarns.

By 1 October we had passed the Azores and I decided to try fuelling again. The weather seemed no worse and the convoy hove to head to sea at about four knots. Captain Edwards added two extra lengths of hose and we had as long a tow as possible. Connecting up proved difficult, but we managed to take in 67 tons in half an hour, before the hose parted under water in one of the extra lengths. We tried again on two successive days, and finally gave up the unequal struggle. While these attempts were being made, *Burdock* screened the convoy from ahead: he did not tell me his asdics had been out of action until we reached harbour! Though virtually hove to, steering and preventing the tow from parting was difficult and the weather was deteriorating. Seas were breaking over the fo'c'sle and despite the long tow, the scend between the ships was an awesome sight. Our hearts were in our mouths every time the towing wire whipped out of the water and came nearly taut, with its serpentine cargo hanging in bights. After the hose parted for the third time, *Abbeydale* signalled that the hoses issued at Gibraltar seemed to be duds. I said: 'The Minister of Production will be informed', at which Captain Edwards replied: 'I wish I had the Minister sitting on the tow now.' (My brother was PA to the Minister at the time.)

This struck me as funny, until we cast off. The First Lieutenant was on the fo'c'sle receiving encouragement from me to hurry up, when a comber landed on top of the party and swept them aft onto the breakwater. From the bridge we could see nothing but a cataract of water, but fortunately no-one was hurt, although a Leading Seaman put his head through the guard rails when under water. Just as well as they were taut.

The question now was, when would *Vimy* have to leave the convoy, with our corvette HMS *Burdock* as the only escort, and go to Ponta Delgada for fuel? I signalled to the Commodore: 'Unless a miracle happens, I will have to leave you tomorrow for fuel at PD.' That night the miracle happened. The gale backed four points to near west on our port quarter and gave us a wonderful opportunity to sail the ship.

All awnings were got up, lower booms rigged and fo'c'sle and quarterdeck awnings set as water sails, like stunsails. These were hoisted and stopped to the wireless yard with light yarns holding the upper ear-ring cringles, reminding one of the leech lines in a Chinese junk. Other sails were used on the fo'c'sle to prevent broaching to, and for over three days we kept station on the convoy at 10 knots, with engine speed for six, using one engine only and trailing the other. The wind gave us four knots and we reached Gibraltar with 35 tons of oil fuel remaining.

The Flag Officer, North Atlantic, and his staff were very pleased to get the oil tankers but were not disposed to dock *Vimy* for a new propeller. I was asked if *Vimy* could go to Casablanca, which would have been interesting in view of the high level of planning being carried out there. But I knew none of this and was only concerned with getting my ship safely home to a dry dock in Portsmouth, some 7,000 miles from Trinidad. Not for some time did we appreciate our contribution to the North Africa landings and the reason why every dry dock at Gibraltar had to be kept cleared for emergencies.

To quote the official account:

> Seven convoys, containing in all some 800 ships carried the Allied Expeditionary Force to North Africa. All our resources were stretched to their very limit to protect this huge Armada.[6]

U-boats were reported breaking out into the Atlantic from Biscay ports and we tried to catch one before reaching Devonport in time for fuel and a welcome night in harbour.

The next morning a tug turned us round and we proceeded, picking up a convoy from Dartmouth and escorting it through a so-called minefield to Portland. I asked for a tug to berth us or for permission to proceed direct to Portsmouth, which was readily granted. A gale was blowing up from the west and we reached The Needles about sunset, anchoring on Solent Banks off Yarmouth after dark. There we spent a jolly night when the fierce tide nearly parted our cable.

It took a long time to weigh at daylight and we went up the Solent at full speed: 15 knots, plus another five with gale astern, making good about 20.

The Yeoman's father-in-law was waiting with his tug to berth us, but we managed to berth alongside at Pitch House jetty ahead of some minesweepers without assistance: our stern missed them by a few feet and we rang off main engines as a flare took the jetty, with the gale blowing on us.

Lieutenant-Commander Stannard VC, RNR relieved me and the ship was fitted with hedgehog, promptly sinking two more U-boats.

NOTES

1. Quentin: later Commander Sir Alan H.P. Noble KCMG, DSC, RN, MP.
2. Pathfinder: Commander (now Captain) E.A. Gibbs DSO, and three Bars RN.
3. Sub-Lieutenant Griffiths DSC, SANVR.
4. Now Carol Donna Hobson of Chicago.
5. Mrs Ethel Bell in *Adrift*: the story of twenty days on a raft in the South Atlantic, as told to J.H. Hunter, edited by J.H. Hunter (Evangelical Publishers, Toronto, Canada and New York, N.Y., 1943).
6. *The Battle of the Atlantic*: the official account of the fight against the U-boats, 1939–45.

Neptune goes to action station

MEN of the 25-year-old destroyer Vimy, now home after a long commission abroad, believe they are the only ship's company piped to action stations during the traditional " crossing the line " ceremony.

As King Neptune was performing his initiation rites a U-boat alarm was sounded.

" I wish we had found a U-boat and had taken prisoners," said an officer, " for they would have been convinced that the British were mad.

"LOVE SUSIE"

" We were all in fancy costume. 'Guns'—the gunnery officer—rushed to his post in all the flowing robes of Neptune; 'Chief'—the chief engineer — was semi-nude. with the words 'I love Susie' scrawled across his chest; and No. 1 —the first lieutenant—in celebration of recently getting married, was hampered by a great mock ball and chain in a rush to the bridge.

"Unfortunately no German turned up, otherwise Neptune could have given them their equatorial baptism with far better realism than usual."

Later the Vimy, commanded by Lieut.-Commander H. G. D. de Chair, did get her U-boat and prisoners.

It was another ramming job. It happened on September 3, third anniversary of the start of the war. The U-boat sank after more than 40 survivors had been rescued.

14

HMS *Tuscan*, to South East Asia Command 1943-44

My next appointment was to stand by HMS *Tuscan*, a new destroyer building on the Tyne, and after Damage Control and Torpedo Control Courses, I was made an Honorary Member and put up at the Northern Counties Club in Newcastle. Swan Hunter, the builders, gave me and my Officers an office, and the work progressed happily until one day on the bridge and looking aft I saw two sterns. Clearly I was not fit to take command with double vision and I reported to the Superintendent of Contract-built ships.

About this time, Pat sent me a telegram announcing our son Colin's arrival. Driving back to the Club, my Wren driver said, 'Why aren't you in a puff-puff?' Evidently the contents of my telegram was common property in the Wrennery. Ian Balfour relieved me in Command of HMS *Tuscan*; I believe she was mined on her first trip.

Our village doctor in Cuminestown recommended me to the Naval Specialist in London, who diagnosed my double vision as a tumour on the eighth nerve. He said, 'I can send you to Faversham Hospital where they have the prettiest nurses, or to Barrow Gurney, the loony-bin, where they have the best surgeons.' I opted for the latter, but it seemed the Naval Surgeons were not too keen on this operation and meanwhile my wife arranged for me to see Mr Norman Dott in Edinburgh, the acknowledged best neurological surgeon. He said, 'I will do my best to save your eye, but I cannot promise', and I said, 'I don't care what you do as long as you get me on a bridge in three months.' Actually I was up and about in a fortnight and after sick leave, was appointed First Lieutenant and Training Officer at HMS *King Alfred* a training establishment at Lancing, Sussex, in the spring of 1943. My promotion to Commander came at the end of the year. With life at Lancing, living in the Headmaster's house, I was soon fully recovered. We were training up to 100 Cadet ratings a week. After a preliminary vetting, they were with us for five weeks before being promoted Acting Sub-Lieutenant RNVR for a further five weeks at Hove.

Instructions took the form of Pilotage, Seamanship, Gunnery, Field Training, Small Arms Drill, Signals, etc. Battalion Drill provided a good set-piece, and for Pilotage we had the football ground surrounded by buoys and beacons. Six ice-cream tricycles, each mounting a Submarine Compass on the handle-bars with a chart on the tray, three boys to each tricycle fixing their position round the field and learning how to apply variation and deviation. Six weeks later, some of them could be driving MTB's at 30 knots.

In the New Year of 1944 I called on the Naval Assistant to Second Sea Lord (NA2SL), who said: 'Now you are a Commander, you are fit for sea.' But this was not to be, as it appeared that my presence in Delhi was urgently required and I would be flown out, my luggage to follow by sea. I took off in a Dakota with a Group Captain and four RAF officers, arriving at North Front, Gibraltar, in time for breakfast, which I missed.

After a stop in a North Africa camp, we flew at 11,000 feet to avoid clouds and bumps beyond El Alamein, and had a strong tailwind to Cairo West. I was awarded a passage onwards in a BOAC Sunderand, leaving at 0430 the following morning. This was luxury, but after breakfast at El Lisan on the Dead Sea, the pilot decided to return to Cairo on account of the bad weather and defects, including flat batteries. The return was uncomfortable and three out of five passengers were sick. I have a vivid recollection of nursing a sick baby who yelled blue murder whilst its mother effected running repairs next door.

The following morning we re-embarked on the Nile, arriving at El Lisan about 0730, with time to walk and make friends with the local Sheikh. Noon brought us by way of the pipeline to Habbaniyah, reminiscent of the exploits of King Col, under General Kingston, earlier in the War. My brother, Somerset, was Intelligence Officer, and covers the exploits in various books.

The next hop took us over the Tigris and Euphrates and a patch of sand alleged to be the site of the Garden of Eden. We circled round the ancient ruin and mud arch of Cestiphon, still intact since 1200 AD, as it never rains there. We reached Basrah about 1700 and after a night in the comfortable Airways Hotel, left at 0430 with a full cargo including Arabs, Iraqis and Indians. Some of these we deposited at Bahrain where we landed for breakfast and two hours later disembarked others at Dubai, still in Arabia, where some fine dhows were drawn up on the beach. Then over the sea to Jiwani in Baluchistan by 1500 and Karachi by sundown, where the comfort of the British Airways Somerset Mess for Officers of field rank was balm indeed.

In an Indian Airways Dakota we touched down at Jodhpur and reached Delhi at sunset after flying at 14,000 feet. There, Lieutenant-Colonel Cowan met and conducted me to South Avenue Camp, where we selected a tent for me to live in. After a day or two this became quite surprisingly comfortable, and I wrote: 'I shall be sorry to leave it.'

My appointment to the Staff of the Supreme Allied Commander, South East Asia, Admiral Mountbatten, is best explained by my letter to Captain Roskill, the naval historian, dated 18 February 1979:

18 February 1979

Dear Captain Roskill,

Many thanks for your letter of February 13th.

I was promoted on 31st December 1943 and reported to NA2SL at the Admiralty. He said 'Now you are a Commander, you are fit for sea.' I had previously been pronounced unfit as a result of an operation leaving me deaf in one ear. Naturally, I asked for another destroyer, but Commander Lovegrove said: 'No. Just the chap, Mountbatten's staff!' I had always had the greatest admiration for Lord Louis who had mounted me for polo in his team when he was a Commander, and Dick Onslow tried to get me as his relief No.1 in the Daring. However, this was war and I felt my contribution to date had been relatively inadequate, so I protested and asked: 'What is the job?', to which Lovegrove replied: 'We don't know. We want you to tell us. He keeps on asking for more staff.' I said: 'Surely you must know something.' He said: 'It's something to do with move-ments', and reluctantly pulled a family tree out of a drawer. My boss was the American General (Spec) Wheeler who turned out to be in Washington, but my appointment was as Naval Adviser on Shipping, Ports and Combined Operations to the Director of Movements and Transportation (SEAC), Brigadier Ronnie Montague-Jones.

155

When I got to Delhi, I found Captain Gill MN of the British India SS Co. (BI) who knew more about Shipping and Ports than I was likely to acquire in a lifetime, and a fully integrated Combined Operations Staff including a Lt-Cdr RNZVR with experience of Combined Operations, of which I had none. So it appeared to me that my appointment to Mountbatten's staff was already covered. After one day I called on Gerald Langley, the Senior Staff Officer (Navy), and said: 'I'm sorry, Sir, I've got nothing to do here.' He exploded: 'What do you mean, nothing to do? Masses to do. Find something to do. Have the Fleet Air Arm.'

Vice Admiral Geoffrey Miles and his staff were accredited to MB by the C-in-C East Indies and his Staff Officer Operations (SOO) was Commander Hewitt. What I did not know and only discovered years later, was that Hewitt had been summoned to attend a conference at five minutes' notice by the Army, and not having seen any agenda, refused to attend. Evidently the Military reaction was: 'We must have our own Sailor who can express the body of Naval Opinion!' For this I was singularly unfitted. Hence my appointment!

Clearly I had much to learn, and proceeded to attend an Army Staff Course for Loading ships (Landing Tables etc.) and visited the ports, reporting fully to Supremo, C-in-C (East Indies) and Director Mov & TN. Much of what I found, particularly in preparations for an assault landing in Burma appeared elementarily unsatisfactorily and my reports did not mince matters. Admiral Miles' comments in the margin of one report read 'Who the hell? What the hell? Why the hell? Poking his nose in again!'

After three months of this, SEAC moved to Kandy, and I was invited to be attached to the staff of C-in-C (East Indies) in Colombo during the move. There I wrote an appreciation of submarine warfare in the Indian Ocean. The Chief of Staff, Captain Gerald Tuck approved it and suggested I take it home to the Admiralty! This of course I could not do without Supremo's permission, being officially on his staff.

The Fleet Air Arm next occupied my attention, and I visited all the FAA stations in SEAC, and also went to the Naaf river in Burma where Wavell's Navy was operating. It was obvious that I, as a 'Fish Head', could not fairly represent the Fleet Air Arm and I requested the appointment of a Fleet Air Arm Officer. Commander Rolfe duly arrived and we discussed our situation, and I asked to be sent home for another appointment.

By this time my friend St John Tyrwhitt had relieved Lovegrove at the Admiralty. Without being disloyal to Mountbatten I could not write much, but Tyrwhitt wrote: 'We never thought you would last long in that job, and if you can get rid of the next one as quickly as you have done this, we might think about sending you to sea again.'

My next appointment was Chief Naval Instructor, Combined Training (India). When the Commanding Officers of Landing Craft at Madh Island heard about this RN Commander, they, having come straight out from assault landings in Sicily etc., said: 'If this fellow comes here, we will all resign.' The occasion did not arise, as I was required to be part of Colonel Lyall Grant's team, lecturing to all and sundry on Combined Operations.

From SEAC's point of view I probably made a thorough nuisance of myself, but evidently it had the effect of sending Rear-Admiral Beevor out with a team to help sort things out. I only met Mountbatten twice to speak to, on arrival and on leaving after eight months. His Chiefs of staff knew I wanted to go and successfully boomed me off. (After reading Mountbatten's biography, I can see why!)

It had been an interesting, if frustrating time. No doubt I could have remained as a Blue Planner with Mike Goodenough, or as Director of Mov & TN Air and Water Section with Acting Promotion, but as my Director put it, my present employment was a waste of an experienced Sea Officer of considerable seniority.

Eventually I wrote out a pass for Air Priority (A) and flew home RAF to be appointed HMS Venus 26th DF. Meanwhile, Mike Goodenough, as an acting Captain, managed to integrate himself with the Staff of East Indies Fleet and so present the required body of Naval Opinion for the Army and SEAC.

Colonel Lyall Grant and Major Gerald Hare invited me to join them in a houseboat on the Dahl Lake whilst on leave in Kashmir. There a Miss Helen Stavrides asked me to inspect the Navy Sheepskin Jackets League HQ. She had been asked by the wife of C in C South Atlantic to get the branch started but was not satisfied with its progress and suspected corruption. It appeared that a flourishing leather goods trade was being carried out all over India in the name of Admiral The Lord Louis Mountbatten. It took over a month to get his patronage withdrawn, and then only because SEAC was leaving India for Ceylon.

The SEAC plan was to mount five divisions in India for the assault on Burma, but thanks to Stalin the assault on Normandy required all our resources, and no one else in India seemed very interested in combined ops. Naturally I was anxious to have operational experience, and the attached signals and letters refer.

The Gordon-Campbells of Butterfield and Swire of old pre-war friends from Swatow, invited me to stay in Bombay on my way home and I succeeded in recovering my suitcase in HMS *Braganza* where it had been sent soon after my arrival in Delhi eight months earlier.

Yours etc.

We spent a month at Trincomalee, lecturing to units of the Fleet, and I called on Commodore (D) in the hope of getting a destroyer, but was told that all appointments must come through the Admiralty. However, Dick Onslow was now Captain (D) of the 4th Flotilla in HMS *Quilliam* and had told me: 'If you ever want a sea trip, let me know.' One lunchtime while walking by Trincomalee harbour, I noticed confidential books being landed from his flotilla, so I went on board to see him and asked if I could come with him. He replied: 'You must go and ask the Admiral.'

Sir Arthur John Power was taking over command of the Fleet from Sir James Somerville and met me on the quarterdeck of the *Renown*. Commander Condor said: 'de Chair wants to go in the *Quilliam*, Sir.' '*Quilliam*, *Quilliam*,' said the Admiral, 'who told you? How did you find out?' I replied: 'Nobody told me anything, Sir, but seeing Confidential Books being landed, I realised there must be an operation on and asked Captain (D) to take me.' 'All right,' he said, 'you go: I'll find out who told you.'

Later I lectured to a packed audience in the hangar of his flagship and the Admiral was there. When I had finished he said

'Now don't get down, I want to ask you a question, but I'll get near the door first.' Then 'Was it, or was it not necessary to have a private Navy for Combined Ops?' I said 'yes', bearing in mind that Mountbatten had been Chief of Combined Operations. The Admiral said 'That's all I wanted to know. I entirely disagree with everything Commander de Chair has said this morning. You've been the darlings of the Fleet, you've always had everything you always wanted and I don't like you politicians.'

With that he walked out with his Flag Lieutenant and the great iron door slammed behind him. I had to start my lecture over again. 'You heard what the Admiral said. I quite agree with what the Admiral said, but he forgets one thing, the Navy isn't sailors any more. Nine tenths of the Fleet are manned by hostilities officers and men. Of the rest trained for Combined Ops the best we can do is to teach them how to put a landing craft ashore.

A year later, I brought HMS *Venus* to Colombo to join the East Indies Fleet and the Commander-in-Chief very kindly invited me to lunch with him alone. By this time the assault on Burma had begun and the Admiral spoke mostly about Combined Operations. He showed that he knew the marks of all types of landing craft and had a thorough appreciation of their functions.

The club run in *Quilliam* was my first experience under fire. Our three destroyers with the six-inch gun Dutch cruiser *Tromp* comprised the inshore Squadron for the bombardment of Sabang in Sumatra. So near the beach were we that at one point our line was straddled by a short salvo from the battleships. I had a grandstand view sitting in the director tower above the bridge, but I heard that the press reporter also in the director tower of the ship astern of us had lost his legs. We were only hit on the quarter by one Japanese shell which failed to explode.

My impression was that we were blazing off into the jungle and could not see the shore batteries firing at us. However, the Fleet Air Arm did good work at the airfield which was the main reason for the attack. It was also in the nature of a farewell to Sir James Somerville who was still on board the flagship.

I felt that my seagoing experience was wasted in a staff appointment, and the correspondence given in the appendices to this chapter show how I desperately tried to obtain an operational appointment at sea.

APPENDIX 1

R.N.A.S. Coimbatore
12th April 1944

Sir,

I have the honour to request consideration to my early release for sea service.

2. There is a shortage of fully qualified Naval officers in the Fleet and I feel that my present duties should be performed by an officer not required at sea. Having commanded destroyers since 1935, including the Hong Kong Flotilla for the first two years of the war, it is hard to reconcile with a clear conscience the effective war effort now permitted to an officer of my staff standing.

3. My promotion to Commander on 1st January 1944 was followed by appointment to Staff of S.A.C.S.E.. for duty with P.A.O. and I was passed fit for sea by M.D.G. on 18th January, to enable me to take up a sea appointment with the Eastern Fleet if required.

4. Since the initial request for a Commander of P.A.O.'s Staff, circumstances in S.P.A.C. have somewhat altered the requirement; moreover several officers with suitable qualifications have reached H.Q. since my arrival on 6th February. They include a Surveyor from Admiralty Plans Division 'Q' Staff and a Civil Engineer, both Commanders.

5. The Movements and Transportation Divs on military officers are adequately schooled in its staff requirements and there is very little office work even remotely connected with the Navy beyond their capacity. P.A.O.'s staff is fundamentally military in character and a "Salt Horse" Naval officer like myself with no military 'Q' Staff or Civil Engineering qualifications can be of little benefit to it beyond taking messages, and is not earning his pay as a Commander.

6. Officers of Eastern Fleet Staff are speedily attached to S.B.A.C. to advise in Naval matters. They are not difficult to refer to but if desired a Military Staff liaison officer could be specially detailed for this purpose.

8. On the other hand my services on Staff of S.A.C. be considered

essential for known projected operations it is submitted that they would be enhanced by sending me to U.K. for the next short Staff course (syllabus attached). This would also enable me to advise Admiralty on the shipping position in the Indian Ocean.

9. It is doubtful whether Operations Division is fully aware of the complexity of this situation partially set out in my report No. 518/ Mov. & Tn. dated 5th April 1944, and opinion is widely held that an officer fully acquainted with it should return to U.K. to explain in person. Having come straight from the Admiralty for training in Convoy and Troop Movements with D.O.D. (F) and knowing the relevant problems confronting Eastern Fleet Staff it has been suggested that I would adequately fulfil this function myself.

10. If not required for duty as a Commander R.N. in the Eastern Theatre of War, it is requested that serious and immediate consideration be given to returning me to the Admiralty for disposal having regard to paragraph 9, and if desired paragraph 8.

I have the honour to be,

Sir,
Your obedient servant

The Deputy Director,   Commander,
Movement and Transportation   Royal Navy.
   (Air and Water)
South East Asia Command

APPENDIX 2

CONFIDENTIAL MESSAGE

TO: ADMIRALTY   FROM: S.A.C.S.E.A.
INFO C. IN C. E.F.
IMPORTANT

CONFIDENTIAL   Reference SEACOS 33 and 36

Commander H.G.D. de Chair R.N., has been carrying out duties referred to in paragraph 2(a) of SEACOS 33 as modified by

161

SEACOS 36. In view of the serious shortage of Naval Officers I have had the complement of my Headquarters Staff carefully reviewed.

2. In view of the presence on PAO's staff of Merchant Navy Officer representing DDST (1) and of closer contact with C in C E.F.'s staff made possible by move to Kandy, this appointment is considered to be unnecessary for the time being. Propose therefore to release Commander de Chair who is strongly recommended for sea service.

3. His experience does not repetition not make him suitable for either Naval appointments asked for in para. 8 of SEACOS 33 but these appointments require filling and I hope will be borne in mind when Naval manning situation permits later in the year.

T.O.O. . . .

(. . .)

Copies circulated to:
A/COS
AD/COS (N)
S.O.E.F.
PAO
COMPTROLLER
SEC. PLANS

APPENDIX 3

SC4/999/C

South East Asia Command Headquarters

25th June 1944

My dear de Chair,

Thank you for your letter of the 3rd June. I shall be going to Delhi with General Wildman-Lushington next week and will ask him to get in touch with D.C.O.(1) to discuss your future employment. If he feels you can do better work elsewhere I feel it is up to him to inform the Admiralty since you are of course no longer on my staff, or, for that matter, even in South East Asia!

Personally I should not be too impatient. The assault phase of the last great amphibious operation of the war in Europe has now taken place, and all others must now be in this part of the world.

Yours sincerely,

Louis Mountbatten

Commander G de Chair R.N.
c/o Directorate of Combined Operations (India)

15

HMS *Venus* 26th Destroyer Flotilla 1944-45

On my return to the United Kingdom in late 1944, I was appointed in command of HMS *Venus* and directed to join her at Scapa Flow to relieve John Richardson. I arrived on board at 1410 on a Saturday and we sailed at 1420 on the same day in company with 36 other destroyers to try and find the *Tirpitz*. Richardson was the Senior Officer of this party and I was glad of the chance to understudy him in a Home Fleet operation.

After a night at sea the doctor reported that the Captain had 'flu and asked me to take over. My immediate reaction was: 'Certainly not. First Lieutenant takes command; I have not taken over the ship yet.'

However, next day the doctor came to me again and said the First Lieutenant had also got 'flu, asking, 'Now will you take over?' So I said: 'I don't mind driving the cab but officially I am not in command until I have mustered the Confidential Books (CBs).'

So it appeared that as a newcomer to the Fleet I was Senior Officer of this search force, until much to my relief we discovered my old shipmate Phillip Powlett in HMS *Cassandra*, then senior to me. We did not find the *Tirpitz* and returned to Scapa where I formally relieved Richardson.

The autumn gales made securing to buoys in harbour difficult, but my main concern was the intense cold during subsequent sweeps in Arctic waters. On one of these when escorting HMS *Illustrious*, the Admiral decided that the weather was too rough for destroyers and ordered a turnround. When stern to wind, I saw HMS *Vigilant* being overtaken and covered by a huge wave which poured down her funnel.

After two months we were ordered to Leith for a minor refit. While there, I entertained Mr and Mrs Norman Dott on board; a pleasant token of gratitude for his successful operation on my eye nearly two years previously.

Two RN officers were appointed as relief officers, the First Lieutenant Peter Meryon and Sub-Lieutenant Hales, and in company with HMS *Volage* we proceeded via the Pentland Firth and the Minches to Devonport.

We left the cold winter waters of the North Atlantic early in 1945, and sailed in HMS *Venus* to join the East Indies Fleet. We called at Gibraltar, Malta, Port Said and Colombo where I reported to the Commander-in-Chief. My first mission was to take Commodore (D) from Trincomalee to Akyab in Burma, whence I proceeded to Kyukpyu with orders to bombard a Japanese position from an anchorage in a tideway; the range was about 17,000 yards, extreme for our guns, but by putting a spring on the cable and so listing the ship in the tideway, it would have been possible to increase the range. However, at 0300 a signal was received from Commodore (D) who ordered *Venus* to be back at Akyab by 0900, and our Japanese were left in comparative peace.

Having arrived at Akyab as ordered, I landed to report to the Commodore who meanwhile had gone on board to see me. Eventually we met on the beach and he explained that HMS *Venus* was there to give a lunch party.

It appeared that he had attended an RAF concert given by ENSA artist Patricia Burke, and as Senior Officer present got up on the stage to thank her, whereupon she kissed him on the cheek. Not to be outdone, he embraced her, to the delight of the audience. Clearly chivalry dictated that further action was necessary and what better way of entertaining the lady than in HMS *Venus*? After lunch it was agreed that we should take Patricia Burke to Kyaukpyu to give a concert for the Army there, and next day she embarked with ten Royal Marines and much luggage. I invited the Petty Officers to entertain her for lunch, after which she sang to the ship's company on the fo'c'sle. 'Pedro the Fisherman was always whistling' went down particularly well and had all the men whistling, knowing this to be the traditional signal for mutiny. We also attended the concert, at which about 5,000 men were present and you could have heard a pin drop before the applause.

We returned to Akyab with the Commodore on board and Patricia Burke flew round us in his aeroplane, her red trousers and blue blouse clearly visible in the open door.

The operations of the East Indies Fleet have been well covered by John Winton in *Freedom's Battle*, *The Forgotten Fleet* and *Sink the Haguro*; the 26th Destroyer Flotilla was part of it all. All these books were very well written, but not entirely accurate in places. As Winton has said, 'New facts are bound to emerge, so I don't think the final story will ever be told.'

During one sweep on 16 April 1945, I was ordered to take *Venus* and *Virago* and sink all shipping on the west coast of Sumatra, but we only found junks inside an island channel, possibly Batu. A warning shot enabled the crews to abandon ship before we set the junks on fire.

My visits ashore in Trincomalee were mainly confined to the dockyard, which had changed little since the days of Nelson. I attended the odd bathing picnic with the Captain and Officers of F.S. *Richelieu*, who were keen on snorkelling in the clear water with its spectacular tropical fish and coral.

We did a lot of sea time, but V-E Day with the East Indies Fleet in Trincomalee Harbour was duly celebrated by the watches ashore. Our flotilla burned down basha huts and men of the 'R' class ships had a fight with the *Richelieu* sailors. I was not surprised when we were ordered to sea in the early hours of the morning; evidently an appropriate punishment and a salutary reminder that we were still very much at war with Japan.

In fact, allied intelligence had reported a heavy cruiser and destroyer due to sail from Singapore on 10th May, bound for relief of the Andaman and Nicobar Islands, and all available units of the East Indies Fleet sailed to deal with them.

That evening, HM submarine *Subtle* reported a Japanese cruiser, painted pink, with a destroyer in the Malacca Straits, steering northwest at 17 knots.

OPERATION DUKEDOM

We steamed for three days across the Indian Ocean; *Cumberland*, *Richelieu* and the 26th Destroyer Flotilla, as Force 61 had been sent ahead on 12 May to be between Sumatra and the Nicobar Islands to intercept the enemy. However, we were spotted by aircraft and the cruiser reversed course back into the Malacca Straits. We then retired to the southwest to fuel, the 26th DF having spent the 14 May searching the Nicobar/Sumatra Channel at high speed.

Having found nothing, they rendezvoused with an oiler at

dusk, and with tanks half empty were queuing up to fuel, when ordered to raise steam for full speed and carry out a further sweep off the northern tip of Sumatra. We steamed at high speed all that night and the following day received orders to cancel operation 'Mitre', the current operation to intercept a convoy, the cruiser being presumed to be in the Malacca Straits. Captain Power queried the signal and, instead of returning, reduced our speed to 15 knots, thereby gaining a valuable 40 miles as it turned out.

Meanwhile, Lieutenant-Commander Fuller RNVR, commanding officer of 851 Squadron Fleet Air Arm, with four Avengers, was at the limit of his fan-shaped search for one of his crews in a dinghy, who had been forced to ditch by gunfire on the previous day. According to Fuller, unbriefed either as to the presence of the 26th Destroyer Flotilla or the possible presence of the Japanese cruiser, and having jettisoned his four bombs to save fuel, he had spotted the Japanese Cruiser *Haguro* and was able to shadow her for twenty minutes, transmitting electrifying signals which were received on aircraft wave by HMS *Virago*.

The Flotilla increased speed to 27 knots with orders to sink enemy ships before returning. The Flotilla was on a line bearing four miles apart, with *Venus* 320° 16 miles from Captain (D). In answer to a query of his, I reported that our radar was working very well. At 2245, when nearing the limit of our search, the Radar Operator on watch, Ordinary Seaman Norman Poole, reported 'Echo bearing 045° 68,000 yards!' I acknowledged with 'Popeye', meaning 'It's a cloud.' He replied, 'No, Sir, it's a ship', and I said 'Plot it.' Five minutes later he reported its course and speed as 125° 25 knots. We were then steering 110° at 27 knots and reported to Captain (D); 'Ship bearing 046° 46,000 yards.' He promptly replied 'Popeye' and we gave him her course and speed as 125° at 25 knots, which Lieutenant Longbottom RNVR, the Navigating and Signal Officer, had quickly worked out.

Years later, Poole wrote: 'I was on the PPI, (Plan Position Indicator) trying to answer the bridge, trying to plot the echo, and trying to get help in the shape of Paddy and Smithy who were crashed down in the flat below.'

Lieutenant Paxton RCNVR, the Radar Officer, who I sent down to the plot, and Longbottom, both supported Poole in his conviction that the echo was a ship, contrary to the opinion of the Petty Officer Radar Mechanic who had been summoned and who

167

had upset Poole's settings. My report stated that Poole had the courage of his convictions to the point of insubordination, for which he was awarded the Distinguished Service Medal.

The great range of detection was due to anomalous propagation, probably off a cloud, and *Venus* lost contact about an hour later. Meanwhile Captain (D) had ordered shadowing sectors which gave *Venus* sector G (320°-000°), and picked up the echo in HMS *Saumarez* at 28000 yards.

Sub-Lieutenant Hales as Torpedo Control Officer had reported earlier 'One of our fish won't angle' and I told him to have all torpedoes set for straight running on the beam, so as not to waste a torpedo in our attack. Torpedoes were normally set to turn 60° ahead after being fired from the tubes set abeam. Captain (D), an ex-submariner, had recently fitted a torpedo sight on his compass which would enable the Captain to fire the torpedoes himself, but we had not had time to fit one in *Venus*, and I had every confidence in my Torpedo Control Officer (TCO) with his sight and firing panel in the bridge wings.

From Sector G we were shadowing the enemy from astern, after Captain (D)'s intention to attack at 0100 had been signalled. She could be seen during occasional flashes of lightning, from which it appeared that we were chasing her from fine on her port quarter, but she was probably zig-zagging.

Shortly before the time ordered for attack, the TCO reported from the plot that the range was closing rapidly, with a small echo to the left of the big one. Clearly the cruiser had spotted our destroyers ahead, turned round and was coming towards us at a relative speed of over 60 knots, with a destroyer on her starboard beam. I told the First Lieutenant that we would aim to pass between the two ships and fire our torpedoes at the cruiser as we passed, hopefully unobserved, at that stage. He gave me rather an old-fashioned look and went aft to his action station as Officer of Quarters, ready to take command if the bridge was hit.

The cruiser appeared from the plot to be dead ahead and I altered course 10° to port to cross her line of advance and keep in my sector G (320-000), her course being roughly northwest and steady, until we passed her.

I told the Sub to come up on the bridge and prepare to fire torpedoes, and reported 'Attacking'. We were obviously going to be in a perfect position to fire torpedoes at very close range, making it impossible to miss, and as an ex-TCO, I had every confidence that, with straight running, this was our golden moment. When nearing the firing position, I called out 'Are you ready Sub?' No reply came and I repeated 'Are you ready, Sub?' By now the enemy was very close, about 40° on our bow, shortly to be tearing past us. Her two funnels completely filled the field of view (in my Barr & Stroud binoculars) and I realised it was time to fire torpedoes (straight running on the beam, as ordered).

The Sub then said to me in a quiet voice: 'We've missed it, Sir.' This could only mean one thing. The torpedoes were still angled in spite of my order for straight running and it was too late to alter the settings. Short of ramming the cruiser or possibly fouling *Saumarez* or *Verulum*, I had no alternative but to turn to port, which we did under full helm, still at full speed, to try and prevent her from breaking out of our circle of the star attack. The Japanese evidently saw the wash of our wake as we turned, and assuming that torpedoes had been fired, turned away to comb the tracks.

This threw him back into the arms of Captain (D) and *Verulum*, who got his attack in unobserved, with three hits. Captain (D) in *Saumarez* found himself with tubes trained to starboard and the enemy on his port bow, but gallantly swung his ship towards, and steaming through eight-inch shell explosions, delivered a torpedo attack under heavy fire, having illuminated with star shell. He also had a brief altercation with the Jap destroyer, who must have passed under the cruiser's stern when *Venus* was attacking.

As soon as *Venus* had reversed course to the northwest, expecting to see the cruiser uncomfortably close and intent on catching her before she could escape to the north, all we could see was what looked like a candle in the darkness on our port quarter. There was a lot of noise from gunfire and *Saumarez* had been hit. We fired starshell rockets and steered towards the action, keeping 'A' arcs open, with all guns firing. The cruiser appeared to be on fire aft and according to our own radar our shooting was very effective. The Chief Gunnery Instructor in the transmitting station, looking at the radar screen, could see our salvos hitting every time, but enemy shells were also apparently hitting us, at which he found himself ducking!

Captain (D)'s order for torpedo depth settings was nine feet, to endanger the enemy destroyers, of which he may have thought there were four, but I felt that this setting would constitute a grave risk to our own destroyers and was not surprised when told afterwards that our engine room staff had heard two torpedoes passing close to the ship.

During one hour of action, not less than 365 signals were made, mostly with radio telephone (TCS). I was quite hoarse from giving orders and acknowledging signals, with so much noise going on which created a continuous roar. Hardly the time to argue with Captain (D) about depth settings and I could not then quote the number of the official document which was the manual for a Nachi class cruiser which I had carefully consulted beforehand; accordingly I ordered depth settings 10 and 14 feet as recommended, but seeing she was heavily hit, I think we increased them to 16 and 20 feet and ordered local control and straight running. This gave the Gunner (T) and tubes crews a better chance, and allowed the Sub to go back to the plot. Besides being TCO he was supposed to be understudying Longbottom as Navigator.

The roar of gunfire was continuous and orders had to be given in rapid succession in a loud voice, and repeated down the voice pipe by my steward. Imagine my relief at finding our Midshipman on the bridge in the heat of action. He had come up to report as Officer of Quarters of 'A' and 'B' guns, that 'A' had misfired. The Captain of the Gun broke rules, ditched the offending cartridge and went on firing. An extra officer on the bridge was invaluable and Midshipman Robathan took over from the steward on the voice pipe to repeat orders.

We delivered our torpedo attack from under 2,100 yards (the Action Officer of the Watch put it at 1,800) and hearing the report 'All tubes fired', retired under smoke. Actually the report was probably 'After tubes fired' (hardly necessary), and we still had two torpedoes remaining. Accordingly I turned back through the smoke to complete the attack, but *Virago* signalled 'Keep clear, am attacking' and we had to wait until she and *Vigilant* were clear, before being ordered by Captain (D) to make a job of it. *Virago* suggested switching on fighting lights, which was a help in avoiding collisons. We had previously asked *Saumarez* to switch on fighting lights for five seconds, to get her bearing. *Venus* closed to within 500 yards and ensured two more hits and watched the cruiser sink, lowering the asdic dome which gave the operator the satisfaction of hearing her breaking up under water. We stopped to pick up survivors and prisoners, as men could be heard shouting in the water, but following a report of aircraft overhead, were ordered to leave and rejoin Captain (D). The Japanese destroyer *Kamikaze* and another ship came out from Penang after we left and picked up about 300 survivors.

During the withdrawal from the Malacca Straits, the flotilla steamed in a tight circle for mutual protection against air attack in daylight hours and was dive-bombed from Sumatra twice. *Virago* suffered severe casualties and I sent our Dr McIntosh and his sick berth attendant, Cattle, by name, over to assist with the dead and treatment of the wounded. John Winton gives a vivid description from *Virago*'s account on page 148 of *Sink the Haguro*.

During these attacks, it seemed best to steer towards each splash, and the next bomb invariably fell the opposite side of the ship.

Responding to my renewed expressions of sympathy over casualties in *Saumarez*, Admiral Power in a letter dated 15 September 1975 wrote: 'I am very sorry you still have regrets about your initial brush, but just consider what my frustration might have been if you had bagged her before I could get an oar in!'

On my return to Trincomalee I was left in charge of the flotilla while Captain Power took *Saumarez* to Colombo to report to the Commander-in-Chief East Indies and no doubt also to Admiral Mountbatten as Supreme Allied Commander South East Asia Command. It was then decided that we needed some relaxation and the 26th Destroyer Flotilla visited Madras before sending *Saumarez* and *Venus* to South Africa for refit.

Sir Arthur Whittaker, the civil Engineer-in-Chief, took passage to Durban in *Venus* and later very kindly took me to Johannesburg in his aircraft, sending me on to Pretoria to visit an uncle. On landing there the pilot swerved to avoid some blasting at the end of the runway. The aircraft lurched over and a wing hit the ground and was broken, but no one was hurt.

Passage from Colombo to Durban was enlivened by having some of the 26th Destroyer Flotilla staff officers on board. Lieutenant Parkinson's alsatian could climb up ladders, but not down, so usually arrived on the bridge. He had a habit of coming up behind me and licking my face. He went ashore at Addu Atoll, got stung in the backside by a bee and went yelping off into the

171

jungle; a lot of signals about this dog resulted before he could be collected. We were very sorry to miss him.

HMS *Saumarez* went to Simonstown and *Venus* to Durban, but after two days Captain Power ordered his damaged funnel to be replaced and proceeded to Durban, sending *Venus* to refit at Simonstown, which suited me since I had relations in the Cape.

The Navy League was very active in South Africa and was most generous in providing *Venus* with gifts. 'Anything we could possibly think of', they said, and I called on the chairman in Johannesburg to record our thanks.

One thing I missed which other destroyer Commanding Officers had was a bath. The officers' bathroom was two or three decks down near the mess deck, so I planned for a bathroom to be built on the fo'c'sle by my cabin, as in HMS *Roebuck*. The Chief Constructor in the dockyard said it would cause excessive topweight and cancelled the order. On return from leave I was annoyed by this decision and called on the Admiral Superintendent who was not prepared to over-rule his Chief Constructor. Accordingly, I went to see the Commmander-in-Chief South Atlantic, Bob Burnett, an old destroyer hand, who said, 'Well, old boy, don't make a signal if it's going to stop you getting your bath!' The Chief Constructor was horrified at my action and the result was a signal, two pages of typed foolscap, addressed to the Admiralty and repeated to the Commander-in-Chief East Indies and Captain (D), among others, from Commander-in-Chief South Atlantic. This missive began, 'I personally consider it essential for the Commanding Officer HMS *Venus* to have a bath.' My cousin Roy Struben was Captain of the old depot ship *Afrikander*, paying off, and we put his bath on the fo'c'sle and had a tile bathroom built round it!

My uncle, Arthur Struben, came out for sea trials and presented a handsome silver cup for which we challenged *Saumarez* to a regatta in Durban, and won.

After the fall of Rangoon and the surrender of Japan, I, being Senior Officer Destroyers at Singapore, was ordered to provide an escort of two destroyers for a convoy from Penang to Balawan Deli in Sumatra. With *Virago* in company, *Venus* embarked a Brigadier to negotiate with the Japanese. A Japanese Colonel in a fishing boat met us and said it was not safe to approach nearer the port than 15 miles on account of mines. Our convoy consisted of a liner, a hospital ship, four LSTs and four LCTs, beside smaller landing craft. Using our mine detector units, we lay dan buoys to mark a channel and led the convoy in single line ahead to within three miles of the port, where we anchored in line. The RAF had laid oyster mines there, which were supposed to be safe as from that day, but I did not trust the RAF mines and accordingly sent a landing craft in empty. It did not blow up, so we started landing stores. The Senior Officer LCTs then agreed to try and get his squadron landing stores and motor transport (MT), but when I asked the Senior Officer if he was willing to risk his 5,000-ton LSTs, he said: 'No b---- fear.' We requested Force 61 of mine sweepers which was crossing the Indian Ocean to report at Balawan Deli; only two of these five electric minesweepers were operational but they nevertheless cleared the channel.

There was an interesting sequel to the investment of Balawan Deli. Commander Armstrong invited me on board the liner to a cocktail party, to welcome a bevy of beautiful girls, obviously selected to restore the morale of the women who had suffered so much in Sumatra. They were to go to Medan and start work there before repatriating the women after their ordeal. A good description of a similar experience is in *A Town Like Alice* by Neville Shute.

Lieutenant-Commander Victor Clark, a survivor from HMS *Repulse*, sunk with the *Prince of Wales*, was in Bangalore on his way home after three years as a prisoner of war and was due for passage to the UK in a P&O ship from Bombay. There were two Wren Officers on leave in the hotel and he asked them how he could go home 'Grey Funnel'; they replied: 'Leave it to us.' So my friend received a telegram ordering him to report to Naval HQ Colombo for interrogation. There he was told, 'There's your ship' and to our mutual delight he joined HMS *Venus* and kept watch all the way home. He said it restored his sanity.

The flotilla was carrying out splash target firing after leaving Aden and the side of *Venus*'s 'B' gun blew out, sending a large splinter through the bridge screen and shattering a man's arm. Our guns were obviously feeling a bit tired by the end of the war and were due for wear measurement. We had to return to Aden and send our man to hospital.

Passing close to the island of Jubal Attair in the Red Sea, I saw an international signal flying from the lighthouse at the top of the island, meaning 'I require a doctor', so out of curiosity we rounded up under the lee of the island while the lighthouse keeper ran the four miles down to meet us. Our Doctor met him and signalled 'Request permission to go to the lighthouse', to which I replied, 'Not unless very urgent.' We were due to join the flotilla entering the Suez Canal and only by judicious cheating on the new fuel restrictions could we do it.

The whaler returned with the Doctor and by the time he reported on the bridge we were on our way at 15 knots. It appeared that the lighthouse crew were suffering from beri-beri and needed yeast and/or potatoes, which was reported to Commodore Aden, the responsible authority. Apparently the lighthouse had not been visited for four years.

The Commodore Aden was not pleased and there was a board of enquiry at Devonport after I had left the ship, at which it was alleged that 'Venus had refused medical assistance to the island of Jubal Attair.' The doctor attended the board of enquiry as I was on leave in Abberdeenshire by then.

I am indebted to Captain John Robatham for the loan of his journal kept as a Midshipman in which he made a record of the action in which the Japanese cruiser Haguro was sunk. He made a copy of Venus's track chart and action narrative from the plot and of some signals before they went over to Saumarez by heaving line. According to Chief Writer Parsons, it was 'a wet, soggy mess'. The following signals were made in the flotilla:

Venus to D26 (R) destroyers:
   'May I express the joint admiration of the flotilla on your classical solution of last night's problem which has caused so many headaches, and our deepest sympathy on your casualties.'
From D26 to 26th DF:
   'Before joining the fleet, I should like to be the first to congratulate you all on last night's excellent performance. Well done and thank you.'

16

HMS *Rosneath* 1945-48

Letters to my parents from the East Indies at the end of the war with Japan show that I was resigned to a shore job on return to England and Their Lordships, presumably realising that I lived in Scotland, gave me one within striking distance of my home in Abderdeenshire.

It took me some time to discover where Rosneath was, and I eventually arrived by Motor Fishing Vessel from Greenock at the little pier at the entrance to the Gareloch, a short run up to Rosneath House, a vast pretentious building formerly the home of Princess Louise. My office was the old drawing-room fitted with its own switchboard by means of which I could telephone to all and sundry. There was a staff office next door, joined to mine by a corridor where I had my bed and a bath. For the next six months I seldom turned in there much before 2 a.m.

HMS *Rosneath* was a Combined Operations base and had recently been run by the Americans, until taken over by Commander Hindley-Smith as Executive Officer, who I relieved. The Captain wisely kept his office upstairs away from the madding crowd and lived out at Portkil by the Naval Hospital. There were five Officers' Messes, some six sections of Nissen huts, a dockyard and over 220,000 tons of shipping, including major landing craft for which latter I was not directly responsible. I was the only RN Officer on the active list, most if not all the others being RNVR Combined Operations Officers and some Wren Officers.

The rackets that went on were unbelievable. Petrol was being sold at Garelochhead in the black market, service transport was used indiscriminately, a Sub-Lieutenant with his girlfriend was elected President of the Petty Officers' Mess, and discipline appeared to be non-existent despite the presence of a Senior Commissioned Master-at-Arms, who was eventually court-martialled on thirteen charges. We had as many as 6,000 people to look after at times, the ratings being accommodated in Nissen huts fitted with American-type space heaters standing on wooden floors with no drip tins. The huts were lined with what looked like cotton wool and the station easily headed the Admiralty list of fires, normally an average of one hut burned down every night. It was not unusual to find Wrens struggling about in the snow looking for an empty hut while their own burned down, and ratings returning from the Far East in batches of 800 to 1600 thought nothing of changing huts if they felt like it. Providing drip tins for the space heaters reduced the number of fires, and a complete reorganisation of the station began. I telephoned my friend, Commander Dereck Holland-Martin in Second Sea Lord's Office and said, 'If you don't send me nine Lieutenant-Commanders by return of post I will have a mutiny in a week.' The Lieutenant-Commanders duly arrived and were appointed in Command of Sections, Captain of the Dockyard, and one, Christopher Bax, as Commander's Assistant, another was selected Transport Officer.

After six months the pressure of work eased sufficiently for my family to come and live at Villa Marina which I bought at Kilcreggan overlooking the Clyde, for £3,000. Some more RN Officers were appointed, including a Staff Engineer Officer, Captain John Illingworth and Commander Bill King DSO, DSC for the Staff Office (intended as a rest cure). Captain Micky Everard relieved Selby and was given a house at Clynder overlooking the Gareloch. After some months I offered him my room as more fitting for the Captain and moved my office to a Nissen hut in the dockyard, having concentrated three officers' messes in one at the old Ferry Inn there. I was not able to persuade the Medical Officers to join the Mess as they said it was important for them to be near the hospital. I struck a bargain with the Surgeon Captain from the Medical Director General to let me have half the hospital huts as Married Quarters if he insisted on the Doctor and Dental Officers remaining at Portkil.

Eventually Surgeon Commander Curjel RN took over administration and a good spirit pervaded the Medical Mess; after several months the Captain moved his office to an accommodation ship alongside in the dockyard. Lieutenant-Commander James Woodward RNVR, the original Captain of the Dockyard until relieved by Abdy, took over as Mess Secretary of the Ferry Inn Wardroom, a very popular move.

Life at Roseneath was never dull. We sold five LSTs to the Greek Navy and allocated a camp near Rosneath Point to the crews where I gave them permission to hoist a Greek flag for colours every morning. They were a cheerful bunch, the best a Captain of one of the LSTs being a Communist. Less satisfactory was the behaviour of twenty-one Egyptian Engine Room Artificers (ERAs) sent for training in running and management of landing craft engines. These Acting Chief Petty Officers called at Malta on their way to the UK, and seventeen of them decided that, as they did not approve of their Government, they should be accorded the status of Officers, and promptly ordered Officers' uniforms from Messrs. Gieve Ltd. The arrival of seventeen Officers in superfine uniforms, each with one thick purple stripe and four ERAs in serge suits posed an immediate accommodation problem until the truth emerged. The seventeen were firmly told that they would not be accorded officer status and would be treated like the rest as ERAs to learn how to handle diesel and internal combustion engines. Accordingly they went on strike, refused to work or attend instruction, and refused all meals, declaring a hunger strike. We informed the Egyptian Embassy and left them in their Nissen hut where it was reported that they were sucking oranges. After four days of this it was decided to send them all to London care of the Egyptian Air Attache.

It was raining and large drops of water from the surrounding trees were pattering on the roof of the Nissen hut in which the American space heater roared its heat, surrounded by the listless figures on their beds. Outside, a squad of Royal Marines presented arms as the Captain emerged from his car accompanied by a Medical Officer and me. We were preceded by the Master-at-Arms and a Regulating Petty Officer who ordered the Egyptians to get out of bed, but they affected to be too weak to move and the Marines were told to dig them out at the point of the bayonet. Of course they did no such thing, but after stacking their rifles with bayonets fixed in their corner, lifted them out of bed and draped them in their pyjamas round the space heater where the Captain, after a suitable interval, entered and told them what he thought of them before sending them back to Egypt. They left by the next train to London, accompanied by a doctor. The Air Attache who met them took them to the Officers' Club for breakfast, but the Egyptian Government was not pleased and we heard that the seventeen got three years' hard labour for their vanity.

Our Administrative Authority was Rear-Admiral Pat Horan whose Headquarters of Combined Operations bases was at Largs. He selected me to lead the Victory Parade through Glasgow, supported by Lieutenant-Commander Raymond Hart, DSO, DSC*, RN, and flanked by two Midshipmen in a sort of diamond. All went well during the parade and there were no incidents that we knew of.

After two and a half years at Rosneath I was successively invited to go to New Mexico, or to Tromso as Resident Naval Officer, and finally to Copenhagen, all of which I declined although with hindsight I should have accepted the appointment as Naval Attaché, Copenhagen.

17

Staff Officer Intelligence (SOI) Hong Kong

Having left Rosneath at the end of July 1948, I duly presented myself at the Admiralty where Commander Horace Law, Deputy to the naval assistant, told me that my next job would be 'make or break' as far as promotion was concerned. I did not take this too seriously at the time, but subsequent events reminded me of it.

With no previous experience of Intelligence work to speak of, I was given one month's briefing at the Naval Intelligence Division with one day at the War Office. There a young Army Captain took me aside and said, 'I think you ought to know, Sir, that the Officer you will be sharing an office with at Hong Kong is a Communist'. Accordingly, I called on MI5 where I was assured there was nothing to worry about and that the Officer concerned was well known and reliable. However, if in Hong Kong I still had doubts, I could go and see the Senior Intelligence Officer, Far East (SIFE) which, after a month or two, I duly did. I considered that a lot of the questions I was being asked were purely technical and of no concern to my opposite number. SIFE gave me the same story as MI5 and probably thought I was a nuisance, and the Army Chief of Staff at my request kindly moved the Army SO(I) upstairs to another office in Combined Services Headquarters.

I was then left in comparative peace with my clerk, an experienced Civil Servant.

The trip out to Hong Kong in the SS *Glen Beg* had been my choice instead of the trooper, as I was keen to learn something of cargo handling in the Merchant Service. At Singapore I was met by my direct boss, the Chief of the Intelligence Service in the Far East, Captain Martin Evans, who kindly invited me to stay and sent me on to Hong Kong by air, as further delay in taking up my appointment was unacceptable. The trooper I could have have gone out in was not due to sail until after the *Glen Beg*.

Evans told me I was to relieve Lieutenant-Commander Crawford and that my parish extended from Shanghai to Indo-China including Formosa and the Phillipines, and that the Director of Naval Intelligence required monthly reports besides anything of immediate importance. My job was overt Intelligence and I was not supposed to know anything about the Secret Service or any contacts.

For the first three months I led a bachelor existence, living in the Senior Officers' Mess at Grenville House, halfway up the Peak and had firmly to decline frequent requests to be Mess Secretary. No one believed that an Intelligence Officer had any serious other work to do. In fact there was not even time to indulge in my favourite sport of sailing races from the new Yacht Club on Kellet Island, despite encouragement from Captain Burr Robertshaw and the Sailing Secretary.

Apart from a lone trip over to Stonecutters on New Year's Day 1949, my only other sailing was to visit a Russian schooner which had been anchored for several weeks at the Northern end of the harbour off Kowloon. Three of us took a 14-foot dinghy over on a windy day and affected to be in trouble alongside, being welcomed on board by the Commissar with vodka. It appeared that the crew of this schooner consisted of Submarine Officers studying our activities and seeing the world.

I had been anxious to get as much travelling done as possible before the family arrived and had covered Macao, Canton, Amoy, Swatow and Formosa when the Senior Intelligence Officer said I should go to Saigon as soon as possible and '*go as a civilian*', since the French were at war in Indo-China. In order to get there I needed a visa from the French Consul who of course knew I was a Naval officer, and I flew in an Air France plane. No sooner were were in the air on course for Saigon than the pilot came aft and greeted me warmly with 'Oh, how do you do. I'm a Naval Officer too', and invited me to accompany him in the cockpit where he left me in the driving seat as we were on George. After five minutes I got up to return to my seat.

The British Consul met me on arrival in Saigon and I was billeted with the Military Attaché. Since my cover had been blown in Hong Kong, I had brought uniform and advised by the Consul, since he had no Naval Attaché, I called on the French Admiral in his flagship where he gave me lunch. The Consul was anxious for the presence of a British Naval Officer to be known, and encouraged his Secretary to take me shopping in uniform before I had time to change. The Admiral sent me up the coast in an aircraft with the crew at action stations and we had a fine view of the Baie d'Along. By way of returning hospitality the Military and

Air Attachés and I invited the Admiral's daughters and the Consul's Secretary to dine and dance at a restaurant. The evening was apparently a success. The Consul then took me up to Haiphong and insisted on driving round the town with me in uniform and flying a White Ensign on the bonnet of his jeep. We also visited Hanoi, but my main concern was to provide some Intelligence with photographs as I wanted to know the beach gradients of certain possible landing places. The Consul reluctantly agreed to wade out, counting the number of paces, until the sea was up to his armpits, while I took photographs. The prospect obviously filled him with alarm and I found him with the Assistant Consul, with whom we stayed in Haiphong, loading a machine-gun, just in case, but anyway I got my photographs.

Soon after I returned to Hong Kong, Captain Evans went to Saigon and thence to Hong Kong. After a few days he summoned me on board HMS *Belfast* and subjected me to a torrent of abuse about my work. The Commander-in-Chief, Daddy Brind, had recently relieved Admiral Boyd and was most considerate. He asked me to sit down and say whether I wanted to go home or stay on as Staff Officer (Intelligence) at Hong Kong, (which obviously was not my cup of tea). The Admiral and Staff remained standing in front of me and I agreed to give up the job.

Rear Admiral Alec Madden as Second in Command had allowed me to attend his staff Meetings and one of the first things the Senior Intelligence Officer had asked me for was an appreciation of how the China Fleet should be organised. It was my contention that the Flag Officer Second in Command should be on board his flagship when the Fleet was away from Hong Kong, and it so happened that he was on his way to Shanghai in HMS *London* when the Yangtse incident started.

The *Amethyst* on her way to relieve HMS *Consort* as guard ship at Nanking came under heavy fire, the Captain was mortally wounded, the First Lieutenant severely wounded, and the ship went aground. Lieutenant-Commander Kerans at Nanking was sent overland with an interpreter to take command of the *Amethyst*, by now under the guns of the Communists. When the news of the attacks reached me, I felt that my Military opposite number should have been able to give warning. With hindsight it is probable that he knew no more than I did, and in the event we were both sent home, probably for different reasons.

181

18

Royal Naval Air Station St Merryn
1949–1950

On 15 July 1949, I took over as Executive Officer, Second in Command of HMS *Vulture*, a big Naval Air Station near Padstow, temporary home of the 17th Carrier Air Group and Observer School. The Captain was relieved in October but it transpired that on account of blood pressure, his relief was required to take pills and was not available for consultation after 3 p.m. The Commander (Air) and I felt quite capable of running the station on our own and were not worried, but the Principle Medical Oficer was, and suggested that we should devise a means of relieving the Captain's anxiety about his health. One day the Captain sent for me and said, 'Commander, I want all the gardeners to build a wall round my house.' His house was a block exposed to the four winds and the request would normally have seemed reasonable as we had ten gardeners, and I might have spared one. However, the Doctor thought this provided just the cure needed, and I said, 'I'm sorry Sir. The gardeners are all very busy. I suggest the Captain build his own wall'! It took him a year but he did it, a fine stone Cornish bank wall.

I was allocated half a block as Married Quarters with a nice garden surrounded by sheep hurdles provided by my friend and predecessor Roy Talbot. There was a constant stream of Senior Officers arriving and leaving by air for which guards had to be provided and drilled. We also ran a band complete with a big drum major and tiger skin which performed for Divisions and special occasions like a visit by the Commander-in-Chief Plymouth.

Our Annual Inspection by the Flag Officer Flying Training was an unmitigated disaster, partly because, in the absence of advice from the Captain, all arrangements were left to me. The weather forecast promised that if it did not rain before 0900 the day would be fine and the Commander (Air) and I decided that it would be safe to get our 2,000-odd personnel out on parade ready for Divisions at 09.30. We were very proud of our turnout and particularly wanted the Admiral to see and hear the band. Soon after the Inspection started it began to drizzle and I assured the Captain that it would soon clear. In any case, we could not stop the Inspection at that stage. However, the rain increased so that the march-past, the only way of getting the troops under cover and away, was a wetting. The band performed valiantly and before many Divisions had passed I signalled for the 'Double' and they all cantered past the Admiral with medals clanking for all the world like the Camel Corps. Meanwhile we were all getting very wet including the Admiral whose only comment to me was 'MAD'. He had to carry out the rest of his Inspection wearing a Burberry.

He then decided to inspect the Seamen's Quarters and the First Lieutenant as Accommodation Officer led the way. Unfortunately he had not checked beforehand and took the Admiral into the only hut which was dismantled and being repaired by some Dockyard workmen from Devonport. The Admiral was not impressed and declined to see any more of the Seamen's huts. In his report he wrote 'enjoyed seeing your Wrens' Quarters'. We had a very good First Officer in charge of the Wrens.

As President of the Officers' Mess, I got to know the Airmen and was always grateful when they took me up in their Fireflies, etc. Sadly there were many crashes, some during test flights, and I had to ask the Ecclesiastical Commision for more burial ground. My wife was driving back from Wadebridge one day and saw an aircraft come in very low before being caught by telegraph wires. She rushed down a lane and was just in time to get the observer out alive, the pilot being already burned to death. For this gallant action the 17th Carrier Air Group were extremely grateful and felt she should have been awarded a decoration, but nothing was done.

Eventually the Captain asked for another officer to relieve me; a sad end to what promised to be a good appointment.

19

Admiralty 1951

Three weeks after leaving St Merryn in 1950, I joined the Chief of Naval Information (CNI) as his Assistant to the Admiralty. There, I was very surprised to receive a certificate from my Captain at St Merryn dated 10 November 1950 which read as follows:

'. . . has conducted himself entirely to my satisfaction. I have never met a more upright, loyal and conscientious Officer.' Signed A.C.G. Ermin, Captain HMS Vulture.

In view of this I wrote asking that it might be confirmed that my confidential report agreed with the certificate, observing that I had been relieved on the understanding that I had not given satisfaction. However, I don't think my letter was forwarded by CNI.

Appointment to the Admiralty meant finding somewhere to live in London and my sister-in-law very kindly let us have the top flat in 92 Eaton Place, providing a nice walk to work through St James's Park.

The job gave me a good insight into the workings of Admiralty and I had a close relationship with the Press Division. The Duty Commanders of Operations Division and I were invited to supper with the Daily Telegraph and put the paper to bed afterwards. We were told that the Duty Commanders were much more helpful than the Board of Admiralty and that editors generally waited until the Senior Officers had gone home before telephoning for Naval information. We provided them with a brief of what they could tell the press, including 'D' notices and what they could not say. On Mondays I represented the Admiralty at a meeting in the Foreign Office at Carlton House Terrace. Guy Burgess and Donald MacLean (of subsequent ill fame) were both on the Committee, I discovered later; obviously most of the conversation was well above my head.

20

HMS *Montclare* Third Submarine Squadron
1951-53

After eight months at the Admiralty and some sailing leave I was relieved by a Supply Officer and given a good promotion job as Executive Officer of HMS *Montclare* and Second in Command, 3rd Submarine Squadron. Admiral Madden, by then Second Sea Lord, was obviously responsible and may have said something to the Captain, a contemporary of mine who certainly did his best for me and I him. But he left after four months, by which time I had been passed over for promotion.

For painting ship, the largest surface area in the service, I took a tip from house painters. Seven sheepskins and innumerable rollers proved far more effective than spray guns and soon became fashionable in the Navy generally.

The Flag Officer Submarine (Shrimp Simpson) came to inspect the ship at Rothesay, and all the evolutions went well. Unfortunately, the Captain was not at the gangway to meet him, so I had to conduct him to the bridge. After 'Out bower anchor' and other evolutions, the Admiral said 'Provide gannet strop'. Not having a notion what a gannet strop was, I piped: 'Provide gannet strop' over the loudspeaker and a bright Leading Hand brought a ready-made wire strop, just the ticket to stop a gannet swallowing a fish. The Admiral, a keen fisherman, then asked me how to make a line float and how to make it sink. This I had learned from the gillie at Forglen, so he did not catch me out.

My small yacht, normally stowed on the boatdeck, happened to be anchored inshore when a gale sprang up and it was blown ashore. At 5.00 a.m. I took the launch and anchored it so that the boat could be hauled out, using a leading block in the launch. While ashore and hauling away on the rope, I was joined by a local fisherman with the spray driving in our faces, and between hauls heard him say: 'Never thought I would be working for you, Sir. My father was Captain of the Maintop when your father was Midshipman of the Maintop in the old *Alexandra*!' (1882).

Two of us attended the Highland Games in Rothesay one day

and took tickets in a raffle. The prize which I won was a pedigree bull calf which all the local farmers wanted. The auctioneer asked me if I wanted it, which I assured him I did, whereupon he said: 'We'll send it off to the ship in the morning.' So I said, 'No, don't do that, leave it with the farmer and I will go and see it.' Once a week we went out to see the bull calf, whose fetlocks were carefully whitened for our inspection and sherry provided on a silver salver.

There was never a dull moment for me as Executive Officer and I found the Chaplain, the Revd Scott, very sympathetic and a great support. He left soon after I did, to become Bishop of Hong Kong. As he put it, 'A less exacting job, that is, on the seat of the trousers!'

21

Commanding Officer Reserve Fleet Rosyth

Commander Moss relieved me in HMS *Montclare* just in time for the Jubilee Review of 1953 which I was able to observe from a motor fishing vessel attached to the Squadron. I could not help noticing the number of deadlights showing in the lower deck ports which I had been so careful to prevent.

Calling on my friend St John Tyrwhitt, by now the Appointments Captain in the Second Sea Lord's Office I heard him say 'rather hard to place'. However he did his best for me and I was appointed HMS *Kenya* in Command and as Commanding Officer Reserve Fleet (CORF) Rosyth. HMS *Kenya* had just returned from the East and was due to pay off into reserve during a refit. Meanwhile I had the Admiral's quarters and retinue and did a certain amount of entertaining while most of the crew were being discharged. When the ship went into drydock I shifted over to HMS *Mull of Kintyre* which was convenient as living ship. My family moved to the top flat of a house owned by Lord Bruce nearby and later I and my Staff were given offices alongside the Captain of the Dockyard. My job as Commanding Officer Reserve Fleet (CORF) supposed to be a nice cushy one to end with, turned out to be extremely busy and interesting, involving as it did some 25 ships in various stages of refit, trials and/or paying off into reserve. Some at Leith and others in outlying ports, besides Rosyth. There were also two large Fleet Carriers, *Indomitable* and *Indefatigable*, out at buoys which I visited periodically. Playing golf with the Flag Officer Scotland at Donibristle one day I pointed to these carriers saying, 'It only needs a strong westerly gale for those carriers to break adrift and carry away the Forth Bridge.' To my great relief they were towed round to the Clyde, one of them in the teeth of a heavy gale north of the Orkneys.

It was decided to move my outfit to living quarters in the newly-formed HMS *Cochrane* at Donibristle. This I resisted for six months but finally had to give in when an Acting Captain was appointed in command of HMS *Cochrane*. This did not suit us at all, being too far from the Dockyard, and soon after I left, a Captain was appointed in Command of Reserve Fleet Rosyth with

HMS *Mull of Galloway* in place of *Mull of Kintrye* as living ship. Eventually HMS *Cochrane* was rebuilt alongside the Dockyard.

Accommodation in HMS *Kenya* proved rather a problem as she was due to be Flagship of the Cape Station. The Director of Naval Construction decreed that all scuttles were to be blanked off in case of nuclear war, but in view of the prospect of hot weather I managed to delay the order until her new Captain should be appointed. I even had a port-hole cut in the stern for the Admiral to look out of, much to the delight of the Captain who soon reached agreement with the Construction Department.

My immediate boss was the Senior Officer Reserve Fleet (SORF) on the Clyde at Faslane. He was also Chairman of the RN Sailing Association (RNSA) on the Clyde and suggested I start a branch at Rosyth, so I became the first Secretary of the Forth Branch and asked the Captain of HMS *Lochinvar* to be Captain of the Branch. We had Dover Strait baulks moored alongside Inter-keithing Pier with buoys opposite, so that the RNSA dinghies could be secured head to the baulks and sterns to buoys (see photograph). I went to Chatham and had a folk boat, the *Jutta*, shipped up to Rosyth and we did some cruising in the Forth in her. The channel into Inverkeithing Harbour was narrow and not accessible at low water, but the sailing in the bay out of the strong tides of the Forth made races and regattas much easier than up the river. My wife and other wives used to bring food and drink and cut huge heaps of sandwiches for the sailing crews on Saturdays, sometimes as many as 100 boys, mostly from HMS *Caledonia* sailing in whalers.

22

Retirement, 1955

There was something rather incongruous about living in my father-in-law's house Teuchar Lodge in Cuminestown and having to register with the local National Service Agency for the dole whilst unemployed after my retirement from the Service at age 50. Naturally I applied for various jobs, always hoping it might be possible to go on living at home, a nice house in the country with a good garden and staff, not to mention many friends of the family, most of whom lived in castles on large estates. The only local jobs apparently open to me were teaching in schools for which I was not qualified, but I did a couple of stints with the idea of teaching French, having been an interpreter. Fraserburgh Academy was more anxious for me to teach religion and arithmetic which I did with varying success to a class of 40 children, at least four of whom, aged 16, could neither read nor write. As fishermen they could earn high wages and their parents saw no point in their compulsory attendance at school.

The Authorities provided all teachers with a leather strap for use on the wrist called a 'tawse', a procedure of which I disapproved. However, an occasion arose when a boy deliberately tried to take advantage of this and in front of the class I said 'put your hand out'. He refused and I took him to see the Headmaster who unfortunately was away in Aberdeen, so I sent for his Deputy. He was also away and I asked the Janitor to come with me and the boy to the bathroom to witness punishment. There I told the boy to put his hand out and again he refused, whereupon I went for him with the strap in the proper place. Somehow the boy escaped during the proeedings and ran home to complain to his parents about this brutal Commander, (a Sassenach at that, who could not speak broad Buchan!). Next day I was invited to the Headmaster's study where the local Police Sergeant had been summoned to hear what I had to say. He thought it was the funniest thing he had ever heard, observing that his wife had also been a teacher at the school and thoroughly understood the position. It seemed to me that having to drive 22 miles on icy roads to this school and back in winter was a mug's game and I asked to be relieved.

The Harbour Master at Fraserburgh was a good friend and was the District Officer for Sea Cadets, I being the Area Officer for the North East of Scotland. Some of the boys were in the Sea Cadets and behaved well; they knew I could get them chucked out of the Sea Cadet Corps if they did not. It so happened that the three-masted schooner 'Prince Louis' was in harbour and I called on the Master who kindly invited me to join him on a cruise. Later, on his advice, I applied to the Warden of the Outward Bound Moray Sea School for a job onboard as his Mate, but was turned down. I learned later that he thought I was trying to get his job. Witness his remark to the Warden, 'The day that bloody man walks on board, I walk off!' The last thing I wanted. However, Admiral Sir Martin Dunbar Nasmith, VC, was a fellow guest at a dinner and asked me if I was interested, and I was delighted to be invited for inter-view for the job of Mate, the Admiral being on the Committee. During the interview it became obvious to me that the appointment of a new Master for the ship was being considered and I was offered the job.

During the previous two years various organisations like the Association of Retired Naval Officers, the White Ensign Association and Officers' Association had tried to find me suitable employment, and I attended interview for the Coast Guard Service and a job with British Petroleum at Swansea where I found the constant smell of oil considerably off-putting, even if a house was provided within the refinery. My father was keen for me to accept the job of Harbourmaster Barbados, but this would have meant separation from the children at schools which my mother's generosity had made possible. My erstwhile First Lieutenant of HMS *Thracian*, then living in Barbados, was very glad of the job and wrote me an interesting letter about his doings there.

TS *Prince Louis*' refit was completed in January 1958 and as there were no boys at the school, I arranged for four Sea Cadets from each of my four units to come as crew for the trip back to Burghead. The weather was typical for the time of year, snowing with a full gale from the South, but after shovelling two feet of snow off the decks twice, we put to sea for engine trials and set sail the following day, arriving at our base in record time. Visibility had been poor on the way round and I never realised that the bow lookouts had been too seasick to call their reliefs, and that our westing after passing Rattray Head had been minus lookouts.

190

However we arrived in bright moonlight about 2 a.m. and all was well.

My permanent crew consisted of two fishermen, (a Bosun and Engineer) and a lorry driver from Glasgow as cook. They all rejoiced in the name of Main. Alec, Danny and Roddy. Danny had been in the Navy during the War and knew enough about diesel engines to coach us in and out of harbour, which was always an interesting if somewhat unpredictable experience. I never used the engine at sea if sailing was possible and my father-in-law said I was very lucky to be paid for my hobby. In fact my £800 a year was a godsend at the time, as our finances at home required considerable adjustment.

We were attached to the Outward Bound Moray Sea School and took about 25 boys for cruises in the Moray Firth and as far as Shetland and the Forth when later allowed cruises lasting a week. For my last year we took the ship through the Caledonian Canal for cruises on the west coast, changing watches in different places every four days. When in harbour I lived and messed at the School.

Two incidents stand out in my mind; the first soon after I took over. Weather forecast was wind west force four to six, and I decided to make a run down the coast to Fraserburgh and beyond where the wind would be off the land. We passed Buckie where my predecessor normally stopped, and gybed to the port tack off Cullen, by which time the wind had increased to force seven and I told the Bosun to start reefing down. He grumbled about being at sea on a night like this and said we did not carry any reefing gear, something I had assumed we had. Being fore and aft rig I considered it necessary to keep the wind about three points on the quarter to prevent risk of a Chinese gybe, and night having fallen, stood out as long as necessary to change onto starboard tack for the run past Rattray Head. By the time this happened the wind had increased to gale force with a heavy sea running, and it was pitch dark. I ordered booms amidships and the foresail came in, with my guest Lieutenant-Commander Evrington and the Bosun in charge, but it was backwinded by the mainsail and gybed itself, so that all those with it thought the order 'gybe-oh' had been given. The shrieking of the wind made it impossible to hear properly. Meanwhile 12 boys assisted by the Mate and Engineer could not get the mainsail in against the wind, so I had to run the ship off a little with dramatic results. A quartering sea lifted the stern, the mainsail still right out gybed all standing, crashing across the deck until the boom hit the port life boats davit, the main sheet unrove, as it had no figure-of-eight knot at its end, the boom caught the Mate a smart clip on the leg and burned the Engineer's hand when he tried to hold it. The cook, having failed to secure his table in the galley despite warning, impaled himself on it and broke a rib. The people forward knew none of this and I appeared to be the only adult left to re-reeve the mainsheet. However this was not difficult as I was pinned against the ratlines with the ship heeled well over to port, and the block at the end of the boom was within easy reach from a good height. For the next two hours the *Prince Louis* averaged 18 knots before rounding up under the lee of Peterhead where we remained stormbound for the next three days. Lessons learned, the Master must check everything normally the provinces of the Mate and Bosun. Another Bosun, also Alec Main by name, soon joined after I found it necessary to give old Alec his congé.

The other occasion was in February the following year. The Warden of the Sea School sent for me after the ship had been stuck in Burghead for over a week, stormbound, and said, 'I can't order you to go to sea, but the psychological effect on boys coming here looking forward to their cruise and then not getting one is unfortunate.' I said, 'Well, I can take them to sea, but they won't like it,' and then arranged with the Harbour Master at Invergordon for a berth alongside the pier. On clearing the harbour at Burghead we hoisted the square foresail and drove before the easterly gale. It was not long before the Mate had nine buckets in a row on the messdeck where all the boys save one, who was enjoying the ride up in the bows, were prostrated. We entered the Sutors into Cromarty Firth on the front of one wave with the rudder out of the water, and had a hair-raising berthing alongside at the expense of our port cathead, remaining stormbound at Invergordon until the weather moderated. At least the boys could say they had a cruise, and honour was satisfied. Admiral Nasmith was very helpful and sympathetic about our crumpled horn.

Normally when gales were forecast I made for Inverness Firth and sometimes into Inverness Harbour, an interesting piece of pilotage, but the best cruises were further afield like the Orkneys and occasionally Shetland. I devised a good way of getting a running fix in fog on the sound signal of a lighthouse by stationing three boys in front of the compass and taking the mean bearing of their fingers when they pointed in its direction! Surprisingly accurate.

Much of our time in light weather was helping Aberdeen Fishery Research Establishment with temperature and salinity readings. This entailed closing the ship's heads so as not to contaminate the water. The Fishery Research Assistant was of course appointed Captain of the Heads with all that work entailed!

Sailing this three-masted Baltic Schooner probably taught me more about weather and pilotage than my 34 years in the Navy, and a close watch was always kept on weather reports. One had to be qualified to operate the wireless set and in first-aid. I ran the ship on a shoestring, £7,000 per annum including crew's wages but after nearly four years my relief wanted new sails, a new engine and higher wages which cost the Trust some £12,000 p.a. which they could ill afford.

Meanwhile my wife took out divorce proceedings and I had to leave my home in Cuminestown. The Chairman of the Moray Sea School, Brigadier Sir Harry Houldsworth, made me welcome at his lovely house Dallas Lodge which I was able to treat as home, a great help when I was able to get away for a day or two.

Lady Harcourt asked me after church in London when I was on leave if I would take her son David as part crew as he was going to Dartmouth, and I agreed to take him as a deck hand for no pay. It was not long before his mother came to Burghead to see how he was getting on and we booked rooms for her at the only hotel in the village. We thought she should see the ship in daylight and went straight onboard, but had not been there more than ten minutes before the wind got up and we had to haul the ship in to get ashore. What happened next is history. Mum diagnosed the noise we heard as a hurricane in the Cairngorms and was quickly parked in her hotel. I found myself rounding up all Instructors and, aided by the school's Matron, closed all the windows in the school before driving our cars down to the harbour. There we found the ship lying well off with the sea and spray being driven across the wide harbour jetty. She was secured with eight four-inch manilla ropes, which we could just see through our windscreens with wipers going, as one by one they parted, until the ship was riding head to wind by just one rope with her stern near the opposite wharf. We drove round and sent for a ladder which was slow in coming, but I was able to jump for the stern and wriggle onboard over the counter in time to let go an anchor as the last warp parted. We dragged across the harbour while others fendered the stern, and I spent a restless night onboard as the ship took the ground with much bumping. Meanwhile Master David went on to tell his mother what was happening, driving my car as the wipers blew off. She felt she should have been warned about Burghead, the pictures in her room were moving as the walls shook and she began to wish she had not come to this dreadful place. However, all's well that ends well, and, to cut a long story short, we were married on 1 April 1961 in London. Clearly this seagoing was not going to be conducive to a happy married life and I started looking round for something more suitable. The Warden, Major Pat Steptoe, Sir Harry Houldsworth, and Admiral Nasmith gave me some nice testimonials and eventually the Officers' Association put me in touch with Lieutenant-Colonel Francis Johnston, the Organising Secretary for the Hertfordshire Association of Boys' Clubs. He asked me to be the Development Officer, a job which I did for the next eight years and found both rewarding and interesting. We formed a very good partnership and I was fortunate in having Antony Tuke of Barclays Bank as Chairman of the Council. In forming new Committees of Management I could generally count on the Manager of the local Barclays Bank to be Treasurer, then added the Chief of Police, a schoolmaster, parson, doctor and some businessmen, possibly the Mayor or a Councillor, and with a good Committee had little to worry about. Finding money to build a club took time and grants worth 25% from the County Council and 50% from the Ministry of Education through the National Association of Boys' Clubs were possible, if the Club could guarantee to find the rest. Many and varied were the schemes devised for fund-raising and I got about five boys' clubs built before Francis Johnston and I handed over to a younger man. I got a pension from the National Association of Boys' Clubs which, together with my Naval and Old Age Pensions, kept the wolf from the door, and I am now a Vice-President of the Hertfordshire Association of Boys' Clubs.

Whilst I was in the *Prince Louis*, my father died at the Kipling House in Rottingdean at the age of nearly 94, where he spent his last days peacefully. Fortunately my nephew Rodney was Flag Lieutenant to the Commander-in-Chief Home Fleet and was able to assist my mother with funeral arrangements and later arranged for HMS *Hardy* to take the ashes to sea for burial. My brother and I attended onboard for the ceremony with the Commander-in-Chief being represented by his Chief of Staff, and by Commodore Neil McKinnon, RAN, for the Government of New South Wales. The sight of Portsmouth Harbour in mourning with all flags at halfmast as we steamed past was deeply moving.

A Memorial Service was later held in St Paul's Cathedral where his KCMG would have entitled him to be buried.

Eight years later I was advised to bring my mother to London and arranged for Mrs Miller, the wife of an old friend, to look after her in the London flat, where I was having afternoon tea with her before going to Watford. My wife broke the sad news to me when I got home that evening that my mother had collapsed entering the dining-room for dinner, and had been found by Mrs Miller later that evening. In view of administration of South African Estate by Syfrets Trust Company and some legacies in Jersey, it took the Executors, of which I was one, six and a half years to get the Estate wound up, by which time there was not much left to distribute of my mother's own capital.

Stella and I celebrated our Silver Wedding Anniversary in 1987 and as I look back on a wonderfully varied and adventurous career, the loving support of my wife is a cause for great gratitude.